THE SECRET TO WINNING

BIG

Published by CelebrityPress™, Orlando, FL
A division of The Celebrity Branding Agency®

Celebrity Branding® is a registered trademark
Printed in the United States of America.

ISBN: 978-0-9857143-3-8
LCCN: 2012944203

This publication is designed to provide accurate and authoritative
information with regard to the subject matter covered. It is sold with
the understanding that the publisher is not engaged in rendering legal,
accounting, or other professional advice. If legal advice or other expert
assistance is required, the services of a competent professional should
be sought. The opinions expressed by the authors in this book are not
endorsed by CelebrityPress™ and are the sole responsibility of the
author rendering the opinion.

Most CelebrityPress™ titles are available at special quantity discounts
for bulk purchases for sales promotions, premiums, fundraising, and
educational use. Special versions or book excerpts can also be created
to fit specific needs.

For more information, please write:

CelebrityPress™
520 N. Orlando Ave, #2
Winter Park, FL 32789

or call 1.877.261.4930

Visit us online at www.CelebrityPressPublishing.com

THE SECRET TO WINNING

BIG

Contents

CHAPTER 1

Getting What You Want

By Brian Tracy

"Personal relationships are the fertile soil from which all advancement, all success, all achievement in real life grows." ~Ben Stein

Cooperation is the key to success in life. Your ability to interact effectively with other people, to negotiate, persuade and to communicate with others in such a way that they help you to achieve your goals is essential to everything that happens to you. Without exception, the most respected and highly-paid men and women in our society are those who have developed the ability to be influential and persuasive in their interactions with other people in every aspect of their work and personal lives.

THE LAW OF CONTROL

There is a "Law of Control" that says you feel positive about yourself to the degree to which you feel you are in control of your own life. It also says that you feel negative about yourself to the degree to which you feel you are not in control of any part of your life.

Psychologists call this "Locus of Control Theory." They say that each person feels that their life is controlled by either internal or external factors. A person with an *internal locus of control* feels that he or she is in charge and is making the decisions that determine the direction of his or her life.

The person with an *external locus of control*, on the other hand, feels that others are in charge, and that he or she is controlled by external factors and influences about which he can do very little. He often feels that his life is controlled by his boss, his bills, his childhood experiences, and his current marriage or relationship.

Having an internal or an external locus of control is the difference between feeling empowered and positive or powerless and negative. And both are states of mind over which you have considerable control.

GETTING RESULTS THROUGH OTHERS

In order to be happy and to enjoy high levels of self-confidence, you have to organize your life in such a way that you feel very much in control of what happens to you. And nowhere is this more important than in your ability to get the things you want through others.

You need the help of other people to accomplish almost anything. To accomplish anything worthwhile, you need the help of lots and lots of other people. To achieve your full potential as a human being, you need to consciously structure your entire life so that you are surrounded by harmonious, cooperative relationships. Your job is to be able to draw upon the organized efforts of many people to help move you in the direction that you want to go.

You really have no choice but to become very good in your ability to deal effectively with others. This feeling of self-efficacy, being competent and successful with others, is essential to your feelings of self-esteem and personal power.

INFLUENCE OR BE INFLUENCED

You have a choice: You can either influence others, or you can be influenced by them. You can learn how to persuade others to your way of thinking and to helping you, or you can simply let yourself be persuaded to the ways of thinking of others and to helping them.

This is the real difference between feeling powerful and feeling powerless. Between being an active agent and being a victim. It is the difference between being a leader or a follower.

Learning how to get what you want through others on a consistent basis makes you feel strong and effective. Every time you achieve a goal with the help and cooperation of one or more other people, you feel more competent and capable. You feel like a winner.

But each time you fail to get results through or with others, every time your efforts are frustrated, your sense of self-efficacy is diminished and your self-esteem and self-confidence go down.

The men and women with the highest levels of self-confidence are those who, through hard work and experience, have reached the point where they have become very skilled in working effectively with different kinds of people to achieve their goals.

RELATIONSHIPS ARE EVERYTHING

In reality, everything in life revolves around your relationships. The quality and quantity of the relationships that you form and maintain will have more to do with what happens to you more than any other single factor. Your relationships will determine your success or failure, and how fast you achieve your goals. They will determine your level of happiness, confidence, and self-esteem. Your ability to influence, persuade and earn the cooperation of others is an indispensable part of everything you become.

The formula is: You x Your Relationships = Your Personal Power

EVERYBODY SELLS

I've been teaching professional selling for many years, and one of the things I've learned is that everyone is *in* the field of sales. Everyone earns their living by selling something to someone. You do not have a choice over whether or not you are in the field of sales; you only have a choice over *how good* you are at selling yourself and your ideas to others. You can be effective or ineffective, good or bad, but you cannot get out of the business. From the time that you take your first job to the time you retire, and for all the days of your life, you are always either selling or being sold to.

Men and women who are good at selling, primarily because they have taken the time to study the field and hone their skills, are much more successful and happy, and feel much more in control of what's going on than those who are poor at selling.

SELLING DEFINED

What is selling? Selling is the ability to *persuade* another person to cooperate with you in achieving a goal. Every act of negotiation and persuasion involves selling of some kind or another. Every act of parenting requires selling your children on good values and behaviors, on cooperating and helping, and even on going to bed at night.

You should approach all your interactions with others from the viewpoint of persuasion (selling) and then learn the skills you need to become very competent in getting your point across and influencing others to your point of view.

There are several areas where your ability to get the things you want can make a real difference in your life. To start with, there is your job, or work. More than eighty percent of people working today would rather be earning more money, doing something else in their same company, or working at an entirely different job altogether. But they continue to stay where they are, earning far less money than they're capable of earning, and working at a job they don't like.

In one study, fully ninety-five percent of respondents reported that they are working below, if not far below their potentials in their current jobs. And this happens because they don't know how to act in their own best interests to change things. We'll talk about this briefly in this chapter.

BUYING, SELLING AND NEGOTIATING

Another area where persuasion skills can make an enormous difference in your life is in the area of buying and selling. The fact is that you are engaged in commercial transactions of some kind all your life. And many people end up paying too much for what they buy and getting too little for what they sell, simply because they don't know how to negotiate effectively on their own behalf. They don't know how to ask for what they want, and to keep asking until they get it.

Another area where selling skills are helpful is in your family and personal relationships. Happy, self-confident people seem to have a remarkable ability to structure things in such a way that they always seem to be getting what they want.

Meanwhile, people who haven't learned how to negotiate in their own best interests always seem to be getting stuck with second-best, or with something that is less than they had wanted or hoped for. And the same techniques that you use to be influential in one part of your life can be fairly easily applied to other parts of your life as well, as you will soon see.

GETTING WHAT YOU WANT

The starting point for getting the things you want is to be very clear about what they are. Then, you start from your goal and work back to the present day. First you visualize, and then you think on paper. You consider all the steps that you would have to take to get from where you are to where you want to go and back again, and then you make a list of all the people whose cooperation you'll require in order to achieve those objectives.

The most powerful tool that you have for improving your life is your mind, and your ability to think. Unfortunately, as Thomas Edison once said, "There is no expedient to which the average person will not go, to avoid the hard labor of thinking."

This is probably true. The good news is that thinking can work to your advantage when you develop the habit of applying your powerful brain to your situation before you start out. Peter Drucker, the management guru, once said that, *"Action without thinking is the cause of every failure."*

The reverse of this is that action preceded by thinking is the cause of every success. This is probably why Thomas J. Watson, Sr., the Founder of IBM, had signs made up with the word "THINK" and had them posted in every office and on every wall in the company. This constant reminder to "THINK" helped to make IBM one of the most powerful, profitable and respected companies in the world.

Once you've decided what you really want, and whose help you will need to achieve it, you think through the basic selling process as it applies to this person or situation, and you are ready to begin the influence process.

INFLUENCING OTHER PEOPLE

The starting point of influencing others is that your must have something he or she wants, needs and can benefit from. You must be clear about what this is before you begin.

You must then establish rapport and trust with that person. Today, the quality of trust underlies all relationships. The most successful people are those who invest a lot of time and energy building up high-quality, trust-based relationships, which they then maintain over time. The smartest people are those who take a *long-time perspective* with other people, and think about interacting with them for many years to come. They think about the third and fourth and fifth interaction with the same person, while they are still engaged in the first, and they behave accordingly.

BUILDING TRUST AND RAPPORT

In the process of establishing trust, you ask questions to find out what the person's needs and problems are, and then you listen carefully and attentively to the answers, as we have discussed earlier on the subject of *attention*.

Everyone is tuned in to their favorite radio station, "WIF-FM". This stands for, "What's in it for me?" The law of reciprocity says that if you want to get people to help you, you have to be willing and able to help them, first. You have to tune into their wavelength and find out what it is that they need and want, or what problems they have that you can help them solve, before you can expect them to help you achieve your goals.

MAKING YOUR CASE FOR COOPERATION

Once you have established rapport and identified problems and needs by asking questions, you will then be in a position to present solutions and benefits. These are the ways that you can help the other person fulfill their needs, or solve their problems. My friend Zig Ziglar says, *"You can get anything you want in life if you just help enough other people get what they want."* And he is certainly right.

If you've followed the steps properly up to now, and you have demonstrated to the other person how you can help him get what he wants, you are in a position to ask for action. You can now ask the person for what you want, and for what you need. All you have to do is ask. Once you have rounded the bases, you cross home plate by asking confidently and expectantly for the things you want.

MOST PEOPLE DON'T ASK

This last part might seem obvious, but, according to studies at Columbia University, fully fifty percent of sales presentations end without the sales person asking the customer to make any decision at all. They just thank them for their time and leave, hoping to be able to come back another day.

If you only learned one thing in this entire book that would dramatically raise your self-confidence and self-esteem and markedly increase the quality of your life, it would be to develop the *habit* of asking confidently for whatever you want from whomever you happen to be dealing with. I have seen very ordinary looking men who have obtained dates with, and even married, beautiful women, because they simply persisted in asking, and the odds worked out in their favor.

ASKING IS THE KEY TO SUCCESS

Many people get outstanding jobs at ridiculously high salaries because they had the audacity to ask boldly for what they wanted, and someone gave it to them.

Thousands of men and women, every day, are buying houses, cars, land and even companies and businesses, far below the original prices because they simply had the courage and confidence to make offers and ask for prices that no one else thought was possible.

When you ask politely and persistently, you cannot possibly lose. Before you ask, you have nothing. If the person says, "no," you are back in the same position that you were in before you asked. You may not have gained anything, but you haven't lost anything either. But if a person says "yes," and eventually someone will, then you are far further ahead than another person who didn't bother to ask at all.

DON'T BE AFRAID TO ASK

A student in one of my seminars started his fortune by going out and making what he called, "sixty percent offers" on houses that were for sale. Whatever the list price was, he would offer sixty percent cash immediately, no questions asked, for the house. He would phone every advertisement in the newspaper and go out with real estate agents to visit every house that was for sale. Of course, he got turned down ninety-nine times out of a hundred, but by calmly persisting, he ended up buying house after house, each of which he was able to mortgage for more than the purchase price, rent out, and eventually re-sell later at a higher price.

Another young man, being new to the city, didn't have any friends, and especially, he didn't have a girl friend. He decided to solve this problem by simply standing on the sidewalk in front of his office building and inviting every girl that appealed to him, out for a cup of coffee. Nine out of ten girls that he asked turned him down, but one out of ten said "yes", and within six months he was happily married to a beautiful girl that he had met on the sidewalk in this way. And all he did was to get up the courage to ask.

NEGOTIATING IS A LEARNABLE SKILL

Some people are good at negotiating in their own interests, and some people are not. One of your main jobs in life, one that will lead to increasing levels of self-confidence, is to become more effective at influencing others by learning how to negotiate more skillfully. In the many studies that have been done on effective negotiators, we find that they all have basically the same qualities and characteristics. These are the same personal attributes demonstrated by the woman in my office when she negotiated and received a fifty percent increase in salary.

Contrary to popular belief, top negotiators are not hard bargainers and tough-minded personalities. They are not aggressive and pushy and demanding. They do not coerce their negotiating partners into unsatisfactory agreements.

The best negotiators are invariably very pleasant people. They are warm, friendly and low-keyed. They are likeable and agreeable. They are the kind of people that you feel comfortable agreeing with. You have an almost automatic tendency to trust them and to feel that what they are asking for is in the best interests of both parties.

TOP NEGOTIATING STRATEGIES

Skilled negotiators are usually quite concerned about finding a solution or an arrangement that is satisfactory to both parties. They look for what are called, "win-win" agreements, where both parties are happy with the results of the negotiation.

Good negotiators seem to ask a lot of questions and are very concerned about understanding exactly what it is you are trying to achieve from the negotiation. For example, in buying a house, both parties might start off arguing and disagreeing over the price. They begin with the position that the price is the most important thing and that is all that has to be negotiated. The skilled negotiator however, will realize that price is only one part of the package. This negotiator will help both parties to see that the terms of the sale are also important, as are the furniture and fixtures that might be included in the transaction. The amount that the vendor might take back as a second mortgage, the interest rates to be charged on the various parts of the purchase or sale, and the time and conditions of occupancy.

SMART NEGOTIATING

For example, a friend of mine was trying to buy a large block of land in Tucson for development. But the owner was asking for one million dollars for his land, even though that was far more than the land was worth. It turned out that the landowner had a friend who had sold his piece of land for a million dollars. Both of the gentlemen were older and both had owned their land for many years. The landowner was determined, for face-saving reasons, not to get less for his land than his friend had received for the other property. The two parties seemed to be at a stalemate.

SEEK AN ALTERNATE SOLUTION

My friend was a skilled negotiator and he realized that the terms and conditions of payment were as important, if not more important than the actual price. So he agreed to pay the landowner one million dollars for the property, and this was the sales price that was agreed to.

However, the amount of the down payment, the annual payments and the interest rates were such that the land was to be paid out over a period of twenty years. In addition, as properties were developed within this larger property, they could be carved out and delivered free and clear to the purchaser.

The bulk of the proceeds from the sale of the land would probably go to the children and grandchildren of the landowner. But both parties were satisfied. The developer got the property on good terms, even though it had a high price, and the landowner got his price and was able to keep his personal pride.

PATIENCE IS ESSENTIAL

Good negotiators are very patient. They concentrate first on getting agreement on all the parts of the contract that the two parties have in common, before they go on to seeking for amicable ways to settle the other issues. They also take the time to get clarity and understanding on each point as they go along, so that there is no confusion later.

The woman in my office did all of these things. She was calm, positive and friendly. She was patient and she walked through the salary negotiations one step at a time. She made it clear from the beginning that it was her desire to find a solution that we would both be happy with, and we would both be committed to living with for the foreseeable future. And she was quite successful.

NEGOTIATING SKILLS ARE LINKED TO SELF-CONFIDENCE

There is nothing that raises your self-confidence faster than to feel that you have been successful in negotiating a contract and that you have gotten a good deal as a result. And there is nothing that will lower your self-confidence faster than to think that you have been out-negotiated into a poor deal that you will have to live with. Therefore, negotiating skills are an important part of your personality development and of your sense of personal effectiveness.

When you are a good negotiator, your self-esteem is higher and you feel more positive toward yourself and others in everything else that you do.

NEGOTIATING SKILLS

In negotiating any kind of contract, whether buying or selling anything, there are some basic negotiating skills that you need to learn in order to get the best deal for yourself and to feel happy about the results.

The first skill in successful negotiating is *preparation*. This constitutes fully ninety percent of negotiating success. The more and better prepared you are prior to a negotiation, the more likely it is that the outcome of the negotiation will be satisfactory.

Preparation requires that you do two things. First, get all the information you possibly can about the upcoming negotiation. Second, think the negotiation through carefully, from beginning to end, and be fully prepared for any eventuality.

The first kind of information you need is about the product or service, and the person with whom you will be negotiating. In this sense, information becomes a form of power. And the power is always on the side of the person with the best information.

DO YOUR HOMEWORK

Begin by finding out everything you possibly can about the situation. If you are thinking of buying a house, go onto the Internet and look at fifty to one hundred houses. Then compare the various sizes and selections and amenities and costs.

If you're thinking of buying a car, or a stereo set, or a product that is available in more than one place, do a detailed Internet search and follow up with phone calls if necessary.

The more different inputs you have, from the greater number of sources, the more knowledgeable and more powerful you will be in any negotiation.

If you are going to be negotiating with a particular person, find out as much as you possibly can about that person. Speak to other people who have done business with that person and ask for their insights and for their advice on how to negotiate most effectively.

THE LAWYER'S METHOD

Use the "lawyer's method" of negotiating. Before you prepare your own position, write out a list of everything that you can think that the other person will want to get out of this negotiation. Put yourself in the other person's shoes and describe the ideal result from his or her point of view.

Lawyers are taught to prepare the case of their opposition in full before they begin preparing their own case. It is amazing how this will sharpen your instincts and enable you to see possibilities and opportunities, and possible threats and vulnerabilities that you had not been aware of before.

DEVELOP OPTIONS

Perhaps the most important form of information is your knowledge of *alternatives* to this negotiation. A basic rule for success and happiness in life is that you are only as free as your well-developed options. If you have only one choice, you are in a very poor position to negotiate in your best interests. But if you have developed a variety of options, not only with this negotiation but in terms of other solutions to your problem, you are going to get a far better deal for yourself than if you had no other choice but to come to terms with this person.

One of the greatest strengths you can have in any negotiation is to be able to get up and walk away. On the other hand, the more intensely you desire to buy or sell something, and the fewer alternatives you have, the less negotiating power you will be able to bring to bear in the discussion, and the less you will be able to walk away.

Excellent negotiators are able to ride the fine line between wanting to succeed in the negotiation, and simultaneously appearing not to really care whether it works out or not. If you seem to want it too badly, or not want it badly enough, you are in a weak position either way. But if you seem to want it badly but are only willing to achieve it on terms that seem fair and reasonable to you, your hand in the game is considerably strengthened.

TIMING GIVES YOU POWER

A key form of power in negotiating is timing. You must give careful consideration to exactly when you will sit down to negotiate. For example, in organizations that run on a monthly basis and which have monthly sales targets to meet, you can always negotiate your very best deal in the last few days of the month. In the first few days of the month, there is very little urgency to compromise or make concessions, but as the time to meet monthly quotas gets closer, the people in charge of sales in any organization become more eager to cut corners and to make deals.

When I bought my home a few years ago, I applied to several places for a large mortgage. The mortgage negotiations seemed to drag on, month after month. There seemed to be very little urgency and a very real possibility that the deal would fall through. The third or fourth company that was considering granting the mortgage was continually asking for additional documents, credit checks and details to support the mortgage application.

Unbeknownst to us however, the year was running out. I began the mortgage application process in August and was still struggling in the last half of December. Then, in the last week of December, as the company's financial year was coming to an end and everyone was eager to get the numbers up as high as they could, everyone seemed to leap into action. There was frantic activity around my mortgage application. I received continual phone calls, and faxes went back and forth between me and the financial institution. Finally, on December 31, at 5:00 p.m. in the afternoon, the final documents were put together and finalized, and the mortgage was booked so that it went into the statements and into the individual quotas before the end of the year.

USE TIMING TO YOUR ADVANTAGE

The same factors apply to cars and furniture and large appliances of all kinds. Whenever you possibly can, give careful thought to the timing of any negotiation and remember, patience always tends to work in your favor.

And here's an important point. Whenever you present people with something new or with an unexpected alternative, be willing to give them a couple of days to think about it. Encourage them to turn over the new price or terms or conditions in their minds, and let them come back to you. If you are patient, people who may be totally opposed to your proposal when you first bring it up, will often come around completely and agree to your price or terms, if you just give them a little time.

NO NEGOTIATION IS EVER FINAL

Remember, no negotiation is ever final. If you find that the situation has changed and that you are no longer satisfied with the terms and conditions of the deal, be willing to go back and reopen the negotiation. Be willing to go back and suggest changes that make the deal more fair and equitable for both parties.

It is amazing how many people stay in a bad situation, working under terms and conditions that they feel are unfair and unreasonable, instead of simply going back, accepting full responsibility and saying, "I am not happy with our arrangement and I would like to change it."

ASK FOR WHAT YOU WANT

It cannot be repeated too often, in all acts of influence, persuasion and negotiation, the keys to success are to research thoroughly, plan carefully, work systematically and don't be afraid to ask.

Develop the habit of asking for a better deal, for better terms, for better conditions, for better prices, both in buying and selling. Ask for a better job or different responsibilities or for a higher salary or for different benefits. Ask for opportunities. Ask your customers to buy. Ask your suppliers for better prices. Whatever you are offered, always consider it an opening bid, and rather than accepting it the first time, ask for something better.

And the more you ask, the better will be your results. And the better your results, the happier and more self-confident you will feel and the more capable you will be of getting a better deal for yourself in every area of your life. You will eventually become an expert on getting the things you want, and every time you succeed, you will feel more like the winner you are meant to be.

ACTION EXERCISES:

1. Resolve today to become an excellent negotiator in every area of your life by asking for better terms and conditions, better prices, and better deals on every occasion;

2. Decide to become excellent in selling. Take a seminar, read a book, listen to an audio program;

3. Review the various areas of your life where you are dissatisfied with your current situation and then develop a plan to negotiate a better deal for yourself;

4. Practice asking for what you want on a regular basis, and if you don't get it, ask again;

5. From now on, ask a lot of questions before you negotiate or make a decision. The more and better the information you have, the better deal you will get;

6. Prepare thoroughly before any negotiation from now on. Take your time and do your homework;

7. Always think in term of what is in it for the other person and then show the other person why agreeing with you is his/her best interests.

About Brian

Brian Tracy is Chairman and CEO of Brian Tracy International, a company specializing in the training and development of individuals and organizations. Brian's goal is to help people achieve their personal and business goals faster and easier than they ever imagined.

Brian Tracy has consulted for more than 1,000 companies and addressed more than 5,000,000 people in 5,000 talks and seminars throughout the US, Canada and 55 other countries worldwide. As a Keynote speaker and seminar leader, he addresses more than 250,000 people each year.

For more information on Brian Tracy programs, go to: www.briantracy.com

CHAPTER 2

"Ask Yourself This..."

By Andy Eilers, CRIS, CMC

"Two roads diverged in a wood, and I took the one less traveled by, and that has made all the difference." ~Robert Frost

HOW DO I TAKE RESPONSIBILITY FOR MY LIFE?

Would it surprise you to know that there are over seven billion people in the world today? Let that sink in for a minute. Think about how many people you know in your entire circle of friends and business contacts. Is it even in the hundreds? Now reduce it down to the number of people you know fairly well and talk to on a regular basis. As the number gets smaller and smaller, take a look at that group and the people in it for a minute. How many of those people in that small group, including you this time, are truly leaders? In my experience, there is one motto that someone either lives by or doesn't, which separates leaders from followers.

Leaders take responsibility and followers don't.

Say this out loud; no matter where you are right now, "I am responsible!" Go ahead, it doesn't matter who is watching. You want to be a leader, don't you? Say it with conviction, "I am responsible!!" When you are earning less money than you could be, who is keeping you from making more money? Remember, no matter what you may have been told all of your life, you are self-employed as a personal services corporation, even though you may only have one client right now. Think about that for a minute.

31

That client might be known to you as your employer or the company you work for currently. However, that is simply your largest. Can you leave anytime you want? Can they let you go anytime they want? If the answer to these questions is yes, then it just confirms that your personal services are only as valuable as you make them under the agreement you have with that client.

Who has the most control over whether you are meeting your career goals or not? You are responsible. If you are out-of-shape or overweight, did someone force you to eat the wrong foods or to stop taking care of yourself? You are responsible. <u>The fact is that you can't lead yourself, let alone others, if you aren't willing to take responsibility for your life.</u>

In my experience, followers are the people who are quick to take responsibility for the things in their lives that are going well. They are equally as quick to blame someone or something else for all of the things that aren't going well. Do you know people like this? Even when you don't have control over everything in a given situation, you are still responsible. When you take responsibility for your life you will be freeing yourself from the chains that making excuses bind you with.

When you look in the mirror and see yourself standing there, say to yourself, "I am responsible and I don't make excuses!" It works and I can prove it to you right now. Has anyone ever told you that you couldn't do something, but you were successful at doing it anyway? One example I have of this in my own life was when my largest client was an insurance agency in Northern California.

When I started working with this company in a sales capacity, I was introduced to an incentive program that required selling $1,000,000 in premium in a rolling 12-month period in order to qualify for a two-tone Rolex Submariner watch. This was with an average premium size of approximately $500 - $2,500 per policy, so I recognized that it would require a lot of work. At that time, that watch had a price tag of somewhere around $7,000. I was told by many of the salespeople who were also working with this company at the time that it was impossible. In fact, there wasn't a single salesperson there at the time who thought this goal could be achieved.

Are you surrounded by people like that in your life? Again, if you are a leader and take responsibility, then you get things done, right? I knew what I had to do. I set my goals, figured out exactly how much premium I needed per policy, per week, and per month. I took ownership of the goals and took responsibility for my results. One policy at a time, one day at a time, one week at a time, and one month at a time, I proceeded to get closer and closer to achieving this goal that nobody else believed anyone could achieve. At the end of my first 12 months working with that company, I had achieved the goal.

Taking responsibility and holding myself accountable for my results made all the difference in the world. Another critical part of this was that I had an income goal that I set that I wouldn't have met if I hadn't achieved this goal. So tying the two together and not allowing myself to make excuses or stop short of achieving these two goals made the burning desire for accomplishment even stronger. After achieving this goal, I went to the owner of that company and confirmed that there was no limit to the number of Rolex watches I could earn.

He confirmed and agreed to offer the incentive again. I decided that when I earned the second one, I would give it to my father. I know that he would never have gone out and invested that kind of money on a watch for himself. I earned the second Rolex in only nine months. I asked the owner if I could present it to my father at our monthly sales meeting upon being awarded the watch. I really appreciated him making that opportunity available to us.

I invited my parents to the meeting, which had never been done before, and presented the Rolex to my father, along with reading an original poem I had written for him. As you can imagine, he was overwhelmed. My mother, who thought she was just being asked to come and stand by his side during the meeting, had no idea what would come next. She had been telling me for years that someday she wanted a diamond tennis bracelet. What a perfect opportunity for me to present one to her, right? I had purchased one that I knew she would love. When I presented it to her she was absolutely stunned.

They were both in tears and couldn't believe this was really happening. When I look back on that day now, I remember it as one of the best days of my life. Every single time I saw my father after that, he was wearing his Rolex and would smile ear to ear when I asked him what time it was. This opportunity to do something special for them had started nine months earlier with me taking responsibility for my results. They have both passed away now and I miss them tremendously. They were special people who fought for what they wanted in their own lives, had incredible relationships, careers, and lives, and set wonderful examples for me to follow.

By achieving a goal for a second time that nobody thought could be done at all, I was then given opportunity to work with many other salespeople in that organization and assist them in achieving that goal. I'm sure you can think of stories when you accepted a challenge similar to this in your life, took responsibility for your results, achieved the goal, and went on to achieve more amazing results because of it, right? A goal can be in the area(s) of education, work, relationships, health, athletics, personal enrichment, travel, something artistic, or anything else that is important for you to achieve.

No matter what you pick though, in order to achieve something great, it is always going to require you being personally responsible for your results. Embrace that fact! Know that when you accomplish something, no matter how difficult it is, that you believed in yourself, refused to make excuses, beat the odds, showed leadership, took responsibility, and achieved your goal. Keep doing that and continue to be a leader by taking responsibility when many others around you will continue to make excuses. Take control of your life by taking responsibility for your decisions so that you can achieve all of your goals!

HOW CAN I TURN LEARNING MORE INTO EARNING MORE?

I'm sure you have heard at some point in your life that "knowledge is power." The fact is that knowledge by itself is not enough. In the book *Think and Grow Rich*, Napoleon Hill notes that "there are two kinds of knowledge. One is general, the other is specialized." He goes on to say that "Knowledge is only potential power. It becomes power only when, and if, it is organized into definite plans of action, and directed to a definite end." Ask yourself this… "Do I have specialized knowledge in the areas I need to in order to be as successful as I want to be?"

Are you getting ahead or falling behind? We all know that there is no standing still when it comes to being a business professional. As a personal services corporation, your objective should always be to increase your hourly rate so that you can maximize your time working in order to enjoy your time away from work. One of the best ways that I have found to do that is to use the ABCDE Method continually. In Brian Tracy's book *Eat That Frog*; he outlines this method based on the idea of focusing on ABC items as what you should be working on in order of priority. Learning and using this method will help you earn more starting today!

This method starts with "A" items being defined as very important or something you *must* do. If you have more than one "A" task, prioritize them on your work list by using "A-1," "A-2," and "A-3" as examples. "B" items are defined as tasks that you *should* do. "C" items are defined as tasks that would be *nice* to do, but for which there are no consequences at all, whether you do them or not. "D" items are defined as tasks that you can *delegate* to someone else. "E" items are defined as tasks that you can *eliminate* altogether, and it won't make any real difference. Look at your task list every single day before you start working and use the ABCDE Method to maximize your time and increase your hourly rate.

This method is extremely useful when you are in the office, but what about when you are on the road? One of my favorite audio programs by Brian Tracy, *The Psychology of Selling*, emphasizes the importance of learning opportunities when you are on the road. Are you listening to the radio when you are in your car, which Brian refers to as "chewing gum for the ears?" If so, make the decision right now to start investing in audio programs in your field of specialization, which will provide learning opportunities while you are on the road so your car becomes a university on wheels. This will be a way for you to keep up with the latest and greatest material in your field that can increase your hourly rate. This is an "A" task that you should plan and complete this year and every year from now on!

Another tip that you will find extremely valuable is to read at least 30 minutes every single day. Read books in your field that will make you an expert at what you do. Remember, as a personal services corporation, you have to take responsibility to learn more so you can earn more. Imagine how much more knowledgeable you will be at the end of the first year you do this. In Scott Alexander's book, *Rhinoceros Success*, he writes that, "You tend to become what you feed your mind. Ask yourself, will the information in this book help me reach my goals?" If so, start reading so you can learn and be able to use the information that much sooner!

Imagine how much more you will know than your competitors if you read 30 minutes a day every single day. That could be a book a week or 52 books a year in your field! What if you walked into an attorney's office to hire him for an important case and you didn't see any law books. Would you think he and his staff were current on the laws that could affect your case? You can ask this question about a number of professions, right? The fact is, if you aren't reading and your competitors are, you are falling behind. Take a minute to get online right away and order these three books: *Think and Grow Rich, Eat That Frog,* and *How to Master the Art of Selling.* This is an "A" task that you should plan and complete this year and every year from now on!

The next step is to attend live seminars with experts in your field. If you sell a product or service, imagine how much better you will be when you learn from people who have invested their lives in becoming experts at selling. Remember, you are responsible for your results, which includes investing in yourself in this area. If you aren't investing in training like this because you are waiting for the company you work with to invest in you, who's in control of your future? Create a budget for yourself that will get you in front of the best speakers and trainers in the country in your field. This is an "A" task that you should plan and make sure you complete this year and every year from now on!

Remember, you are a personal services corporation, not an employee. That means you are responsible to yourself and your client(s) at all times for providing the best possible value for each dollar you receive. Don't stop there though, because we aren't finished yet. Napoleon Hill notes in *Think and Grow Rich,* "Success requires no explanations and failure permits no alibis." If you are focused on success and want to take the fastest route to eliminating failure from your vocabulary and life, take these steps right now.

1. Start focusing on where your time is being invested and how you can maximize your hourly rate.

2. Use the ABCDE Method to prioritize your time and tasks throughout the day.

3. Start listening to audio programs instead of the radio when on the road.

4. Read 30 minutes a day so you can become an expert in your field and always be a step ahead of your competitors.

5. Attend seminars and training sessions that will bring positive change to your life and business.

Take responsibility, follow these steps for improvement, and watch your life and business change forever!

About Andy

Andy Eilers is the Director of Sales & Marketing for First Service Insurance in Roseville, California. First Service specializes in construction and transportation insurance in multiple states with over 2,000 current and active clients. With over 20 years of sales, sales management, and sales training experience with a multitude of companies, Andy's goal is to assist people and companies in achieving their personal and professional goals through teaching, managing, training, and personal and professional coaching.

For over 20 years Andy has studied the material of many of the great trainers and teachers of our time including: Tom Hopkins, Brian Tracy, Zig Ziglar, and Napoleon Hill. He has earned top sales and sales management awards throughout his career. Andy is also the reigning "Champion" of the Tom Hopkins 3-Day Boot Camp held annually in Scottsdale, Arizona. In addition, Andy has consulted for many companies in the areas of motivation and sales training throughout Northern California.

Andy has a BA in Economics, with a minor in Communication Studies from CSU Sacramento. He will complete his MA in Psychology with an emphasis in Organizational and Business Psychology this year. Andy plans to begin his Doctor of Psychology program in 2013. Andy is also in the process of completing an audio program including all of his "Ask Yourself This…" material and other sales and motivational instructional information.

Andy Eilers is also Co-author of the Best-Selling Book *In It To Win It* with the legendary Tom Hopkins, and is a member of The National Academy of Best-Selling Authors®.

Andy is an accomplished martial artist, holding a 1st degree black belt in Tae Kwon Do. He is also an avid reader, golfer, tennis player, singer, poet, and wine enthusiast.

For more information on Andy Eilers, email him at: andy@firstserviceweb.com or love2live@mac.com.

CHAPTER 3

Finish It

By Donna Darlington

"Yes Lord, another morning," Gahiji muttered after he spat the rinse water from his mouth. He shuffled over to a window. He looked out. It was still dark but the big trucks, with their uncovered trays, were rolling out of the landfill. Gahiji stared into the darkness and cleared his throat. "Today makes it thirty years I've been working in this labasse—this dump," he said loudly. "A man's gotta do what a man's gotta do." Gahiji went outside and joined others who were already sitting on the dew-drenched grass, eating bread, drinking tea and playing cards by flambeau light. He did not understand why he was feeling so disenchanted. "We'll just have to wait to see what today brings," he muttered.

Everyone was waiting. The men. The women. The children. The dogs… and the vultures. Then, just a little before eight, horns honked and the first truck was seen in the distance. The horde stood up and closed in. Amidst the trucks wobbling back to the landfill, and the shouts hailing their arrival, men, women, children, dogs and vultures stampeded on the garbage as it tumbled out from the trucks. Every man knew the more aluminum cans, cloth, plastic bottles or glass bottles he could hoard, the more money he could get, in exchange, to take to his shanty at the back of the landfill.

The melee continued for hours. It seemed like the sun revved up to degrees bordering on 'incinerate', but the desire to make a living burned much fiercer, so no one noticed. Around 2 pm Gahiji straightened up and lifted his arm to mop the sweat leaking into his eyes. Then, as though it was the first time, he noticed the multitudinous, incompleted piles of trash, safeguarded by children warding off bullies with sticks and broken bottles. By habit, he mentally calculated the number of dollars certain plies would fetch but this time he also counted the putrid smells and the number of incompletes in his own life.

It was around that time news reached that Chong, the top gangster on the landfill, had been maimed by rivals. News had it that they caught him retailing their drugs and had chopped off both his hands. Chong had always looked down on Gahiji because of his scavenging. Nevertheless, Gahiji went to visit him, partly to see if the news was really true and partly because in sickness and death, you were supposed to forget all the bad blood that existed between that person and you. During their conversation, Chong told Gahiji that he regretted that he had neither finished things he had started nor realized his dreams. Without hands and money, he wondered if it was too late. He wanted another chance.

Gahiji's heart flip-flopped. He had felt that sensation before, but it was long ago when as a boy he had tagged along with his father and others to the city. When they arrived, the heat and the meandering lines made Gahiji stray into an office where a fan was blowing cool air. There he met an accountant who told him about his profession. On his way back home, Gahiji disclosed that he was interested in numbers and wanted to be an accountant. His father and the others laughed and told him that nobody on the landfill could be an accountant. Gahiji felt stupid and never brought it up again.

Gahiji looked at Chong's stumps and made up his mind to finish his own incompletes and dreams. That night, Gahiji decided that he was not going back to work in the landfill. He had no money and just about the same amount of education. He did not know what he was going to do next or how he would earn a living but he was sure he was not going back. As time went on, Gahiji took free adult education classes in the neighboring village and graduated with a high school diploma. Shortly afterwards, the principal announced that an agriculture recruit was coming from America and those who were interested in going overseas to work on farms should stay for a meeting. Gahiji stayed and was eventually drafted. Late in the evenings when the other exhausted agriculture workers were playing cards or sleeping, Gahiji, just as exhausted, would attend a small accounting class. He was good with numbers but it took him eight years to get his qualifications. He was determined to finish. One of his classmate's father hired Gahiji on trial and then on contract.

At the company's Christmas party, one year, Gahiji met a co-worker called James and the two became fast friends. He told James about his previous life on the landfill. James was fascinated and became interested in knowing what took Gahiji so long to make that critical change. They talked for hours. James realized it was not that Gahiji had not tried to better himself before, but it was just that he gave up when he felt the weight of the incompletes and failures he had amassed. Gahiji had mentioned that he did not know how to begin the overwhelming task of finishing the things he had started, because he had not seen anyone he knew do that before. Added to that, Gahiji told James that he did not think he was smart enough to do anything else and even if he thought he could, he was afraid that he would look silly and people would laugh. Gahiji had come a long way since then.

About three years after that conversation, Gahiji asked James to accompany him to the handing over of his new house. James was thrilled. When Gahiji opened the welcome package that the home developer had given him, he pulled out a key chain and she told him to count the keys. He counted eight. He smiled and said, "Eight. You know, God took six days to create the world and when He saw that everything was good and complete, He rested on the seventh day, so day number 8 represented a new beginning."

"Yes, a new beginning," she said. "There is a key for everything. One for the front door. One for the mailbox. One to access the swimming pool and tennis court. One for…"

Gahiji smiled. He realized that he now owned keys to unlock and open all the doors to successfully access everything he needed in his new community. Gahiji singled out key number 1, walked up to his new house and opened his first new door.

Successful people understand that, just like Gahiji, taking advantage of the new beginnings requires being equipped with keys to unlock and open new doors. In order for you to effectively acquire, unlock and maintain the kind of success that opens up new doors, you will need your own set of keys.

Here are the 8 keys you will need to unlock and open the new doors to success in your life:

FINISH IT

1. F = Find Out
Before achieving success, we need to be absolutely sure to find out what goals we are interested in. Knowing your "what " attracts your "how." Be decisive. Don't waste time, energy and resources on 'maybes' because statistics prove that those aspirations eventually fizzle away. Successful people stop starting new projects before completing those already in existence. They specify key performance indicators they want to achieve and file new ideas away until ready to act on them.

Considerations: List goals that interest you. Find out and cherry-pick only those you are passionate about. List them separately and create a folder for each. Read your list at least twice daily. Find out what is your most important goal and begin there.

2. I = Initiate a Plan
Time management guru, Dr. Alec Mackenzie once said, "Action without planning is the cause of every failure." So true. Research has found that if someone invests one hour a week into planning, it actually saves that person at least four hours of performance time. That one hour need not be used all at once but may be fixed into 5-10 minute chunks over the course of the week. Time taken to plan equates time rescued for executing your goals. Now, four hours of "extra time" per week may not seem significant but scale that up to a month. A year. Using one hour to plan per week, frees up 208 hours per year, which equates to about 8 days. So, looking at the big picture, if you consistently plan for 1 hour a week you would have redeemed 8 days per year to use as you like. Remember 8 is the number of new beginnings, so with this amount of free time, you can begin learning new skills, begin a new project or language, and the list goes on.

Considerations: Expectations—what should your end-result look like? Conclusion—what is a reasonable wrap-up time? Time and energy investments—how much do you need to put in? Resources—what do you need? Make an outline.

3. N = Negotiate Alternatives

While planning is crucial, there is a military axiom that says, "No battle plan ever survives first contact with the enemy." Just like combating real-life military enemies, finishing tasks and goals require changing your plan strategically as your execution advances. Sometimes, in life, things happen beyond your control and they may have a direct impact on your plans. Your Negotiate Alternatives key comes in very handy here. After you have found out what needs to be done and have initiated your plan, you now need to negotiate your plans to accommodate unexpected occurrences. The more in-depth your plan for the initiation stage, the more flexibility you will have to negotiate change tactics to accomplish your goal.

Considerations: Don't be a perfectionist, revisit your plan continually to make adjustments, tell others about your plan, acquire accountability partners, itemize and break plans into smaller steps.

4. I = Imagine

If you have confidence in what you hope for and assurance about what you do not see, the Bible, in Hebrews 11:1(NIV) calls it faith. In common terms, it is believing what you imagined. Albert Einstein said, "Your imagination is your preview of life's coming attractions." It is crucial then, that you imagine or see your goals as being completed. Your subconscious mind does not discriminate what is real or imagined, it simply goes to work on what it is fed. According to Robert G. Allen, "The future you see is the future you get." Added to that, Paul of the Bible said, "… God shall supply all your need according to His riches in glory by Christ Jesus." When you imagine and believe that you successfully completed your goals, your mind procures this visual and an alert is sent out. According to Paul, God then makes available every resource to assist you in realizing your goal. Your imagination draws attention and launches your needed resources.

Considerations: Successful people know that if they can imagine success in their mind, they can hold success in their hands. What are the thoughts in your mind?

5. S = Start Now

This is one of your most important keys. Don't ever lose it. The legendary archer, Howard Hill said, "Unless you know your game's feeding, sleeping and daily habits, unless you plan your hunt in great detail and follow your plan with precision, you are not hunting at all…you're just walking in the woods," and Nike® summarized it for us: **Just do it**. Once you start doing things that move you in the direction of your goals, the doors of resources, strategies and ideas will open up to help you achieve those goals. No matter how focused you are on your goals, it is your action that brings results. Act. Start now.

Considerations: Start your most important task first. Oprah Winfrey, Bill Gates, Mary Kay Ashe and, Bishop T.D. Jakes did not acquire success by magic. No. They stepped forward to pursue their goals. They started. And the rest of their acts continue to fill our history books daily. Don't just take a walk in the woods, *start to hunt*.

6. H = <u>Hang On</u>
Shift happens. But, no matter what change happens, you need to hang on. Doing the everyday job of committing to plan, negotiate and start may become tiring, but you will become proficient to do that everyday job. Persist. To accomplish your goals, do not fall into 'if only' traps. No! In spite of the shift, hang on and focus long enough to realize your dreams.

Considerations: Continue to itemize and keep breaking down tasks into little steps. Write that email. Clean out that drawer. Make that call. Cultivate stick-to-it-ive-ness.

7. I = <u>Irrigate</u>
Statistics from the Food and Agricultural Organization show that irrigation water has enhanced food security and raised the quality of life in many impoverished developing countries. Without irrigation, food shortages and mass starvation would be commonplace. Just as food crops need to be irrigated, so too your body, paradigms and goals. When you nourish and take care of your body you are better able to think clearly and achieve success. This in turn improves your standard of living. When you are constantly 'watered' by positive people and your mind by positive thoughts you begin to believe that you can be, do and have everything that was designed for you. Irrigation intensifies your confidence and this leverages your capabilities in achieving your goals.

Considerations: Engage in positive self-talk. Celebrate both small and big accomplishments. Keep a little book of the successes you have achieved and revisit it periodically to boost your self-confidence. You deserve it.

8. T = Track It

According to Darren Hardy, "Winners are trackers." Tracking your advancement, no matter how small, makes you accountable and helps you accomplish your goals. It is the little things that count and separate the ordinary from the extraordinary. Tracking your goals, time, energy and money helps you to understand why you succeeded or failed, and this information sharpens your decision-making. Successful people stay on track, but they also recognize when it is the wrong door and then make an executive decision about it.

Considerations: Reassess your goal folders weekly to track your progress. What is working? What is not working? What actions do you need to take? Have you used all your keys?

Using these keys positions you in the strongholds to achieve any goal.

Now, go FINISH IT!!!!

About Donna

An "Above and Beyond" award-winning Pastor and also referred to as "The Empowerment Conduit" by colleagues, Donna Darlington is known for her service to God and to others. Inspiring Speakers Bureau-represented speaker, author, former teacher, and entrepreneur, Donna is the founder and president of It Is Possible International®, a firm which trains individuals and organizations, to tap into their greatness and realize their highest potential. Donna is also the founder and president of His Virtuous Intentionally Empowered Women International® (His V.I.E.W. Int'l®), an establishment which equips and builds women to be, do and fulfill their life's supreme purpose.

Donna is a CTA Certified Coach. She is an international keynote speaker at health seminars where she inspires audiences and also addresses attendees on the mechanisms and treatment of neurodegenerative diseases such as Alzheimer's disease. Donna writes across many genres. Her work has appeared in publications of the Brooklyn Tabernacle Church, the *Trinidad Junior Express* (Trinidad, W.I.), *The Collegian, The National Library of Poetry, Sparrowgrass Poetry Forum,* and *The Poetry Guild*. Donna has also published articles in medical journals. Donna has been interviewed by Curley and Pynn-The Strategic Firm and, as a consequence, has been pictured in the *florida.HIGH.TECH* 2012 magazine. She has also been featured on Radio Isaac 98.1 FM (Trinidad, W.I.). Donna is a member of the Christian Medical and Dental Association, the Golden Key International Honour Society, and Toastmasters International, and has earned honors in tertiary level degrees. She is the author of the soon to be released book, *Suddenly Significant®*. Donna may be contacted at Donna@ItIsPossible.com.

CHAPTER 4

Six Steps To Building A Winning Team

By Jeff Bonham

The year: 1992. The setting: Barcelona. Who? The Dream Team. Arguably the absolute *greatest* basketball team ever assembled. Michael Jordan, Scottie Pippen, John Stockton, Karl Malone, Magic Johnson, Larry Bird, Patrick Ewing, Chris Mullin, David Robinson, Christian Laettner, Clyde Drexler and Charles Barkley. At the Olympics, opposing teams were blown out of the water by the superior skills of the Americans, losing by an average of 43.8 points per game. The team is one of only eight in the Basketball Hall of Fame.

It's obvious what this has to do with Winning Big, but what does it have to do with taking your life to the next level? The most common challenge I see coaching real estate agents is seen in any business that starts with just one person: the greatest obstacle is not product knowledge or an ability to generate leads and convert those leads into customers. The greatest challenge is learning the skills necessary to take their career from a successful individual producer and turn it into a business that provides a stream of predictable income whether they are personally engaged in it daily or not. Most professionals I work with are already great at branding themselves or their product; they are great at generating leads and converting those leads into customers; they are great at closing transactions. As a result, most of these professionals have a great income, but they don't have enough hours in the day to handle all the business that comes their way; they tend to lose their life balance attempting to keep up with servicing the business.

If you are great at generating and converting leads, it's virtually impossible to keep up by yourself and have a personal life. Isn't that what it's really all about? At the end of the day, the only reason for earning more money should be to fund our life mission. Money in and of itself is worthless; it's what money can do for us and our families that makes having more of it desirable. I've seen too many peers who have been so focused on their earnings that they have lost the most valuable things in their life: the people they love. As a result of having watched so many people around me wind up with nothing but a bank account, I have become determined to help them discover a path that provides both financial independence and the time to enjoy life.

Below you will find my 6 Steps to Building a Winning Team:

1. ADMIT YOU HAVE A PROBLEM

So at some point in your career, after mastering selling opportunities, you must evolve into the next stage of business development: hone your management skills, and master the art of attracting and retaining incredibly talented people. That is a big, hairy spider for many people, and they are, quite frankly, afraid of taking the leap into hiring. Here's the thing—if you want to gain freedom in your life and win big, the only way it will happen is if you create a business model built on a foundation of duplicatable, delegatable systems run by people perfect for their individual team roles. Back to the basketball analogy, it does no good for the coach to design amazing plays if he has no one to execute them. He needs to know how many players he needs. He needs to know how to recruit and train players, and how to hold the players accountable for desired outcomes.

Often times we are so caught up in our own egos that we honestly believe our clients will not be willing to work with anyone else. Seriously? Are you that special that you can't be replaced? Here's the good and the bad news: people don't choose to do business with you because you are the only person in the world that does what you do or because of your amazing charm, wit, and intellect. The reason people do business with you is because you have been able to meet their particular need in such a fashion that they enjoyed the experience. It's not about you; it's about the standards you represent. Can your Standards be replicated? Absolutely. Do you have a specific way you generate your business:

Specific marketing techniques, scripts, and ways you follow up with clients? I bet you do. Even if you are not 100% conscious of the way you do it, you will find you probably have 3-4 main sources of generating business in your life, favorite phrases you use to close the transaction, and ways you respond to the most common objections your hear. Again, can this be duplicated? Can you teach someone to market the same way you market or respond to clients' concerns the way you respond? Absolutely.

Remember, it's not about you; it's about the standards you set, the ability to deliver a predictable experience over and over. Your delivery allows people to trust you, to believe that if they send someone your way that you will handle the referral with the same care as you did when they worked with you. Your ability to duplicate this approach will allow you to win big thereby gaining freedom. Having mastered the basics of generating sales in your business, your focus now needs to shift to leveraging yourself to sell more.

2. DESIGN YOUR PERFECT WORLD

Where to start? The first thing to do is to figure out what your perfect organization would resemble. In real estate sales, there are two main areas of your business: the sales division and the support staff. One drives the sales while the other handles the follow up—including the minute details that most sales people abhor. As an individual producer, you handle all sides of the transaction. What I typically see happen is: (1) the sales person starts filling up his pipeline with orders then must slow down handling the proper paperwork to service the customer. This means they go into servicing-their-customer mode thus not creating as many sales. This results in the roller coaster sales cycle causing their income to do the same; (2) the sales person creates so many leads staying in selling mode he neglects paperwork and issues arise because service was not delivered. Eventually, customers get angry and do not repeat or refer business anymore. Either of these modes can result in serious burnout and/or seriously limit your income potential.

Therefore, to go to bigger levels in your life and your business, you need to look at all the possible divisions in your business and figure out what the perfect organizational chart will look like someday if you waved a magic wand. Would you have salespeople who focus only on specific niches? In real estate sales, you may have sales people on your team who focus only on working with buyers while others focus only on working with sellers. You may have some that specialize in working with investors or only with banks or institutional sellers. If you had the perfect amount of sales being driven to create the ultimate income you want with time off, what support staff would you have? Would you have someone focus solely on the transaction after you consummate the sale making sure proper compliance is done? What about someone to manage your customer database or do all of your marketing like clockwork? When you can begin to visualize your business in this fashion, all you need to do now is start attracting the right people to fill those roles, create an environment that allows them to thrive so they will stay with you long term, and provide them with the right tools to do their job at the highest level possible. Does this seem easy to you or does it seem overwhelming? The good news is people have lived before you and can provide you the guidance you need. Visit my website for The Real Estate Masters Institute (www.theremi.com), view a sample organizational chart for the real estate business. This is a chart that can be emulated in many service-based businesses.

3. PERFORM CPR

The next decision you need to make is who to hire first. This is an interesting question. Do you make more money selling your product or by doing data entry after you sell. Right! You make more money by generating the sale. One might think the first thing he needs to do is hire another sales person. More sales equals more money. Even though that may seem logical, the challenge with taking this approach is that even though you may be generating more sales you have simultaneously created two side effects: 1) more transactions and customers that aren't being serviced properly and 2) you have just created a position that is incredibly expensive to your business. Most sales people are commission based; they love it because they know the more they sell the more money they make. Perfect! Except for you. No matter how you skin it, you will eventually have to hire proper support staff to handle the customer service side, which drives repeat, and referral business. Also, you're going to have to have someone to handle transactions and the compliance side of your business. Therefore, the answer to the question of who to hire first is support staff.

Look at it this way, if you didn't have to worry about any of the details, could you do more deals every year? Heck, yeah! When do you make your money? You make your money generating the business negotiating the sale. The cost of support staff is going to be much lower than hiring a commissioned sales person. Depending on your market area, you can find someone who will be great providing support costing between $15-20/hr, which is nothing compared to your potential sales. The key is to find the *right* person. When you are generating so much business you feel like you're about to die from work overload, you need to perform CPR for the sake of yourself and your business. CPR means, in this case, creating a Candidate Profile Report ASAP. Figure out who you need – what technical skills they will need; what are their personality traits (upbeat, energetic, or calming and detail oriented); how many years experience do they have? Again, view some sample CPRs by visiting: www.TheREMI.com   for both sales people and support staff traits.

4. RECRUIT YOUR DREAM TEAM

Now that you know what positions you need to fill and have a candidate profile, the next step is to find the people to fill those roles. This is not an area that should be done in times of high stress and urgency; you are more likely to compromise your standards out of desperation. This is a process that takes time and multiple states. When done right, this approach will increase your money in multiples buying back an immense amount of your own time. The people you bring on your team are a direct reflection of you. Everything they do will have your name attached. If they don't deliver at a high level to your clients and colleagues, then you will be judged by their results. This is not a step where you can apply the "fog-a-mirror" principle that so many use…meaning if you're within three feet of me, can spell your own name, and can fog a mirror then I'll make you my assistant. The good news is that today is a relatively soft job market. There are many people with amazing skills caught in the downsizing of our economy. Choose wisely. We recommend a specific hiring process to our clients that help them make the right decision when interviewing candidates and making offers; first, you have to have candidates. You should be running ads on classified websites, working with a recruitment firm, letting everyone in your database know what you need. Remember, when the right person comes along, pay well. A bad hire will cost you six figures; a good hire will make you an additional six figures.

5. DEVELOP YOUR PLAYERS

Steps four and five are usually the two steps where sales people struggle when building a team. They tend to make a hire and say, "Here's your desk, here's your phone, good luck." A proper transition to help a new team member become self-sufficient and empowered will take about 90 days of consistent training activities. DO NOT read into this that you will not be selling for 90 days. DO READ into that that you need to have a solid plan in place that educates your new hire on your standards, tools, and processes. Then, once they've mastered that, they should have the ability to work your systems and free you to do what you're best at doing.

6. DON'T LOSE YOUR PLAYERS TO FREE AGENCY

You've built a great team, you're knocking it out of the park, and all seems well in your world. Bang! One of your star players says they're leaving the team for a better offer. This can throw you into an emotional tailspin and set you back dramatically if you aren't prepared for that scenario. Also, it will make you wonder what you could have done differently to keep them. The interesting thing is very rarely does someone make a move strictly because of better compensation. Usually, it is because someone else has made them feel more important and more valuable than you have. If you build a great culture that focuses on helping them meet their life goals and truly commit to caring about helping them achieve their dreams, no one will be able to take them from you.

At least once per year evaluate where they are personally and professionally; find out what their top goals are for their life this year. Provide them the tools they need to achieve those goals. Do they want to lose weight? Help them set up meetings with a nutritionist and a personal trainer. Do they want to pay off their debts? Set them up with a credit counselor and financial planner. You build trust and loyalty helping people reach their goals; in return, they will be committed to helping you reach yours.

For more in-depth information on our 6 steps to building a winning team, visit www.TheRemi.com.

About Jeff

Jeff Bonham began his Real Estate career in 1996. He discovered there has to be a better way to succeed than traditional real estate broker methods and became a student of Leadership and Business Development. He joined Keller Williams Realty in 1998. In 2000, Jeff opened The Bonham Group. After three years of successfully operating his brokerage, he realized his business reached a plateau; it was time to find a coach to break through this ceiling. He then had the good fortune to rejoin Keller Williams as a franchise owner/broker in Springfield, Missouri.

Jeff is now a partner in multiple Keller Williams Realty franchises, including Keller Williams Realty Greater Springfield, Keller Williams Realty North Mississippi, and Keller Williams Realty Coral Gables-Coconut Grove. He has played an integral role in opening KW offices in Miami Beach, FL, Syracuse, NY and Albany, NY. Jeff has also served in the role of CEO of The Jackie Ellis Team in Boynton Beach, FL, a team recently recognized by The Wall Street Journal as being among the top 200 of all Realtor Teams in North America. Since joining Keller Williams in 2003 he has recruited over 450 agents and trained thousands focusing on helping them fulfill their life mission. He has received Keller Williams Realty International's Team Leader "Black Belt" Award and is an Approved Trainer for Keller Williams University, an honor held by fewer than 150 associates of the 78,000+ associates in Keller Williams Realty International.

Jeff has discovered it takes a third party with an objective perspective to analyze the gaps in your business structure, what systems to implement, how to hold your money accountable to driving results, database management, direct response marketing, and Team Building, so that you may transition from individual producer into someone who owns a business that provides income – whether you show up every day or not. This is why he founded The Real Estate Masters Institute, a coaching company dedicated to helping top producers develop their business to such a high level they are able to live a balanced life and focus on fulfilling their personal life mission. He offers one-on-one coaching for agents and one or two day seminars on a variety of topics designed to give you action plans for immediate implementation and significant results.

You may visit The Real Estate Masters Institute online at: www.TheREMI.com. For coaching, consulting, or speaking engagements, you may contact Jeff via email: jeff@theremi.com

Testimonials

Jeff Bonham has taught several classes for our Market Center. He is well versed... and has excellent presentation skills. He is able to deliver material in a clear, concise manner and paces classes well for the skill level of students. His style is engaging, interactive and fun. We always pack classes when Jeff is teaching; he's a great teacher! – Marc Weiss, Owner/Broker, Keller Williams Capital District, Regional Director Keller Williams Upstate NY Region

CHAPTER 5

Put Clients First

By Edward Biernat

"So, how can I save <u>my</u> clients millions of dollars?"

I met an old friend, Jim Bennet, in the waiting area at Charles De Gaulle airport in Paris. He was on his way to a new client and I had just finished a successful engagement in Africa.

"So let me get this straight," Jim replied after I told him a little bit about the project. "In a few short months you established a strong management steering team, engaged the workforce through projects and saved the client nearly $3 million. And you accomplished all of this in a foreign culture and in spite of language issues. So, how can I save my clients millions of dollars?"

"The process is pretty straightforward and can be summed up in one phrase – **Put Clients First**," was my reply. "We abbreviate it to three letters – **PCF**. Each letter has a framework around it that we use in all of our deployments."

P – Prepare for a successful outcome well in advance

C – Communicate in a way that brings out the best in every conversation

F – Forthright and honest in everything

Our company has used these three concepts around the world in a variety of businesses that include heavy manufacturing, healthcare, banking and government. **PCF** acts like an accelerator for the change effort, solidifying the improvement for maximum sustainability. That impact alone excites most clients. **PCF** not only works for consultants like us, but several clients have used it in their entire organizations to dramatically impact their continuous improvement cultures.

Since we have focused on this approach:

- The results for the client have increased dramatically, at times doubling the expected outcomes.

- Key changes are sustained both during and after the end of the engagement. (We measure this through metrics and client surveys or follow up calls.)

- The engagements flow much smoother with noticeably less friction between the key parties.

- Our referral business from clients recommending us to other clients is up significantly as well.

I pulled up a screen on my iPad that had an article I was reviewing. "I asked one of our team to write a paper on the PCF framework, and I was reviewing her draft. Let me know what you think," I said as I handed it to him to read.

THE 1ST PRINCIPLE: (P) – PREPARE FOR A SUCCESSFUL OUTCOME WELL IN ADVANCE

This is an important step, because it sets our mental framework for success.

1. We are prepared. If something comes up, we can adapt and change, but we have spent time thinking about exactly what we want from the change effort.

2. Focus on the successful outcome. While you might need to look at contingency plans and other tools to minimize risks, a key to a successful change-effort is to focus on success the majority of the time. (That is success as defined by the client.) And focusing on successful outcomes generates the energy that we will need in the process.

3. And we do this from the first meeting with the client to scope the project through project completion.

Here are a few key points regarding the first principle.

Define the change methodology you will use.

- There are many proven change methodologies out there – pick one that resonates with you and your specific circumstances. For complex change efforts, some organizations use Lean (derived from the Toyota Production System), Six Sigma (popularized by Jack Welch and General Electric Corporation) or a similar methodology in which they have expertise. For simple processes, we follow a 5-step model:

  1. Select the process we want to change.

  2. Understand the current state of the process

  3. Generate a 'picture' of what the optimum process could look like

  4. Compare the two and generate an improvement plan

  5. Implement the plan and track results

Identify the key people that are affected by the process and understand what they need.

There are people associated with every process. Write down who they are (we call them stakeholders) and what they want out of the process.

Here are a few questions to help identify stakeholders:

- Who owns the process? (Who will be responsible for maintaining the new system?)

- Who works intimately in or with the process?

- Who monitors or reports on the process or its outputs?

- Who is affected by the process? (This group is often neglected, but is critical for long-term success.)

For team-based change, we recommend selecting team members from several of these stakeholder groups. The new process that they develop will not only have fewer problems, but also have their buy in.

Build a model of each stakeholder group

Consider making a composite model of each stakeholder group. This model, often called an avatar, has as much detail as can be generated and is then personified with a name and even a face.

EXAMPLE: Management is often a key stakeholder for change. We can construct an avatar named Benson that has among his attributes:

- *Needs to see bottomline-results*

- *Talks accounting terms (payback, ROI, etc.)*

- *Averse to significant negative feedback from his group regarding the change*

- *Wants to be perceived well by his peers and superiors*

- *Etc.*

Then, as alternatives or processes are developed, the team can ask how they think each avatar would react to the change, how to best communicate the changes to them, how involved do they need to be in the change, etc. This gives a personal feel to what is sometimes an amorphous group.

THE 2ND PRINCIPLE: (C) – COMMUNICATE IN A WAY THAT BRINGS OUT THE BEST IN EVERY CONVERSATION

One of the most common complaints from employees is that the company doesn't communicate enough, yet most managers would say they communicate a great deal. While this is annoying and problematic in a stable environment, it becomes crippling in an environment of ever-increasing change.

Change the dialogue to focus on what is working, not always on the problems.

- Something has to be getting done right in order for the organization to still be around and to still have clients.

  o Problems often follow the 80/20 Rule: they make up less than 20% of the output of a given process (often much, much less), but take up 80% of the organization's focus.

o So 80% or more of what organizations produce are totally correct. The best question we can ask isn't "What's wrong?" but instead "How can we increase the percentage of things that are going right?"

- Recent studies in neuroscience indicate that negative thoughts tend to shut down our ability to think things through (we go to a fight-or-flight response), while positive thoughts actually stimulate the portions of the brain that we use to creatively improve processes. To be very responsive to change, organizations need to be able to creatively improve processes, which is best done in a positive environment.

Ask better questions

To a third party observer, questions in most companies are phrased more like we are searching for the guilty than trying to improve. "Who is responsible for this?" "What went wrong?" "Why did it fail?" All of these start moving the mind away from creativity and towards defensiveness and survival. These types of questions, called Negative Inquiry, do have their place and are effective when:

- There is real danger

- Immediate actions are necessary

- And we are in a command and control mode ("I tell, you do")

An often unintended outcome from Negative Inquiry is that, when a person is in that mode of operation, it is hard for them to think things through, to have creative thoughts. And they tend to compound their errors.

An alternative is a framework called *Appreciative Inquiry*. Appreciative Inquiry was founded by John David Cooperrider of Case Western Reserve University and is built around looking for what is working in an organization instead of focusing on what is not. For example, many organizations conduct regular customer satisfaction surveys. If a typical organization found that 96% of the customers were satisfied, many would immediately look at the 4% that were not and try to find out why. Appreciative Inquiry would suggest that you approach the 96% and find out what you did that made them satisfied, then try to do more of it.

While there are a variety of research papers on the topic, here are a few key points for consideration:

- Appreciative Inquiry is not a Pollyanna approach to life. Issues are dealt with from the point of view of what is working, but they are still addressed.

- Every organization has assumptions regarding how the group acts, and these assumptions set the framework for accepted behaviors. These assumptions are often not visible to the members of the organization because "that's just the way we are." Assumptions can be identified and, if they no longer serve the organization, modified or discarded.

- In every organization or group:

  o Something works.

  o We get more of what we focus on.

  o If we focus on what is working, we get to have more of what is working.

- Language has an impact on how we perceive reality; if we change how we talk and what we talk about, we can have an impact on our perceived reality.

A major component of Appreciative Inquiry, as the name implies, is how to ask questions.

- Rephrase questions to get at what is working.

  o What is the best performance we ever received from this process?

- Tie into emotion

  o When things worked great, how did that make you feel?

- Look for how to do more

  o What made that outstanding performance possible?

- From this dialogue, develop statements of what the new reality will look like o These are called Provocative Propositions, and are different from other visioning methods because these are based on something that really happened, not something imagined.

Celebrate Successes

Celebrating success, on the other hand, seems a natural outgrowth of business, but in sad reality it is not. Perhaps it is because we are so intent to get to the next problem. Companies, groups and individuals seldom stop to say "Thank You" and recognize accomplishment.

- Plan for the celebrations. The first principle sets up the process for success, so add in where and how milestones or completions will be acknowledged.

- Tie the celebration to success. The success doesn't have to wait until the end of the project. Completing a difficult audit or presenting the draft plan to management can be used as an incremental success worthy of celebration.

- Keep the celebrations consistent. One client gave out nice jackets for one team and, later, inexpensive tee shirts to later teams. This devalued the later teams' contributions.

- Money is not the only motivator. Something as simple as management or leaders saying a heartfelt thank you and citing what the person or team accomplished is very motivating to most people. *Think out of the box.*

THE 3RD PRINCIPLE: (F) – BE FORTHRIGHT AND HONEST IN EVERYTHING

The Merriam-Webster dictionary defines forthright as "free from ambiguity or evasiveness: going straight to the point." Being forthright and open makes the rest of the process work and cements trust and confidence in the process and the individual.

Forthrightness also means reporting the good with the bad. Errors, missteps and mistakes need to be shared as openly as successes, but slightly differently. While it may be acceptable to point out the contribution by individuals and groups when celebrating, the process should be the focus of the failure unless there is a clear person responsible. The best thing to do then is for that person to take responsibility, make the necessary corrections and move on. No change effort is ever perfect.

Understand the key behaviors and model them

It is important to identify the key behaviors that need to be modeled in the new process. If you are working to streamline meetings, for example, having everyone in the room prior to the start of the meeting might be a key behavior. But if the person leading the initiative is always late, this disconnect from stated expectations has an immediate negative impact on both the leader and the change initiative as a whole. So select the key behaviors and model them from the first meeting until the project concludes.

Encourage an environment of forthrightness through open feedback

The term 'feedback' has taken on a negative connotation because individuals sometimes use it to hurt or demean others. But, if we are to have people really change their behavior, we all must be open to feedback so that we can course correct and improve outcomes.

Here are a few keys on how to set up an environment for giving and receiving feedback.

- Focus on the behavior, not the outcome.

- Forget the 'sandwich' approach. (Tell them something good, then tell them the thing that needs to change, then tell them something good.) Once people figure out the pattern, they ignore the positives and brace for the negative.

- Be tangible and specific. 'Always' and 'never' should be avoided in giving feedback. Be specific, and make sure it is something that indeed can be changed.

- Don't limit it to improvement only. Tell people what they did well.

- And when you receive feedback, realize that it is from that person's point of view. If it is valid, accept it. If not, ignore it. However, if the same feedback comes from different sources or repeats over time, it is probably valid.

Jim looked from the screen. "There are some great points here that I can apply with my next client," he said.

"What are you planning to apply?" I asked.

"Well, we always plan for success, but we don't always spend enough time identifying the key stakeholders and making sure we meet their needs. And, regarding communication, I like the Appreciative Inquiry toolset. I will be rewriting some of my presentation to probe for what is working and build for more of it. And finally, I can see specific areas that I can be more forthright, especially when it comes to modeling critical behaviors. I will be thinking about what I know of this client and start to develop an avatar of how a successful manager would act in the improved process and how I could begin to model them from the first meeting."

"Thanks for sharing this with me. Any chance I can have this so that I can share it with the rest of my company?"

I thought about it for a minute. "I'll make a deal with you." I replied. "Try out those ideas that you really liked. Let me know your results, and I'll be glad to send it out to you."

The announcement system had just announced Jim's flight. We both stood up and he shook my hand. "It's a deal," he said. And as he strolled toward the gate, I heard him say to himself, "And I think these are some of the keys I have been looking for."

About Edward

Edward Biernat is the founding partner of Consulting With Impact, Ltd., a consulting firm with an international client base specializing in implementing sustainable improvement systems. A former Navy nuclear power officer, he held a number of management and corporate positions including Vice President of Corporate Quality prior to founding Consulting With Impact, Ltd. in 1998. Consulting With Impact has helped more than 100 clients change their business and achieve measurable returns on their consulting investments, often at a 10:1 return ratio. Edward's clients include companies on Fortune's 125 list as well as many small to mid-sized companies seeking rapid, lasting change. He has implemented transformations for companies in India, Africa, China, Southeast Asia, and numerous locations in North America – in a variety of industries.

A major tenet of Edward's change process is that 'change happens at the individual level.' His proven approach combines established improvement methodologies with the latest research in neuroscience and organizational development, building a behavioral model that reinforces and locks-in the enhanced process. Once the key behaviors are identified from the model, they can be reinforced through coaching and feedback to assist the individual through their personal change process. "Lasting change happens with people, not to people."

To enable the reader to receive the greatest benefit from the content in this chapter, Edward is making available additional resources for downloading at his corporate site: www.consultingwithimpact.com/briantracybook. Edward is available for one-on-one executive coaching and corporate speaking engagements. If you or your organization would like to work with him directly, please refer to his personal website: www.edwardbiernat.com.

CHAPTER 6

This Ain't Your Father's Retirement

By Peter J. D'Arruda

"The boomers' biggest impact will be on eliminating the term 'retirement' and inventing a new stage of life...the new career arc."
~Rosabeth Moss Kanter

I remember picking up a copy of USA Today a couple of years ago and seeing the headline: **"First of 77 Million Baby Boomers Coming of Age"** and wondering exactly what that meant. Upon reading the article, I was to learn that by "Coming of Age", the writer meant that the generation that was nicknamed "the baby boom generation" because of a spike in the birth rate following World War II, was now – can you believe it—turning 65. Yep, the generation that invented rock and roll, grew up on black and white television and fought the Vietnam War… the generation that watched Howdy Doody and gave us Woodstock… the generation that put a man on the moon and saw both the beginning and the end of the Cold War…was now ready to retire. And, statistically anyway, they were doing it in the same manner with which they entered the world—with a boom. How would the country adjust to one-fourth of its population stopping work and lining up for Medicare and Social Security?

Officially, to be a baby boomer, you have to have been born between 1944 and 1964. On January 1, 2011, the very first baby boomer turned 65. For the next 18 years baby boomers would be turning 65 at the rate of 8,000 per day. Let's face it. As this unique bunch gets older, they will likely transform the institutions of aging dramatically, perhaps even redefining what retirement means forever. After all, they have done that to just about every other aspect of American life.

Some who have been looking forward to retirement and now find themselves at its doorstep have that 'deer in the headlights' look, as if to say, "What do I do now?"

Growing up in Laurinburg, North Carolina, I was a Boy Scout. The Boy Scout motto is, "Be Prepared." Some added the words, "and not surprised!" to the motto. That has always stuck with me. As a financial advisor now, it is my job to keep my ear to the ground, as it were, when it comes to matters of financial preparedness. In my work as the host of a nationally syndicated talk show that deals entirely with financial matters, I take questions and have on-the-air conversations with literally thousands of people each year. What I hear sometimes frightens me. Many of the burgeoning horde of seniors in the stampede toward the green meadows of retirement are in line for a harsh dose of reality and some are totally unprepared for the shock. Exactly how it will affect the economy is hard to say. Will the country's healthcare and Social Security systems survive the strain? That remains to be seen. One thing is for sure: these boomers, as a societal class, are wealthier and healthier than any generation before, and statistically, as a group, they can look forward to an active old age.

LONGEVITY

Just what is the life expectancy of the baby boomers? Well, life expectancy works in a strange way. Every year you live extends your life expectancy a little further. I suppose the people who analyze this say, "Well, if you've made it this far, you must be made of better stuff than we thought...so we will tack on a few more years." I like the way one octogenarian put it when asked his age: "At the rate I'm going, I'll be 100 before long." The life expectancy of a person who makes it to 65 is 83.6 years. That's an average. It's a bit lower for men and a bit higher for women. Life expectancy gets even better at age 75. If you make it to age 75, then life expectancy becomes 86.5 for men and 87.5 for women.

WEALTH

For wealth, the outlook is not as good as the health picture. It is true that boomers are wealthier than their parents, but inflation has driven up both prices and wages dramatically on their watch. Real median household income is 35 to 53 percent higher (depending on their age) than in their parents' generation. And 27 percent of baby boomers have four or more years of college, making this the most highly educated generation in U.S. history. On the whole, however, baby boomers do not feel that they have saved enough money to cover the costs of retirement for the longevity they hope to enjoy. If retirement starts at age 65, and your nest egg must last another 18.6 years, then as Odyssey said to Houston in the movie Apollo 13, "We have a problem here."

What are boomers looking to for support during retirement? Defined benefit pensions have almost become extinct, and 401(k) plans, which could do no wrong in the heady 1990s, went backwards in the 2000s. Home values took a substantial hit when the housing bubble burst. Adding to the uncertainty are higher energy costs, higher health care costs and the recession that began in 2008 and is still going on at this writing. Baby boomers were raised in affluent times and imbued with high expectations. The first crop of this wave of retirees, however, now faces the ironic prospect of living longer but more crimped lives.

GLOOM MEETS BOOM

According to a USA Today/Gallup Poll taken in early 2012, two-thirds of baby boomers say they are less optimistic about retirement than they were 10 years ago. The Insured Retirement Institute recently surveyed a cross-section of individuals from 50 to 66 years of age, and found that only 40% of them were confident of having enough to cover basic expenses in retirement. Sixty percent believed that their retirement security would be worse than that of their parents. Even the pollsters were surprised at how much the pendulum of public opinion within this group had swung toward the negative in just 10 years. One ray of sunshine in the gloom—74% said that their retirement picture would get no worse, and would probably improve.

When asked from what source their retirement income would come, most of this sampling of boomers, 46%, said 401(k)s, 403(b)s and similar defined contribution plans. Only 37% listed traditional pension programs as their main source of income during retirement. The older the boomers get, the more these programs drop off.

The 2008 market downturn took a toll on wealth; inheritances on average won't be as big and many shop-till-you-drop boomers simply haven't saved enough money to last through their retirement.

Apparently, some of the baby boom generation are the embodiment of the attitude espoused by that dubious spokesman of their youth, Alfred E. Neuman of Mad Magazine – "What, me worry?" According to Annamaria Lusardi, Economics professor at the George Washington University School of Business, there exists a general lack of financial literacy and planning among "a sizable group of the population that has not even thought about retirement." She points out that many people see retirement as a distant stage – even if it's only five years away.

With all that in the wind, it's not surprising that a significant number of those polled said that they expect to postpone retirement past age 65. Does that mean that the old 30-something gang will still be showing up for work at 70-something? So it appears, if they hope to enjoy a retirement that enables them to continue the lifestyle to which many of them have become accustomed. It is a fact that more and more boomers are either working or beginning a second career after "retirement age."

One thing is for sure – seniors in the music industry aren't retiring. The Rolling Stones are still together at an average age of 65. Check out this list of "mature" citizens from the top ten grossing music concert tours for 2010:

- Bon Jovi (age 48), #1 music tour with $201 million worldwide

- AC/DC (lead singer Brian Johnson, age 63) #2 (tied) music tour with $177 million worldwide

- Roger Waters (age 67), #2 (tied) music tour with $90 million worldwide from a mid-year start

- Dave Matthews Band (Dave Matthews, age 43) #4 music tour with $72.9 million

- The Eagles (singer Glenn Frey, age 62) #6 music tour with $64.5 million

- Paul McCartney (age 68) #7 music tour with $61.8 million

- James Taylor (age 62): #8 music tour with $50.7 million

Hey, it looks like old age is cool…and profitable!

WANTS VERSUS NEEDS

The media bombards us daily with things that are attractive and appealing. Advertising moguls are paid millions to find new ways of making us want the things they dangle before us. Credit cards make them easy to purchase. It is no wonder that some think there is a giant conspiracy out there, the purpose of which is to prevent anyone from saving anything! I know my mother would see it that way. "It's a game," she used to say. "And it goes like this. You have money in your pocket, and everyone around you is trying to get it out."

Those words still come back to me every time I leave a Best Buy store with some new gadget that I felt sure I could not live another day without. I get that little tingle of conscience they call "buyer's remorse."

DEBT VERSUS SAVINGS

America these days is addicted to credit the way drug addicts are hooked on narcotics. The actual number is hard to nail down, but one source recently stated that the United States owes more than $2.5 trillion in consumer debt. Even if it is off a billion or two, that's a lot! How much is a trillion?

- Our standard nine-digit calculator can't display it. It's a one followed by 12 zeros.

- A trillion one-dollar bills, laid end to end, would reach the sun.

- A trillion dollars amounts to $3,333 for each of America's 300,000,000 people.

David Schwartz, a children's book author, says in his book *How Much Is a Million?*, "One million seconds comes out to be about 11½ days. A billion seconds is 32 years. And a trillion seconds is 32,000 years."

With that in mind, here are a couple of staggering statistics. As of this writing, the United States federal **deficit** stands at $1.7 trillion. The national **debt** stands at over $15 trillion. The debt is incurred when the government spends more than it takes in. It is the debt that creates the operating deficit that resets annually. These deficits are paid for by the government selling interest-bearing Treasury securities.

This is where you gulp and swallow hard. **If** the federal government were ever to **default** on its promise to pay periodic interest payments or to repay the debt at maturity, the economy would spin into chaos and collapse. It is the interest on the national debt that gives the shivers to those who track this and understand what it means.

That's why the question is often asked, "Will Medicare and Social Security be around when I retire?" The answer is "yes" if you retire before 2024. The answer is "maybe" if you retire after that. According to the trustees who report on those programs annually, Medicare's trust fund will run dry by 2024, and the Social Security will hit that same dry gulch in 2033. We say "maybe" those programs will still be here because steps will probably be taken to preserve Medicare and Social Security. But it remains to be seen what form those measures will take, and how the face of Medicare and Social Security will change as a result.

SPARSE SAVINGS

According to the Employee Benefit Research Institute, about 60% of American workers say their household savings and investments total less than $25,000. According to the book, *The Narcissism Epidemic*, published in 2009, average credit card debt in the United States exceeds $11,000—triple what it was in 1990. That's just **credit card** debt and doesn't include what we owe on our houses, boats, and cars, etc.

How much are Americans saving for retirement? Not nearly enough. The average American worker spends 94% of disposable income. The EBRI's report breaks down by age group the retirement savings of America as follows:

• Under 35: $6,306

• 35 – 44: $22,460

• 45 – 54: $43,797

• 55 – 64: $69,127

• 65 – 75: $56,212

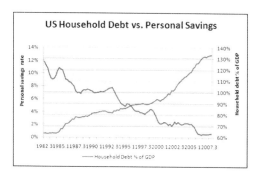

IT'S ALL A MATTER OF PRIORITIES

I do not recall ever going out to eat as a kid. Even after our belts were a little looser and we no longer ate government cheese, my father and mother were both too conscious of laying a foundation for our family's future to waste money on something so frivolous as ordering from a menu. To this day, regardless of my financial situation, my eyes still go to the right side of the menu first. I can't help it. It is a habit I learned from my frugal parents, who knew the value of a **dime**, let alone a dollar. Any surplus was to be used as a foundation for our future, not wasted.

Today, when I see young people eating out in a fancy restaurant, I can't help but wonder if they have taken care of the necessities of life first. If not, then they are eating on borrowed money that will eventually have to be paid back by someone. I don't mean to sound like the curmudgeon who resents seeing others' joy. It just makes me wonder if we are perhaps headed in the wrong direction as a people – a pampered society, not one of industry and thrift. Could it be that retracing our steps back to those taken by an earlier generation might be the best way to move forward to the rich lives we all envision for ourselves?

BABY STEP ONE: TAKE A LOOK AROUND

Yogi Berra is credited with saying, "You've got to be very careful if you don't know where you're going, because you might not get there." To get to a ridiculously reliable retirement income, you first must take stock of where you are. Understand the economic environment around you.

If you are young, start saving now, even if it hurts. Lose the movies and evenings out if you have to, but save at least 10% if not 20% of your income. A dollar saved today and invested properly will be worth five dollars when you need it for retirement. Your parents had more guarantees than you do. Learn this chant, "If it is to be, it's up to me," and say it every time you want to buy something you don't need. Credit card debt is your enemy, not your friend. Get rid of it ASAP. Get a life insurance policy now with a death benefit of at least five times your annual salary while the premiums are low.

If you are in your middle years, take full advantage of any tax deferred retirement plan at work. If your company has a 401(k) and they provide matching funds, contribute the maximum, even if it hurts. If you are self-employed, create your own IRA and pump as much as you can into it. Live within your means. Adjust your needs/wants priorities to provide a foundation for the future.

If you are approaching retirement, recognize that you must change gears from accumulation to preservation. Follow the rule of 100 when it comes to investing. Take your age, subtract it from 100, and that's the amount of money you should have at risk. The rest must be in an absolutely safe place. Take a look around. There are ways for you too to have a retirement income that is ridiculously reliable.

About Pete

Peter J. "Coach Pete" D'Arruda, a Registered Financial Consultant, Certified Financial Educator and Investment Advisor, is President and founding principal of Capital Financial Advisory Group, LLC. He is also the author of several personal finance books and hosts the nationally-syndicated radio program, *Financial Safari.*

Every week, the Financial Safari is broadcast on nearly 100 radio stations across the country. During the program, with the help of his co-hosts and first-rate guests, "Coach Pete" equips individuals with the knowledge they need to navigate through the financial world successfully. He helps many nationally with income planning and can be found online at: www.TheKingofIncome.com

During his career, Coach Pete has gained national attention for his financial insights and expertise. He has appeared on CNBC and Fox Business, and has been quoted in *The Wall Street Journal, Newsweek, AARP* and *Kiplinger's Retirement Report,* among many others.

CHAPTER 7

Employee Motivation

By Ralph Thompson

Zig Ziglar says, "If you can dream it, then you can achieve it. You will get all you want in life if you help enough other people get what they want." This can be done by giving to charities, but the most common and effective means to help others get what they want is by building businesses that employ these people and developing them so that they are able to achieve their dreams. Build a culture of success for the employees of your business, or under your supervision and your financial and career dreams will manifest before you. By establishing the proper progression policies at your site, you are able to increase production, efficiencies, increase morale, motivate your staff, and also ensure proper discipline is enacted.

In times where competitive advantage at the best value runs king, the fact that most managers do not look to their own personnel to gain market growth is a missed opportunity for success. By increasing efficiencies and production you are always able to increase your bottom line without increasing manpower expenses or additional equipment costs, if applicable to the job. Instilling your employees with the abilities to make minor decisions frees you to focus on bigger picture items while your employees are keeping a watchful eye over the day-to-day operations. By allowing your employees to gain the skills and knowledge to run more of the day-to-day operations frees you to focus on business growth, or spend more time with outside commitments or at your home.

How critical is it to discover your employees' goals or create goals for them? There is no lack of documentation that points to the power of having goals, and how the majority of people do not have goals in place for their development. To get your team to success and in turn achieve your own success, you must have a game plan for your employees.

Knowing your employees capabilities and knowledge base is critical in order to analyze your business and recognize windows of opportunity for profit increases and maintenance losses. More importantly, breaking down the key components of the different jobs forces you to really analyze all of the jobs and what is required. Bringing in experts also helps in this process as they can identify high return areas for improvement. Unfortunately, the reason the consultants make so much money is that they are able to identify areas for increased profitability but don't provide a process to fix it, except for an additional fee, and leave it up to you to create your own, or the company does not continue the practices recommended and the numbers go back down after the consultant leaves. Many attribute this to employees working harder while being watched and evaluated, so why not use this proven concept to increase your bottom line. Once a knowledge and skill-tracking process is established, you are able to get real time answers to concerns.

Money is always a great motivator, so by having a progression policy in place that is as objective as possible by incorporating a number of different areas for improvement. As employees know these criteria are what is in line for them to increase their earning potential, and you, as their employer will receive the benefits and profits of their best actions. Highly performing employees allow you to spend less on manpower; it increases productivity, improves better customer service, and generates a work environment that everyone wants to work in.

The five areas we will focus on for our progression policy is skills, knowledge, human resources, safety (or attention to detail), and supervision. Each area will be explained and some examples of the monetary differences these areas mean for a company.

1. SKILLS SETS

The secret is to sit down and identify all the skills required to do an assigned task. Once that is completed look for ways that these tasks can be measured. Most common can be times, line of code, average ticket size, but make sure your measurement tool is one that increases your bottom line, not just a measurement accepted by the industry.

In the mining, construction and military arena the dollars are astronomical, utilizing the proper braking procedures can save hundreds of thousands of dollars in maintenance costs not to mention preventing the cost of losing a life if the brake system fails due to improper use. I have visited many locations that put up 'band aid' solutions to help prevent the issue without truly addressing the issues behind the problem. In the meantime, their operators were scared to operate the equipment and extra manpower was spent trying to come up with a solution.

A mine site in Chile was experiencing a rapid amount of brake wear in their new trucks that they procured. Because these were new trucks, the site blamed the manufacturer and demanded money to replace the brake pads that were worth in excess of 25,000 dollars. But as is often the case, the damage was due to improper operator practices that were causing unnecessary brake wear; while proper use would have actually reduced the cost of brake repair as the new trucks braking systems were superior to their old trucks. Lack of training and knowledge of the new braking systems cost hundreds of thousands of hours in replacement costs and down time. How much is the cost of documenting skills worth now?

Checklists work for everyone—whether they are airline pilots, aircraft weapons loaders in the military, or cooks. A study presented in the Wall Street journal stated that hospitals could save millions and reduce deaths considerably just by having checklists. These checklists also work to determine what task skills your employees require, and how to evaluate your workers.

2. JOB KNOWLEDGE

To successfully make your employees able to make correct decisions they need knowledge applicable to their job, do they understand the processes, how the equipment works, and case studies of how people react under emergency situations? When things are on fire is not the time to teach your personnel about critical decisions.

The military is famous for this style of training. Not only do they require constant repetition of tasks to make sure the individual can perform the task under stress, but there is also a lot of background knowledge passed on to ensure personnel understand why certain tactics or maintenance practices are performed. Personnel in the military are trained to be able to fill in when either their leader or specialist goes down. What happens when one of your employees call in sick or quits?

In the military, personnel are trained to perform their jobs under high stress and to find innovative ways to overcome a problem – because not overcoming the problem can result in the cost of lives in the battlefield. Being unable to get an aircraft in the air due to a lack of tools and/or lack of trying could cost the lives of ground troops requesting their help. Finding solutions to problems is the product of training and increasing their knowledge of the systems and procedures.

3. HUMAN RESOURCES

During my deployment to Bagram, Afghanistan, we were the first F-16's to be deployed to the location. Of course, finding parts compatible were few and far between as the unit worked to get the aircraft up in the assigned times to support ground troops. The effects of training are evident in military operations as instead of complaining and refusing to do the jobs without the proper tools, maintenance personnel adapted and were able to get the aircraft airborne at the assigned time. Most of our jobs were not life and death, but the culture of workers becoming creative to solve tasks and get the mission completed. These are the opportunities that can bring your business to greatness.

Talent isn't the only attribute that is critical in employees, the Human Resources part is another contributing factor. It doesn't matter how talented an employee is, you don't get anything if they aren't there at work. It's also critical to monitor the workers who never take time off or work considerable overtime. By comparing skills vs. attendance you can play detective and analyze work if the operator's performance is affected. You can only solve the case if you have all of the clues.

An employee needs to be present to deliver the requirements your company needs, so the Human Resources and attendance are a key part of this progression policy. Many talented people receive higher pay though they always seem to be absent for various reasons. They still collect annual raises, maybe do well on testing, or they may be superstars but everyday they are not there, the "super star" isn't helping either of you succeed.

4. SAFETY & FOCUS

Safety is easy to document when there are mistakes but are you looking at your workers to see if they are truly being safe even though no safety instances have been recorded? A better phrase can be attention to detail if you're in an industry that may not be affected by loss time accidents. An accident often has the same symptoms as equipment damage, misspelled words in documents, incorrect entry data, or incorrect accounting. All are symptoms of not paying attention to their tasks and focusing on outside details. Are your employees focused to do the job?

The military is so concerned about this there is an assigned individual in each unit whose focus is to identify those who may have financial, family, or personal issues that may injure or endanger other service men. This responsibility often falls onto the supervisor, but if your supervisor does not have the tools to properly identify those employees who may have issues, either mentor the supervisor or find someone in your organization who can. It doesn't seem important until your cook, who is going through a messy divorce, spills hot oil on a server because he is not paying attention to what's going on around him and focusing on his job. It should only take one such accident to happen to make this a priority. Hopefully it becomes a priority prior.

Each accident tells a story, and after studying and documenting many organizations that used a strong knowledge and skills-tracking formula for their workers, the safety incident rate was almost nil. Was there a correlation with training operators to a high level so that they had no choice but to focus on their jobs? The same formula worked with cooks in showing efficiencies in getting food out quicker. You can't defy the physics of the stove to make the food to heat to the proper temperature quicker, but you can train your staff to have the plates ready, condiments for the menu item lined up, and cleaning areas up to allow a better work space and flow. All of these steps allowed my cooking staff to focus on their jobs, and a time to measure how well they were doing. If this works for aircraft maintenance, heavy equipment operators, and cooks, it can be adapted to all fields.

5. SUPERVISION

Supervision is your frontline tool to make sure your employees are achieving their best, but how much time have you spent doing reports that don't tell the whole story? You can measure tons of dirt and the expense of moving the dirt, but without knowledge of your operators, how can you decide if the maintenance increase this month is due to equipment failure or improper operating techniques? If it is due to improper techniques, is it deliberate or due to a lack of training? Your supervisors are the ones to provide you with this information, but if you are not making it a priority for your supervisor to look at your operators, these trends can run rampant.

Heavy equipment isn't the only field to which this applies, I own a restaurant and like all business owners, couldn't wait for the opportunity to find a good manager and spend more time with my family. What I found that was without a supervisor willing to enforce the standards and systems in place, the food quality decreased and in turn so did the service—as the servers knew the food quality wasn't good because the customers weren't tipping. In a matter of weeks, recipes were changed and the level of consistency dropped. Revenue dropped almost 50%!! The difficult part was deciding whether to punish the employees for deliberate mistakes or if it was due to a lack of training. With proper documentation of their training, it would have been easier to show where their skills were measured, and if they were tested competent, then it is much easier to instill the proper discipline. It only took a short time to get back on course, but what if I took a safari in Africa – that might have been the end of the business.

Self-improvement is one of the most important tasks you can do to help those around you, but you must also focus on improving those working for you. By coming up with clear requirements that are objective and fair to be accomplished before your employees can be promoted, you will have a highly motivated workforce with high morale. It takes some work in the beginning, but if it is maintained properly, it requires very little work to keep up and the reports are very telling on how to improve your business and deliver the success you are seeking.

About Ralph

Ralph Thompson has been the owner of several businesses in differing fields – include Heavy Equipment Training, Restaurants and Car Sales. He has also spent portions of his career in new product development engineering and has dedicated over 20 years in the Air Force Reserve Command where he has deployed in support of several operations, including the most recent deployment to Afghanistan. His successes during his career in the military have resulted in many decorations and honors primarily due to the high performance of his units.

The majority of his career in the civilian and military sectors has been in the development of personnel and preparing them for success in high stress fields that require working in dangerous conditions, or where close attention to detail is mandatory. Properly preparing these individuals has led to many mission successes and improvement to bottom lines.

More information on progression policies, and training templates can be found at: www.OperatorPerformanceDevelopment.com

CHAPTER 8

Employment Made Simple

By Rodney Diekema

I love the title of this book "The Secret to Winning Big." An alternative title could be: *Learning From The Mistakes Others Have Made*. Well hopefully that's what you'll get out of this chapter, because having been an entrepreneur from a very young age, I have made multiple small business mistakes. Some of them I've made multiple times, some of the lessons have cost me dearly.

My passion and meaning in life for the past 20 years has been in the PEO industry. A PEO is a "Professional Employer Organization." The name of the industry may be a bit confusing, but I try to explain it by defining my company and companies in our industry as "Employment Process Experts."

If you are business owner, or if you're thinking about starting a business, many of you either have employees or will have employees. Now the entrepreneur in you is most likely what inspired you to go into business, and whether you open a bagel shop, a manufacturing company, auto repair center, or any other business, what you may not have realized as you started your journey is how having employees would impact your dream of being an entrepreneur.

Most entrepreneurs have a great passion for the product or service they decided to choose as their business. Those entrepreneurs are typically either outstanding from a technical aspect, or great salespeople who want to share their love for the product or service they are offering. And then as they start growing their business, they become employers, and employers typically don't have a choice. Employers have to find and recruit outstanding employees. Once they find an employee, they need to collect the necessary tax forms for the Federal, State and local governments they are involved in. Another step is to verify that the employee is even eligible to work in the United States. Now all that paperwork needs to be completed properly and then put into an employee file. And even if the employee only last two weeks, those employee files have to be retained for several years. And then there's the issue of workers compensation. In most states, workers compensation is mandatory and if for some reason an employer fails to put in the correct protection, any injuries that occur become the liability of the employer. Another area to consider is benefits, and depending on your industry, benefits could be health insurance, 401(k) retirement accounts, dental insurance, vision insurance, disability insurance, and the list goes on and on. And what about payroll? Payroll has to be done, done correctly, and it has to be done on time.

When I started my first business, I wasn't a very good employer. I mean I found some great employees, but the paperwork and the process made me crazy. I mean my vision was on creating an outstanding business, and what you find is that although you have good employees, in most cases their vision is on having a great job with good pay and nice benefits.

There had to be a better way to manage employment, I knew I couldn't be the only employer that was frustrated with the minutiae of doing the day-to-day tasks that being an employer requires. That's when it came to me, and it was interesting how it happened, I ran into a former salesperson of mine and he was telling me about how he was selling a product called employee leasing, and the first thing I thought of was manpower. No, the services manpower offers are temporary in nature —where the employee leasing concept was a way for an employer to partner with a company that would help manage their employment. He went on to tell me that the process included everything from the administrative side of employment – the paperwork, the employee files, the payroll, workers compensation, benefits, human resources. This is a dream, I mean the company he works for to do all the things that I hated doing as an employer.

30 days later, I found myself working for the employee leasing company that my former sales person told me about. I mean if all of this stuff that

I hated as an employer was available through the service, I knew that the employers in the world would be lining up to do business with me. Well it wasn't quite that easy, it took me a year to really break into the industry, and to educate businesses on how the process worked, and how it could benefit them.

What started out as employee leasing has been replace by an industry referred to as Professional Employer Organizations, the acronym is PEO, nationwide there's somewhere close to 1000 PEO's. Industry has matured and grown and become more professional, there are PEO's that offer nationwide services, regional PEO's, and specialty PEO's.

Let's go back to the concept of "Employment Made Simple." That's what a PEO can offer you. As a business owner, set yourself free and allow a quality PEO to deal with the administrative side of employment for you. A PEO acts as your outsourced human resource department. PEO's can assist you in locating quality candidates; once you decide you want to hire, the PEO will handle all the enrollment paperwork. The concept between your business and the PEO is called co employment, where the PEO handles the administrative side of employment, and you and your organization handle the worksite employment issues. You control who gets hired, the rate of pay, the benefits offered to your employees, while the PEO handles the paperwork involved in being an employer.

Well, that all sounds great, but this sounds way too expensive. Most business owners learn about the concept and feel that while the idea is great it has to be way too costly for them to afford. What's interesting is that when I meet with prospects to discuss the concept of using the PEO, I'll often ask them what it costs them to manage employment. Now most of these business owners could tell you exactly what it costs them to make a bagel, to manufacture a widget, to change the oil in the car, they know what the cost of their product or service is. But ask them how much a $10 an hour employee costs and they don't have a clue. There some parts of that question that are easy to answer. Tax calculations like FICA, state unemployment tax, federal unemployment tax, and workers compensation are relatively easy to determine. But how much does the administration costs them, how much do they spend on the hiring process, how much does it cost them to maintain employee files, to create and maintain an employee handbook, to research benefits, to deal with annual Worker's Compensation audits, to do payroll, to answer employee questions regarding payroll and benefits. Most employers don't have any idea what it costs them to administer employment.

I explained the services the PEO offers as simply a better way to manage employment. If a business has employees, PEO helps consolidate the processes required to manage them, including human resources, Worker's Compensation, benefits, payroll and more. The PEO concept shares technology, expertise and services all while taking advantage of pooled purchasing power. PEO's create employment practices and benefit offerings designed to attract and retain the best employees.

Let's explain that a little deeper, the PEO invests in a payroll system that they can share with multiple employers. So as an example, the payroll system that may cost a PEO $50,000, would also cost a single employer $50,000. But by sharing the technology among multiple employers the PEO can provide an outstanding payroll system and technology for its customers and the customers' employees at a fraction of the cost the client would pay if they purchased it themselves. Most small businesses can afford an experienced human resource manager, but by taking advantage of the services available through a PEO, that business can now share an experienced human resource manager with the other clients of the PEO giving the client company the human resource expertise at a fraction of the cost. The time savings a PEO provides its clients is also substantial, the time it takes to research Worker's Compensation or benefit programs is substantial, this is another example of how using a PEO can reduce the cost to a single employer.

An ideal client for PEO is typically an employer with five to one hundred and five employees. As an industry, the average client for a PEO has 19 employees. What's interesting is over the past several years, more and more larger employers are taking advantages of the services of professional employer organizations. These larger employers would rather outsource the human resource responsibilities to a PEO where they have a fixed cost, rather than building the human resource department internally that creates no revenue for the business and in many cases has a hard time in defining their costs.

Currently the PEO industry has about 3% of its potential market. When you consider that 89% of all of the companies in the United States employee fewer than 20 employees, PEO's have a lot of opportunity to grow over the next several years.

Why should a business use a PEO? It's simple; a quality PEO will provide the majority of the employment services that are required by most employers. The service typically costs the employer less than they can do it for themselves. The PEO helps keep the business complaint with federal, state and local employment laws, the PEO can help find the benefit options necessary to attract and retain quality personnel needed to grow their business.

Would you like to learn some more about what a PEO can do for your business? Here's what you need to do, go to: www.PEO.com, the website will give you more information on the PEO industry and answer some basic questions for you. It also will provide you a listing of PEO's in your area. I would suggest taking the time to find a great PEO in your area and inviting a rep. to do an analysis on your business. This process typically is done free of charge. The PEO will review your employment practices and the costs you currently have regarding employment. Typically, the PEO will take the time to learn a little bit about your business and what your objectives are. The PEO will perform an analysis and return with pricing for your organization. What you'll find is that in most cases, what the PEO has to offer is a very cost-effective approach to managing your employment. The bigger benefit by utilizing the services of a PEO is that you can now focus your attention on growing your business.

One last thing to consider and something that I'd like to point out is that by utilizing a PEO, you're outsourcing your human resource functions. Outsourcing, think about this for a moment, you may have a human resource attorney on retainer, you most likely have an insurance agent for your workers compensation, if you offer health benefits you would typically have an insurance agent handling the health benefits, and what about a 401(k) – those two are typically handled by an outside group, payroll in many instances is outsourced either to a payroll company or your accountant. I think the concept of outsourcing is not a change for you. Rather, by outsourcing to a PEO, you reduce your points of contact from multiple organizations to one organization. You and your employees will have fewer points of contact to deal with, and the PEO can handle all of the services for your business.

About Rodney

Rod Diekema has spent 20 years becoming one of the Nation's leading "Employment Process Experts." Since 1992, Rod has been involved in the PEO "Professional Employer Organization" Industry. PEO's are simply a better way to manage employment. If you have employees, we help you consolidate the processes required to manage them...including Human Resources, Workers Compensation, Benefits, Payroll and more. The concept shares technology, expertise, and services, all while taking advantage of pooled purchasing power. PEO's create employment practices and benefits offerings designed to attract and retain the best employees.

To learn more about Rod Diekema, connect with him on LinkedIn at: http://www.linkedin.com/in/roddiekema or call him at 616-606-0763.

You can also visit his business websites at: www.eecap.com or: www.peo.com

CHAPTER 9

Are You Willing?

By Kevin Neff

Are you willing? Seems like a simple question, maybe even a little silly. I mean you did buy this book. But therein lies the problem. It's such a simple question to ask, but yet can be the most difficult to answer. Let me explain…

I was raised by my grandparents in a small town in rural southeastern Ohio, deep in coal country. To say it was humble beginnings would be an understatement. Because of my father's travels, he was a Marine Corps aviator, I rarely, if ever, got to see him. After graduating high school, my father chose to have me attend college in Virginia where he then resided, so as to be closer to him. I quickly learned that college just wasn't for me. After a few months, I dropped out to save my father the embarrassment of me being kicked out, (which I was well on my way to being). What made my decision so difficult was that my father was raised in a time that believed you could only go as far as the higher education you obtained. After leaving school, I kicked around with the typical, as some would describe, "blue-collar" jobs. I worked for brick layers, tile installers, carpenters, even as a gas station attendant. I also began working at a local health spa. Basically it was for the free membership as I loved lifting weights, but found that I had a knack for selling memberships while there. My father was always concerned about my future, asking me things like, "Is this what you want to do with your life?" I could always sense his concern or even worse, lack of conviction about my future. I'm sure that it was because of my disinterest in continuing with my higher education studies. When asked what I wanted to do with my life, I remember answering more than once, "I'm not sure what I'm going to do, but I know I'm going to be great at it!" I ALWAYS believed that. I just **couldn't see what it was**, I had NO idea. I was, however, good at selling those memberships.

With a lack of a college degree, I discovered that I was limited in my corporate career options. I want to stress that I was limited only in other people's eyes, not mine. That being said, it seemed that a job in sales was my way into the "professional" world. I got hired as a salesman by a family-owned boat dealership. I found something that I was not only good at, but enjoyed as well. I became their salesman of the year for four straight years. But, as is the case with any family owned business, well you know the saying, "blood is thicker than water." With really no room for growth, (did I mention they had three sons?!), it was time to take my newfound success in selling and find the next challenge.

I found it when hired to sell Yellow Pages for the phone company. At that time, it was the most coveted sales job you could have. I wondered if I would be able to cut it in such a large company. This was a very, very long way from a family-owned boat dealership. Well, I almost didn't find out. Three months into the job, I was literally at the bottom of the sales rankings of the hundreds of reps selling for the company. I remember going to the annual sales banquet and taking in the extravaganza. The room was packed, probably about 400 people or so. The funniest thing that I remember about the evening was that my seat could not have been any further from the stage. I was literally sitting in the entrance way for the servers who were coming in and out. I'm not kidding. I remember one moment in particular though. A teammate of mine was on stage receiving an award and I was awestruck by the spectacle. Huge video screens on either side of the stage, all the lights, it looked as if it were the Oscars. I remember sitting there thinking, "I want to be up on that stage next year." What I probably should have been thinking is "am I going to have a job with the company this time next year?"

Well, that evening drove me to performances that in the coming years garnered me many accolades and awards with the company to include a chair on the President's Council. And yes, I did stand up on that stage the following year receiving an award. I remember looking out in the crowd and seeing the seat where I had sat just the year before. It was surreal to see literally, how far I had come. I had done it. I had actually accomplished that 'something great' that I knew I would, or so I thought.

In the years of selling Yellow Pages I had become a big fan of sales and motivational material. I remember always having a tape of Tony Robbins or Brian Tracy playing while driving to and from appointments, (yes, I said Brian Tracy!). I'm not sure what it was but I was always intrigued by motivating people. I just seemed to have a passion for it. Of course, I would always get that "buzz" from a sale but it paled in comparison to what I felt when able to motivate an individual or a business to achieve success. I had my own ideas and dreams and wanted to pursue them. It finally got to the point that I couldn't ignore them any longer and I handed in my resignation. The funny thing is that initially it wasn't accepted because they thought I was crazy...literally. Basically, nobody ever left that job. Well, I did.

I immediately began looking for opportunities to share my ideas. Individuals, groups, businesses, it didn't matter. Basically, anyone I could get in front of. A friend of mine in the salon industry mentioned they needed a speaker for an upcoming event and wanted to know if I would be interested. I told him that I welcomed the opportunity, (never mind I had NO BACKGROUND in the industry). Next thing you know I'm in front of several hundred stylists and salon owners and rocked it! I had done it, or so I thought. It was soon afterwards I realized that something falling into your lap as opposed to actually going out and **earning** the opportunity were two very different things. I saw very quickly that this was going to be much more difficult than I had anticipated. Could I actually make the kind of living that I was accustomed to? Was I **willing**, and able, to stick it out and find out? Frankly, having no money sucked.

Eventually I went back to what I knew and got another advertising sales job. This cycle repeated itself I can't tell you how many times. The industries might change but the results wouldn't. I would be an award winning sales rep, but it would always be from selling the ideas, services or products of others. That wasn't a bad thing, it just meant that someone else was always going to tell me what my time, knowledge and services were worth. I began to wonder if the entrepreneurial blood running through my veins was a blessing or a curse. During that time I had an idea for a clothing line. It would be a way to spread the message that you don't have to be limited to other people's ideas or thoughts of what you or your own life should be. The irony is that I was never totally **willing** to do what was necessary to live those dreams myself. This went on for probably over 10 years. And next thing you know, I'm full circle, back in advertising.

I had aspirations and ideas, but was never fully **willing** to do what was necessary to see if any of them could actually succeed. Then one day I mentioned to a friend that I would enjoy speaking about marketing and showing businesses how to track the results. (Surprisingly I had never really spoken about the topics or things **that I knew best**). She made me aware of an event she was promoting and needed someone to speak about that very topic. I jumped at the opportunity. The day that I spoke I was never more in my element. I delivered the message they all needed to hear, the way they all needed to hear it. The response was overwhelming. And that's when it happened. I finally realized that this was what I was meant to do. It was at that time I made the decision to do these 8 things:

1. **Look in the Mirror** – Decide what your definition of "winning big" is. Why? Because winning big is a state of mind. Everyone's definition is different and what matters is <u>yours</u>. It is your life. Determine what you are good at, great at and willing to succeed at. If you mentally can't see it, you can't be it. If you can't believe it, you can't become it. Make the decision to become focused on who and what you want to be.

2. **Trust Your Gut** – I know a lot of people say follow your heart. Don't. Business decisions made with the heart are driven by emotion and usually aren't good ones at that. I know because I've experienced it myself. My gut however, is usually dead on. I remember pitching my clothing idea to a very good friend of mine in the advertising industry. Someone I really looked up to and admired. When told the concept, his reply was…"Kevin, I don't get it." I was devastated. It would have been easy to give up after that meeting but I knew in my gut I had a great idea. That clothing line, Slave No More®, is now sold to motorcyclists & racing enthusiasts around the world.

3. **Swim Upstream** – Don't be afraid to go against the current. I know it's easier to just go with the flow, and guess what? It's easier to be just like everyone else too! Many people want a fresh perspective, so

provide one. Share <u>your</u> opinions based on <u>your</u> experiences. Don't be afraid to buck the system. That is how great things are achieved. Make sure to always have your opinions backed up by results, experiences or both.

4. **Become Relevant, Remain Relevant** – If they don't know you they can't do business with you. It's that simple. Become the go-to person on a topic or an expert in your profession. Offer to speak every chance you get. Remember, sharing is caring, plus it's a great way to "audition" for new business. Write an online newsletter, blog or ezine and offer free subscriptions to customers so as to remain "top of mind." I have found Constant Contact to be an excellent tool for this is. You can even try it free for 60 days using this link: http://www.constantcontact.com/index.jsp?pn=kpngroup

5. **Be the "Grain of Salt" in the Pepper Shaker** – Now more than ever, the status quo is no longer acceptable. You must stand out, be seen and be heard. Be creative in getting your message out to the masses. I don't care if it's a business card or your website, be memorable. Once we created a marketing piece making light of business owners crying about business, but yet were not willing to do anything about it. We stuck a miniature pacifier on the back as a "cure". That piece was very successful in getting my company noticed…as well as getting our point across!

6. **Old School is the New School** – The fact is, many business owners became "order takers" during better times. Potential customers, patients, clients etc., all now understand that this is a buyers' market. They are looking longer, shopping smarter, and are asking, "What are you going to do to earn my business today?" Think about it, I'll bet you are doing the same things in your personal life. I know I am. New business is not a right, it is earned. And repeat business is earned through follow up and great customer service. If there is a problem, take care of it. If you're gonna talk it, then walk it. Say what you mean, mean what you say.

7. **Embrace Technology** – Don't be overwhelmed by it, embrace it by educating yourself on it. Pick a topic or subject that is of interest, (don't get caught up in trying to be the "Jack-Of-All-Trades" as you **will** just be the "Master of None"). There is an abundance of

free information, such as whitepapers, case studies and examples available online. Another way is to subscribe to free newsletters like I mentioned earlier. Believe it or not, most of my knowledge was learned by educating myself and then applying it. By not learning you will always be at the mercy of the opinions of others, or those who are trying to sell to you. Empower yourself through knowledge.

8. **Track the Results** – If you don't track, you don't know. Period. Too many people mistake activity for progress. If you are going to make an effort, then know the cause and the effect of that effort. With technology there is nothing that can't be tracked. RCF phone numbers, (remote call forwarding) are a great tool for tracking advertising results. Many times they can even be obtained for little or no charge from advertisers themselves. I offer a free tracking pad, and even though it is basic at best, it proved to be an invaluable tool to one business that saved itself over $30,000, simply by using it. Email me and I'll send you one for free: info@KevinMakesSense.com

Today The KPN Group works with businesses of all sizes helping them to become and remain relevant with creative marketing ideas. In addition, I do business consulting & speaking to inspire and motivate businesses and their owners. The best part is that I am well-compensated doing the things that I love and am passionate about, everyday. And it started with the 8 points above that I became willing to do. That may sound simple enough, but would you be shocked to know that the majority of businesses I meet with do none of the above? Crazy, I know. Which is probably why you are asking, "Why don't they?" As I said at the beginning, it can be a difficult question to answer. But let me ask this … **are you willing?**

About Kevin

Kevin Neff is a sales & marketing professional of twenty years, an entrepreneur and visionary with remarkable clarity and a sound understanding of how and where to reach people. Kevin has an uncanny ability to mentor, motivate and educate, all in the same message. He founded his marketing and consulting firm, The KPN Group, to give businesses owners a chance in the ever-changing world of marketing, to make decisions that actually grow business and expand prospects based on his *"Smart Marketing"* and *"Blunt Force Trauma Marketing"* techniques. An expert in R.O.I. marketing strategies and tracking technologies, Kevin shows that thru' measurable results you will have a more honest analysis of your current marketing performance – thus allowing for better marketing decisions. It's no wonder that people are always saying…."Kevin makes sense!"

Amongst his many accomplishments, Kevin is a former member of the President's Council of Bell Atlantic Yellow Pages. He is the creator of *Slave No More® Clothing Company*, an international hit amongst motorcycle and performance enthusiasts worldwide. He has earned Google certification as well as being SEMPO Institute SEO certified. He is also certified through Constant Contact's Experts Program as well as being named an Authorized Local Expert for them. In addition he has earned the title of SoT.

To learn more about Kevin and his insights, you can subscribe to his complimentary eblast "Kevin's M.A.D. Thoughts" by going to his website: www.KevinMakesSense. com or by simply texting **KPNGROUP** to 22828. You can even join by scanning the code provided below with your smartphone.

CHAPTER 10

Leveraging your Passion and Strength to Achieve Massive Success

By Nate Miller

In your life, you have likely been given the advice to choose your career or activities based on your passion. This advice only goes so far because doing what you are passionate about might exclude an important key to success, your strengths. Instead of focusing only on what you are passionate about, for maximum results you should focus on what I have come to call Passion Plus. Passion Plus takes what you are passionate about to the next level by isolating, then incorporating your strengths. Passion Plus is the sweet spot where your strengths and passions overlap. When you combine your passions with your strengths, you are harnessing a very powerful force to usher in waves of success.

Let me share with you the story of how I first discovered this principle. When I was in 10th grade, my new high school coach moved me from fullback to tackle. I was livid. All through junior high school, I played fullback, and I loved this position because I got to run with the ball and score touchdowns. I relished reading my name in the paper, how many yards I carried the ball and how many touchdowns I made. Scoring a touchdown was my greatest joy, and now this new guy was going to take it away from me. No more running the ball, no more touchdowns, and no more glorious newspaper articles about my accomplishments. You see, an offensive tackle is a lineman that blocks for the running backs. They never receive the glory of scoring a touchdown and rarely get their name in the paper. When they do, they are barely mentioned. I decided I was going to sit down with the new coach and set him straight about why I should be a fullback. He allowed me to state my case, and then bluntly told me that I was playing tackle for two reasons. First, my strengths were better suited for tackle and, second, I would have a much better chance of earning a college scholarship at tackle.

As it turns out, he was absolutely right. I went on to earn a scholarship to the University of Central Arkansas, where I collected All Conference, All District, and All American honors as an offensive tackle. You see, I was passionate about scoring touchdowns, but this wasn't my strength. As it turns out, once I played the position of tackle, I realized that I was just as passionate about this position because it was really the game I loved. When I played tackle, it amplified my joy of the game because it was where my passion and my strength overlapped, resulting in greater successes.

THE FOLLOWING EXERCISE WILL EXPLAIN HOW TO DETERMINE YOUR PASSION PLUS ITEMS:

Take out a sheet of paper and draw a line down the middle. In the left column, list all the items that you are passionate about. In the right column, list your strengths. Set aside for now.

People typically can list what they are passionate about with ease, but can encounter difficulty identifying their strengths. Peter Drucker, who is known as the father of modern management says, "Most Americans do not know what their strengths are. When you ask them, they look at you with a blank stare or they respond in terms of subject knowledge, which is the wrong answer." A strength is much deeper than your career or your hobbies. It is what makes you unique and special. A strength is a pattern of thoughts, feelings, and behavior that brings forth gratification and pride, generates emotional and/or monetary reward, and demonstrates quantitative progress towards excellence. Here are some questions to help you determine your strengths:

What do people come to you for help with?

What have you learned that you caught onto quickly and were able to do with ease?

What do you do that makes you feel alive and energized when you do it?

What do you like to learn about or read about?

What do people tell you that you're good at?

What was the best day you had at work in the last three months? What were you doing and why did you enjoy it so much?

Answering these questions will help lead you to your strengths.

Another great resource that will help you isolate your strengths is the input of your family, colleagues, and friends. Here is a sample email you can modify to solicit this feedback:

"I am seeking to discover my strengths, the things that come naturally to me. This will allow me to be more productive in my personal and professional life. Since you understand me, I would really appreciate your assistance. Could you please take two minutes to reply to this email and tell me what you think are my greatest strengths? Your feedback will be very beneficial and I truly appreciate your help. Thanks for taking the time out of your busy schedule to help me. I really look forward to reading your comments. Yours truly, (Insert your name here)."

Once you have received all the responses back on email, print them out. Take a highlighter, and highlight all the common strengths listed. Now, take these and place them into your strengths column. Once you have listed your strengths, then look for the items you have listed on both sides. These are your Passion Plus items on which you should focus to achieve maximum success.

Now that you know your Passion Plus items, it's time to show you the secret to leveraging your strengths. Most people spend a lot of time working on their weaknesses to improve their performance. In reality, focusing on your weaknesses will only provide you with mediocre results. Your strengths are what make you unique. Your greatest ability to grow is in the areas where you already excel. Here are a few examples to drive this point of view home.

Tiger Woods is one of the greatest golfers of all time. Recently, he's been known for other things, but he is still one of the greatest golfers of all time. He has great swing mechanics and the ability to drive the ball long distances down the fairway, but did you know he rarely ranks in the Top 100 in sand saves? The focus on weakness approach would mean that for Tiger to be the best golfer, he should spend a lot of time working on his sand saves. What Tiger actually does is spend his time working on his natural strengths, his great swing, and ability to hit the ball far off the tee to avoid his weakness in the first place. He does practice his sand saves, but just enough to have some level of competence so it doesn't cost him the whole tournament if he makes a mistake.

The winning coach of the Chinese Olympic ping pong team describes how his team focuses on perfecting strengths eight hours a day to overpower their weaknesses. "Our winning player plays only his forehand, even though his competition knows he can't play a backhand. His forehand is so invincible it can't be beaten."

Vince Lombardi, arguably one of the greatest football coaches to ever live said this about reviewing game film, "From now on, we only replay the winning plays." Coach Lombardi understood you don't win by making your weaknesses just a little bit better. You win by making your weaknesses irrelevant.

To leverage your strengths, we are going to use a proven law of the universe, the 80/20 principle. The 80/20 principle will apply to all areas of your life. It is pervasive in every area. . The 80/20 rule was discovered by an Italian economist named Vilfredo Pareto in 1897. He discovered that 80% of the wealth was owned by 20% of the population. This was the case no matter what country or time period he researched. The 80/20 rule is commonly referred to as the Pareto Principle. The Pareto Principle was commonly ignored until in 1951, a quality expert named Joseph Juran revived the Pareto Principle and referred to it as The Rule of the Vital Few. He surmised that the majority of quality issues could be resolved easily by focusing on the 20% or the vital few. He instructed people to ignore the 80% or, as he deemed it, the trivial many. This is so important because the overwhelming majority of individuals focus on the trivial many.

The 80/20 principle states that 80% of your results come from 20% of your activities and, conversely, 80% of your activities only lead to 20% of your results. Look at these statistics:

- 80% of automobile accidents are caused by 20% of the drivers.

- 80% of healthcare costs come from 20% of the diseases.

- 80% of your business will come from 20% of your customers.

- 80% of the value of all crime comes from 20% of the criminals.

- 80% of the divorces come from 20% of the people that get married.

- In your personal life, 80% of your happiness will come from 20% of the people you associate with.

- You will wear 20% of your clothes 80% of the time.

The 80/20 rule states that there is an imbalance between effort and outcomes. We customarily accept that there is a direct relationship between effort and reward and that an equal amount of effort results in an equal amount of reward. This is not the case in life or business.

The 80/20 rule applies to our efforts and outcomes as well. This imbalance means that 80% of our rewards are the result of 20% of our efforts. Think on that a moment to fully understand how powerful this law is in leveraging your strengths. Here it is in a nutshell; **80% of your current effort is only resulting in 20% of your results**. This imbalance can lead to frustration, overwhelm, and more importantly, lackluster results. In business and life, you do not get back equal to what you invest. Sometimes you get more and sometimes you get less. This means that right now it is possible to dramatically improve your results with less effort. The trick is achieving understanding of what causes you to get a lot more and what causes you to get a lot less. Once you understand what these items are, you can use them to your advantage.

I first discovered the power of the Pareto Principle as the Director of an outpatient rehabilitation clinic. I realized that the majority of our patients came from just a few doctors. Instinctively, I thought that if I could get the doctors that were sending fewer patients to our clinic to increase their referrals, that our business would increase. I spent most of my time marketing to these doctors. What I noticed is that while we were getting a miniscule increase with these physicians, our referrals from our top physicians were declining.

At first, I was baffled because I thought I was focusing my efforts on our greatest opportunity. I then began spending the majority of my time on our top-referring physicians and then occasionally marketing to all the other doctors. In a matter of months, our business doubled. I have used this approach throughout my career as a healthcare executive and have had phenomenal record-breaking results at every facility I worked by focusing on the vital few.

This is the same approach we use in our personal development. We intuitively want to improve our weaknesses because we feel like this will improve our performance. The opposite is true: to improve our performance, we must really place our focus on improving our strengths. For a long time, I spent a great amount of effort trying to improve a weakness of mine. I have always struggled with organization. My desk is always a mess. People consistently comment that they have no idea how I find anything. I have even been scored down on performance evaluations because of it.

Early in my career, I spent a lot of time, energy, and effort to improve this weakness. It became my personal mission. I attended numerous seminars, purchased every type of planner pad, and even several electronic organizers, all to bolster this weakness. I tried creating alphabetical filing systems and filed everything on a daily basis. This all led to a high level of frustration and disappointment. I repeatedly lost my planner pads and never could remember where I filed important documents. After all the effort and time I placed into this endeavor, I was no more organized than before. Once I realized that I was never going to be highly organized, I began placing that energy and effort on the things at which I naturally excelled, and my career began to soar. What are the vital few in your performance?

80% of what you achieve comes from 20% of your time and effort. Do you know what these activities are? You must know them to harness the power of the Pareto Principle. Let's refer back to your Passion Plus items you discovered in the previous exercise. These are the items that were common in both your passions and strengths columns. Prioritize these items based on which of them would provide the greatest results. Start with the Passion Plus item you placed at the top of the list. This is the strength on which you should focus all your effort and energy.

Be totally committed to developing this strength. This is how you will achieve excellence.

Hopefully, by now you can see the importance of being clear on your strengths. In summary, understand and practice the 80/20 principle. Identify where 20% of your effort provides 80% of your results. Focus your time and energy here and you will be amazed how you grow your success tremendously.

About Nate

Nate Miller is an Author, Professional Speaker, Entrepreneur and Healthcare Executive. A product of the success principles he teaches, Nate had a highly decorated collegiate football career at the University of Central Arkansas earning All-Conference, All-District and All-American accolades. There he learned the value of hard work, discipline and focus as well as the ethic of continual improvement. He carried these principles into his professional career where he became one of the youngest hospital Chief Executive Officers for HealthSouth Corporation. There his hospital received the highest honor the "President's Circle Award." Nate then took the CEO position at the Surgical Hospital of Jonesboro. During his time there, the Surgical Hospital of Jonesboro received the Joint Replacement Excellence Award and Spine Surgery Excellence Award from Healthgrades. They were one of only 13 hospitals in the country to achieve both these awards. The Delta Group also placed the Surgical Hospital of Jonesboro in the top 2% of all acute care hospitals in the United States. Nate has spoken at many national events and enjoys sharing insights into personal and professional development and assisting people in putting these insights into practice to multiply success.

Nate's belief in and passion for maximizing personal development is the core of his business and life philosophy. He founded Championship Success because he is committed to help others achieve their potential in order to live richer, more fulfilling lives. Nate gives you the tools you need to achieve championship levels of success in your personal and professional life through workshops, webinars, teleseminars, books and video training.

To learn more about Nate, visit: www.successchamp.com

Or contact him at 870-268-9944.

CHAPTER 11

The Secret To Shocking Your Audience

By Greg Rollett

Jill is getting married. It is the biggest day in her entire life. It is a day that she has been dreaming about since she was 7 years old and playing with her "Wedding Day Barbie" set.

Now Jill is planning her wedding. From looking for a great venue to catering, sorting through invitations and programs, flowers and cakes, she has seen more companies, proposals and ideas than would fit in a giant scrapbook.

Nearly every company that Jill has reached out to has kept things relatively simple. The flower company told Jill to "check out our website for floral arrangements and pricing."

The cake company invited her in for a quick tasting, as did the next cake company and then the next. None of which followed up with Jill to see how the tasting went and if she had more questions.

Her request for invitations led to emails loaded with PDF files and more links to check out.

The bridal shows presented her with more tri-fold brochures than a local printing company could handle in a week!

Through the entire process, everything was good, but nothing shocked Jill. Until one day she received a package from a photographer. Photos are the one-thing that truly last a lifetime from your wedding and Jill was not taking the decision lightly. She knew the style of photos she wanted and starter scouring the web to find photographers that had online portfolios of the styles she envisioned.

She filled out a few forms online to request meetings and appointments. But one company took Jill's breath away. Not only did they have a great gallery online, with sample photo albums, stunning imagery and depth that made the images come to life, but they also had a clear call to action. Jill entered her information on their website on a Tuesday afternoon. On Wednesday when she arrived home from work she had a FedEx box on her doorstep. Upon opening it she saw the logo of the photography company.

Inside Jill saw a stack of printed photos from recent weddings, a postcard that was used as a 'save the date,' a cigar and matches for her fiancé, a business card, a DVD with a video introducing the photographer and showing off his personality, his gear and highlights from some of his biggest and best weddings.

This left an impression on Jill that immediately led her to forget all of the other photographers that sent her links and brochures.

On her wedding day, the photographer that got the job had won the job because of their ability to break through in a crowded and seemingly cluttered marketplace. It's time you did the same in your business.

THE MYTH OF TOO MUCH COMPETITION

In nearly every market there is more competition now than there has ever been. More people are advertising, working search engine or social media strategies, attending events, putting on their own events, writing books and doing what they think it takes to get in front of their target audience.

In the fitness market for example, there are 67,068 "weight loss" books available on Amazon.com at the time of this writing. By the time you are reading this there will be substantially more.

That means people are still entering the market at record pace. There is a huge demand for health and fitness information, products and services and it is not going away anytime soon. But just because there are 67,000 books out already doesn't mean that you need to stop before you get in the game.

What about personal injury attorneys? Using a search on Google Maps for "personal injury attorney orlando" there are 2,219 results! Over two thousand personal injury attorneys just in little old Orlando. That sounds like a lot of competition. Yet there are accidents everyday and someone is going to be fighting to win their case. Don't you want that to be you?

On the surface, it looks like there is a lot of competition. But when you get the prospective call, be it from the Yellow Pages or your website, it's up to you to deliver a first impression that they will never forget and give you their business. And this is where most businesses give up and start their complaining about too much competition.

In fact, their entire strategy now depends on sending out a link via email, pointing to a YouTube video and maybe sending out a brochure and welcome letter. And they do it at their convenience, not right now and without the urgency of the situation.

We have become a society of instant gratification. Why do you think we wait outside of the Apple store for hours on end when we can order the same phone from AT&T and get it in a week?

When you are given the opportunity to impress a prospect, to win their business and take them away from your competition, it is your duty to do everything in your power to do so. Let's break down how you get that done.

MARKETING LIKE A CELEBRITY EXPERT®

Once you have someone interested in your services, it's time to shock them with something they would never expect from a company like yours.

The first step is to set up your own system internally so that this process happens like clockwork. There can really be no delay from the time someone is interested till the time you get your Celebrity Expert® machine rolling. This means looking for automated tools and alerts, finding the team members and giving them defined roles and responsibilities and having a plan to track and analyze where a prospect is along the chain of your Shock-And-Awe Campaign.

The best system triggers pre-populated, automated pieces of media that are instantly sent out to your prospects as they come into your business. Many fulfillment companies can integrate with your customer relations software or download spreadsheets from your server that activates their printing and shipping teams.

The next step is to decide what a new client is worth to your business. This number is crucial as it will determine how much money you are willing to spend to convert a prospect into a customer. Look at the initial sales price, the frequency of recurring purchases, the referrals they bring into the business, any affiliate revenue they generate and ultimately the lifetime value of that prospect. Getting this number will give you a clear as day number that you and your business will be comfortable to invest into this marketing system in order to attract, shock and secure them as a customer.

Now it's time to plan out your Shock System. This is where the true Celebrity Experts® are made. They have the number they are willing to spend on each prospect and they craft a plan to maximize that dollar amount through a series of high value and hyper-responsive pieces of digital and physical media.

Every business will vary in the length of time that you will continue to actively market to a new prospect, however the heaviest concentration should be right up front, right when they have expressed interest in learning from you and your business, or have raised their hand for more information to help their decision- making process.

In our business, this is a 30 day campaign with a heavy physical media push during the first 14 days. As the campaign continues on, we resort to email and digital communication.

The first piece in your Shock System needs to happen immediately. This will be the most expensive and most vital piece of any media that you send out. While your competition sends out a link to their website or even a brochure in the mail, you are going to tell your story, the story of your clients and support your mission and vision through multiple pieces of content. This is your instant Shock-And- Awe Package.

The idea here is to FedEx a package to a warm and interested prospect and get it to their doorstep or office the next day. This step alone, before they see what's inside, will impress them and get their attention.

FedEx boxes and envelopes often get past the red tape and the gatekeepers that keep many general mail and marketing pieces from ever reaching their hands. You now have a leg up on the competition that is mailing out standard brochures or welcome letters.

Next you want to carefully choose pieces of media that tell the story of your business. It can be a CD from an interview you gave that highlights some of your work, it can be a signed copy of your book, or a DVD that shows your face and voice in an engaging light. You should include testimonials, case studies or special reports that frame your products and services as the solution for your prospect. You can also choose to insert little knick-knacks that are associated with the brand, as did the photographer in the story at the beginning of this chapter.

The goal is to give them so much stuff that they are literally "awed" at the amount of things you are doing in your business, and that even if they never listen or watch or read, they see you as the definitive expert and would feel really bad without giving you a call back. This goes back to the Law Of Reciprocity, as taught by Robert Cialdini in his breakthrough book Influence. People tend to return a favor, or feel like they must now give back to someone that just gave them a gift. It's why we buy presents for people that buy presents for us. We need to return the gesture that was shown to us. This "big ol' box" of stuff helps you kick off this law of reciprocity and win the trust of your prospect.

After you send the box, there is a chance that you might not get a call right away. In that event, you need to be ready with a few more steps in your Shock System and really create a campaign around the actions you want your prospect to take.

The sky is the limit on what you can send next, but you want to make sure that you begin sending multiple messages in multiple formats. If you are talking about one particular service that they may be interested in you should be sending some post cards, emails and packages. These messages should be filled with audio, video and text. Your market is going to respond differently to different messages and you need to ensure that one of your messages matches the way they want to receive communications at the exact time they are looking for those communications.

Hitting them with a postcard in the mail may trigger them to open an email that is sent in the evening. An email in a cluttered inbox might spark action and familiarity when a package shows up at their doorstep. These media pieces need to work together and all need to center around a common call-to-action that will take the prospect from interested to client or customer.

For many of our clients that have books, you can send gift cards for a cup of coffee with messages that say to "have a cup of coffee on us and enjoy a complimentary copy of our Best-Selling Book." When you finish, I'd love to hear what you thought and how we can help you apply the concepts from the book into your own business."

With every piece of content and media sent, you want to continue to build on the 'shock-and-awe' factor of the first box. At every corner you want them to think of you and only you.

When you get this right, there will truly be no more competition. Even with 2,200 local competitors or 67,000 other authors trying to get the attention of your market. Why? Because no one else is taking the time to truly get and keep their attention. That is what separates you, the Celebrity Expert®, from every other business owner in your market.

What are you going to do to shock the Jills in your market when she calls your office or fills out a form on your website? There are Jills all over the world waiting and someone is going to win her business. Let's make it you.

About Greg

Greg Rollett, @gregrollett, is a Best-Selling Author and online marketing expert who works with authors, entertainers and entrepreneurs all over the world. He utilizes the power of social media, direct response and personality-driven marketing to attract more clients and to continue to do business together long-term.

After creating a successful string of his own educational products, Greg began helping others in the production and marketing of their own products. He does this through 6 proven steps in the Celebrity Expert(R) Marketing System.

Greg has written for Mashable, Fast Company, Inc.com, the Huffington Post, AOL, AMEX's Open Forum and others, and continues to share his message helping experts and entrepreneurs grow their business through marketing.

Greg's previous clients include Coca-Cola, Miller Lite, Warner Bros and Cash Money Records, along with hundreds of entrepreneurs and small-business owners. Greg's work has been featured on FOX News, ABC, and the Daily Buzz.

Greg loves to challenge the current business environment that constrains people to working 12-hour days during the best portions of their lives. By teaching them to leverage technology and the power of information, Greg loves to help others create freedom businesses that allow them to generate income, make the world a better place, and live a radically-ambitious lifestyle in the process.

A former touring musician, Greg is highly sought after as a speaker, appearing with other well-recognized speakers as well as at events such as the Affiliate Summit.

If you would like to learn more about Greg and how he can help your business, please contact him directly at: greg@productprosystems.com or by calling his office at 877.897.4611.

Greg offers a free download report on 'How to create your own educational products' at: www.productprosystems.com

CHAPTER 12

Expand Your Life: Seven Ways to Find Greater Fulfillment and Happiness

By Deborah Hightower

"The biggest human temptation is to settle for too little."
~ Thomas Merton

What are you passionate about?

What gets you out of bed in the morning, energized and ready to go? What makes your toes tingle the second you think about it?

Now, answer this. How long has it been since you felt that way?

If you're like a lot of people, your answer might be, "A long, long time." While a little sad, it can be totally and completely normal. Most of us lose sight of our passions as we climb the ladder of "success." Often we choose the "regular" path; we choose the safe one. We expend our energy with work and plans for success. We do the "right" thing, the "smart" thing, and the "practical" thing.

Often, as a part of that process, something gets lost.

But what if you could get that "something" back? And what if that "something" enriched not just your personal life, but your professional life as well?

I'm here to tell you it can. All through a process I call "Expansion."

FINDING MY OWN EXPANSION

You could say I'm the poster child for Expansion. "Deborah, you are never satisfied," is a comment I hear frequently. But I view that as a *good* thing.

When I was a kid, I had two passions—singing and finance. Yes, I realize those two go together like peanut butter and motor oil, but those were the two things to which I felt an immediate connection. Ironically, I was introduced to both in the same place— church.

Church was the first place I had a "job"—not only did I get paid to dust the pews; I also helped my father manage the offerings. That simply meant gathering the collections at the end of service, preparing it for deposit the next day, and making the appropriate ledger entries.

It was then I discovered my knack for numbers.

But singing…that was something else. I spent many days and nights pretending to be a country star—knowing in my soul I was meant to sing. Sundays proved to be the fertile ground on which I began to sprout my wings. Music has a way of transforming the heart and mind—and singing became a passion that has stayed with me since.

So, when I "grew up," which path do you think I chose?

By default, I chose finance. I entered the world of financial services at the bottom of the totem pole— albeit with one of the nation's largest financial institutions. My road to success wasn't exactly a straight shot, but the potholes along the way taught me perseverance, and laid a foundation that would pay off in the long run. I made a plan, focused my energy like a laser, and started climbing the ladder. I began the climb with a high school diploma and two college classes and ended up a senior vice president. Along the way I obtained several industry designations and graduated summa cum laude with a bachelor's degree in Business and a master's degree in Organization and Management.

I was a success. Or was I?

Every now and then, the other passion, would tap me on the shoulder.

While music was never completely out of my mind, I hadn't given much thought to expanding it past the proverbial party, wedding, or funeral. Until one day, the "something" spark showed up and I let it ignite.

And guess what happened?

I embraced it. My financial career continues to rock on. A couple of albums and award nominations later, I can now say my music is rocking too. I have lived a life Expansion! I can manage both passions, enjoy the financial rewards of both, and give back to others.

Expansion has afforded me the opportunity to be in the company of a beautiful tapestry of people – from the homeless to world leaders. Music has given me a platform to bring people together whose path would likely not have otherwise crossed. It allows me to bridge gaps in communities, support social causes and encourage others to launch their own Expansion project.

We get what we give – in business and in life.

That's the power of Expansion. I firmly believe that life can be more fulfilling and happy when we expand ourselves -- and expand outside ourselves for the good of others. When you move past the boundaries you've set up in your life, when you allow yourself to embrace your passions, amazing things can happen.

And they can happen as easily for you as they have for me.

SO...WHAT EXACTLY *IS* EXPANSION?

Expansion is just what it sounds like – it's "going bigger." It's about going beyond the boundaries in your life to include the things you care about the most and feel the most passionate.

If you have confidence, drive and perseverance, it can work anywhere and everywhere. You can expand within your current business or career by growing your skills, reaching out to new and different prospects, or connecting on a deeper level with the culture and community in which you currently do business. You have the power to profoundly enrich the lives of others and by doing so, your life will be enriched.

Perhaps your current business or career no longer sets your heart on fire. Sometimes a job is just a job and a means to get you to the desired end. You can begin to expand your talents and passions outside your job and who knows—the expansion project, your expansion project, may advance you from your current place.

Personally, my financial services career continues to be a priority. Over the years, I have helped people plan their financial future, provide for their family, and leave a legacy. On the other hand, music is also my passion. When the spark ignited and I fanned the flame, doors opened that benefited both career areas. When you pursue your passion, you never know where it will take you. You will meet new people and gain a new perspective all the while gaining a higher level of confidence that will carry over into everything you do.

Expansion for you could mean supporting a cause you feel strongly about. Perhaps it's an organization that helped you along your path. Studies have shown that giving to others, paying it back and paying it forward, produces an incredible psychological boost for people at all levels on the ladder of success. When you do good on the outside, you feel good on the inside.

Of course, the ultimate is to expand in every area of your life—because every area of Expansion has a way of enriching the other.

For example, I use my musical gifts to give back by working with kids and adults who otherwise would not have the opportunity to explore the field. So while music enriches my life and work, it enriches those around me. As a bonus, meeting other professionals who share my love of music has led to business outside the music arena.

That's the power of Expansion!

Which leaves just one more question...HOW?

Trying to make a dream or a passion come true without some sort of plan is an invitation to chaos. But if you approach the idea of Expansion with diligence and planning, you can master it and start experiencing the incredible rewards.

And the best news is, you can start right where you are—at what I call your neutral data point. That's where the plan begins.

THE PLAN

• Evaluate and define.

The first step in the process is to look at the big picture. That starts with taking an honest look at where you are right now and the life you dream of. What is your perfect state and place? What makes up your DNA for fulfillment and happiness? Is there something inside that has been lying dormant? Have you forgotten what it's like to wake up in the morning fired up to start your day and make things happen? What does success mean to you?

Finances are an important component of this equation. Changing your life may change your financial situation, in both expected and unexpected ways. However, life is about more than money—prosperity comes in many forms.

• Let the spark ignite.

There are always excuses for not moving forward with your dreams and passions. Maybe you feel like you have too little time and too many obligations. Or maybe you were totally inspired to act, only to have that spark die as you got bogged down in daily to-do lists and concerns about the bottom line. Clear a space in your mind for inspiration and allow it to blossom. Make it a priority. It could ignite the spark that starts the fire that fuels the passion that—and here's the good part—actually gets things done.

When I finally allowed my music spark to ignite, I found a renewed energy – not just in music, but in everything I pursued. Instead of daydreaming about what might happen, I started working it. The excitement and renewed energy spilled over into other areas as well.

• Diversify.

You've no doubt heard the old adage, "Birds of a feather flock together." This is the step where you throw that adage out the window. Expansion requires building new relationships—an essential component to opening doors and creating opportunities. Expansion opportunities can lie outside our comfort zone, away from business colleagues, friends, neighbors, and contemporaries with whom we spend our everyday lives. Don't be afraid to stretch.

In the financial world, my gender typically makes up less than 10 percent of financial planning executives. The same can be said for African-Americans, Asians, Hispanics, and basically everyone else in the field who isn't a grey-haired white guy. So it can be said I started my financial career in Expansion territory!

Expansion requires diversity—a moving beyond traditional boundaries and actively seeking out new opportunities, new people, and new experiences in new places. Don't miss an incredible opportunity by doing business with only people who look like you.

So, get outside that bubble, seek out diversity in people and experiences! There is a world of possibilities where expansion is waiting to happen.

• Commit to learn.

In order to really do something well, no matter how passionate you may be about it, it is critical that you have a thorough understanding of the organization and the people with whom you will be working. Be willing to listen to those with experience in the area and examine your short-comings—knowledge gaps and beyond. Identify any formal education or training that may be necessary. If you are working with a particular group, think about how well you understand who they are, what they value and issues specific to their community. Remember, you need to expand yourself before you can effectively spread Expansion to others.

For example, if you plan to grow your business by expanding and diversifying your client base by offering products or services to another culture, you'll have a much better chance of connecting with them if you have a working knowledge of their belief systems. I'm not talking about stereotyping, in fact, I'm talking about the exact opposite—acquiring *real* information covering the basics of how things are done and what really matters in their particular community.

• Plan to show up.

Whatever your dream, whatever your desired expansion area, always strive to give of yourself. I'm not talking about simply writing a check, or just going through the motions. I'm talking about giving your heart. I'm talking about relationship and fellowship. When you make that in-vestment—you can be guaranteed a return.

Whatever your goal and wherever you feel led to invest, do it from your heart. The more deeply you connect with others, the bigger your ultimate return—in the form of fulfillment, happiness, and, yes, Expansion.

• Engage the spiritual.

Often times, we get in our own way, questioning our impulses and decision-making abilities—paralysis by analysis as it's often called. Let the 'unction'—the gut feeling you have inside—guide you. This inner voice will lead you in a direction; your job is to take a deep breath and follow it.

Ask yourself—"what am I passionate about—deep down inside?" Most often when I ask people that question, they don't need a lot of time to ponder the answer. Almost everyone has a cause they believe in or a dream they have put on hold in favor of more "practical" pursuits. Follow your heart, and it will lead you in the right direction.

• Love. Inspire. Empower. Share.

The greatest catalyst for Expansion is the ability to love. When you have a genuine love for others, it comes across in the interaction. Love allows you to inspire and empower. It allows you to promote the growth—the Expansion—that comes from sharing.

It will be obvious when love and concern for others is real and obvious when it's not. For true Expansion to take place, be genuine in your thoughts and actions and encourage others to do the same.

When you get out of your bubble and let yourself expand, I promise, whoever you are and whatever you do, you will find yourself re-energized and your passions finally engaged. So don't hold back any longer. Whatever you love, whatever makes your toes tingle, embrace it! Break through the old boundaries and expand. That's where you will find true fulfillment and happiness.

You'll be amazed at where Expansion takes you.

About Deborah

A thought leader in the area of Expansion, Deborah Hightower has found success in the unique multi-faceted areas of finance, speaking, writing and music. She believes the components of fulfillment, happiness, and prosperity can be found by expanding our horizons past self-imposed limitations.

Deborah holds a Bachelor's Degree in Business Administration, Master's Degree in Organization and Management, and professional designations in the field of Finance. She assists individuals, corporations, non-profit organizations, and trustees with financial plan development and investment planning and has received awards in that area.

Speaking, writing, and music play a big part in Deborah's personal Expansion. In turn, she helps individuals find and develop a plan to pursue their passion, and assists organizations with expansion in the areas of employee work/life balance, client development, and team motivation. Her writings can be seen in industry print and online magazines. She celebrated four Top 10 radio hits and award nominations from her latest album.

A proponent of living life to its fullest, Deborah encourages others to be motivated, uplifted and renewed by broadening their horizons, engaging their passions, and seeking genuine expansion in all areas of their life.

To learn more about Deborah Hightower, and how you can receive your personal *Expand Your Life* guide, visit: www.deborahhightower.com

CHAPTER 13

Courtesy System For Success

By Dr. Matt VanderMolen

THE UNCOMMON SUCCESS SECRET

It is no secret that successful people commonly choose to do the uncommon. If they did what was common, they would be, well, common. Given this choice, it sounds simple enough to choose uncommon routes as a means for attaining success. But, is it easy? The decision to follow uncommon methods often becomes difficult. Most can identify successful people who have invented whole new products, systems or services that no one else chose to do. Innovation is a lot of work and seems to often require superhuman powers to accomplish the uncommon.

But I have a good secret. And like any good secret, I just have to tell somebody. It is really great news. In our fast paced, high tech world, there is an uncommon choice that was once considered common: courtesy. "Common courtesy" was a social norm routinely expected of others, even including young children. Today, you have the unique opportunity to win big in your business and personal life by simply choosing to do something once expected of a child! Practicing "common courtesy" is the big secret to success in our world today. It is a simple concept that can bring great gains to your life.

What happened to courtesy? Why is it not common anymore? Most importantly, what does courtesy have to do with success and winning big in our world today?

Somewhere and somehow, someone decided courtesy was inconvenient, time-consuming and even financially draining. Basically, why would you inconvenience yourself, spend time and therefore money (time is money—right?) just to act courteously? Our society has become one that pushes courtesy to the wayside.

With all the demands on our schedules, courtesy just does not seem like a productive use of our time. Our society generally equates the amount of time spent on production with the amount of success you have in life. Thus, it seems logical to not even bother with courtesy.

Certainly, courtesy can be still be found and appreciated in our world and economy. But, think about it. Where do you find it the most? Have you checked into a five-star hotel or dined in a five-star restaurant lately? If you have, you were given superior courtesy—that is partially why these businesses earned a five-star rating. As you probably expected, you were also given a superior bill. After all, you rationalized that courtesy costs money. You have been conditioned to believe a successful business that spends time on courtesy should be highly compensated for their productive time lost.

So, in order to be successful with courtesy, do we have to find a way for people, customers, clients to provide us extra compensation? The answer is "no." We can all agree that when courtesies are extended to us, we appreciate them. And the more courtesy we receive, the better it is. So let's do more! The perception of courtesy costing time or money is just that—a perception. The reality is courtesy does not really cost time or money. A deeper secret and the key to winning big with courtesy is using this very perception to set yourself and your business apart.

COURTESY STARTS WITH "PLEASE" AND "THANK YOU"

So what is "common courtesy?" Where should you start? Let's start at the beginning. When courtesy was common, children were taught to say "please" and "thank you." These are two very powerful words that are second only to the use of a person' s name when communicating. Does it cost anything to say them? Does it take extra time? They really do not. Is it now society's perception that these two words are special words meant for special people, occasions or circumstances? Absolutely, it is! Simple statements of "please" and "thank you" present a perfect opportunity. It will cost you nothing to implement, and everyone wins.

When I first went into private practice as a dentist, I said "please" and "thank you" to my newly hired assistant as she passed dental instruments back and forth to me. At the end of our first day together, she stopped me and said she had never worked for a doctor who said "please" and "thank you." She said it actually stunned her to hear it, but she appreciated how I treated her as a professional. She went on to say she knew my office was going to be a special place to work. I could not believe what I just heard. I was stunned too! I learned two lessons that day. First, "please" and "thank you" would always stay in my vocabulary . Second, courtesy counts the most when it is unexpected and these days it is almost always unexpected.

Of course, "please" and "thank you" should always be used with your customers and clients. It makes a huge impression—if you do it right. "Please" should always be vocalized in a helpful and respectful tone instead of a more demanding and instructional tone. "Would you please sign here?" Translates better than "Sign here please." When you thank your customer, look her in the eye and say "thank you" in an appreciative tone. You can even say, "Thank you, I really appreciate your business." This is so much better than saying "thanks" while looking away to see who or what is next in your day. If you are providing excellent goods or services, and also using "please" and "thank you" correctly, most of your customers or clients will actually thank you. When they do, your outward response should be a smile and "my pleasure" or "you are very welcome." Your inward response should be "Yes! That was a win!"

SMILE

A necessary tool for winning big with courtesy is situated right beneath your nose. It is your smile. Infinite volumes of literature have been published about the power of a smile, but it is not commonly understood. Here is your chance to easily be uncommon again! Here is yet another powerful secret. Smile and the world smiles with you. I know you have heard that before, but do you really understand it? When anyone smiles, they always feel at least a little better about their situation. Start with yourself. Go ahead and force a smile right now. How do you feel? Psychologists have shown even a forced smile will elevate a person's mood. Furthermore, your smile will elevate the mood of others around you. Do you want happy customers or clients? Smile at them! But, as in "please" and "thank you," it must be done right.

A great smile starts in your eyes, moves to your lips which raise like a theatre curtain to unveil the stars of the show—your beautifully framed white teeth. It is important to smile with your eyes and with your teeth. Anything less is a discourteous smirk. On the other hand, an overdone "cheese" type smile showing top and bottom teeth is typically perceived as insincere and even disrespectful. What you want to project is a relaxed smile with your teeth apart and showing mainly the top teeth. Look at print ads of people smiling to see what I am describing. Those people are professionals, but you can be every bit as good as them. Go look in a mirror and practice your smile and see the difference.

If you do not like the teeth in your smile, you can get them fixed. As a dentist, I have to tell you that most everyone can have a great smile. The two things that stop people from getting a great smile is their fear of dental procedures or their unwillingness to commit the finances to get the treatment. If you fear the treatment, find a dentist who provides sedation dentistry. It could literally change your life. If it is the money, an investment in your smile will return a thousand fold in personal and professional success. The only regrets I ever hear from my patients is why they did not fix their smile sooner.

Smile as a courtesy to others and as a necessary tool for your own personal and professional success. It won't cost you a thing, and pretty soon you won't be able to stop!

TELL THE TRUTH

Another uncommon courtesy that can separate you from the crowd is to simply tell the truth. Think about it. You can usually tell when someone is not being honest. How does it make you feel? Do you find their action to be discourteous and maybe even offensive? When people tell you untruths, essentially they are indirectly saying that you are not smart enough to know the truth. How do you feel about that?

Nobody is perfect. There will be times when negative events or outcomes occur in your business even when you are doing everything to the best of your ability.

Courtesy dictates that you tell the truth to your customer. Instead of insulting your customer's intelligence, go ahead and tell them what really happened. Then tell them what you can do to make it right. More often than not, your customer will immediately recognize your integrity and appreciate your courtesy. They will even continue to be a loyal customer and they will refer others to you as well.

ASK AND LISTEN VERSUS TELL AND TALK

No one likes to listen to someone who is always talking about themselves. Unfortunately, it seems to be a natural tendency to talk about oneself. Courtesy demands you to ask and listen to others instead of telling and talking about yourself. However, the fact is people like to tell and talk about themselves. This is a positive thing for you—as long as you are not the one doing it. The more you ask and listen and then ask again, the more positive your interaction will be with other people.

Studies show people are strongly attracted to people who give them the opportunity to talk about themselves. The more they can talk about themselves, the more they will like you—even though they do not know much about you. How can they? They have spent all their time talking about themselves.

Again, it is not natural to ask questions and listen. So make a game of it. When you converse with someone, make it a point to do very little telling and use mostly asking. Try to even respond to questions with a question. You will be amazed at what you will learn, the positive response you will get and the inevitable success you will achieve.

THE COURTESY SYSTEM AT WORK

A system of courtesy starts from the top. The CEO must be courteous to employees, vendors and customers. The common thought is the customer is number one. Actually, your employees should be number one. Your employees should be treated as well as your best customer. Tell your customers and vendors how fantastic your employees are whenever there is an opportunity.

Courtesy given to your employees will tend to be reflected by your employees to your customers.

As always, your actions will speak louder than words. However, it is very important to actually train courtesy in the workplace. Remember, courtesy is not commonly known or used. So it must be trained. You are only as strong as your weakest team member or employee. Fortunately, courtesy is easy to train. Use this chapter as your guide.

Once you have trained the courtesy system, expect courtesy within your organization and to be given to your customers. Then, verify courtesy is actually happening everywhere in your business. Verifying something is occurring throughout all aspects of an organization is usually a tall order. However, verifying the courtesy system is in action is fairly simple to observe.

Here is what the ultimate verification will be. A work environment where people are polite and speak to each other in a friendly way. Employees and customers laugh and smile a lot. Constant complaints from customers and employees are a thing of the past. Employees come early and stay late because they want to be there. There is no gossip or backbiting. Instead, employees are positive and complimentary about each other. They make it a point to edify each other in front of the customer. They know what the customer wants because they asked and listened and always with a smile.

Your customers are frequently asking, "Where do you find such good people?" Other business owners and vendors are baffled with the same question. And, best of all, your customers are returning, doing more business with you and sending even more your way.

UNCOMMON ACTION

Commonly, after everything is said and done, more is said than ever done. If you desire success, be uncommon and take action with the courtesy system. I suggest you begin with extending courtesy to those you love. Simply start with "please" and "thank you." You and everyone else around you will be glad you did.

About Dr. Matt VanderMolen

Dr. Matt VanderMolen practices at his office, Advanced Dental Care of Springfield, in Illinois. He has provided 27 years of friendly, courteous, comfortable and highly personalized care to his patients. Advanced Dental Care of Springfield received the Most Outstanding Performance Award from a national dental organization in 2010. His practice has been recognized as the Best of Springfield every year since 2009 by the United States Commerce Association.

Dr. VanderMolen is also listed as a Top Dentist in Cosmetic and Sedation Dentistry in the United States. Recently, he was nominated for Small Business Person of the Year in Springfield for 2012.

As a member of the Pierre Fauchard Academy, Dr. VanderMolen is a recognized leader in dentistry. He is a Fellow of the Academy of General Dentistry and the American Dental Implant Association. He is also a member of the American Dental Association, Illinois State Dental Society, Chicago Dental Society, International Congress of Oral Implantologists, Crown Council, Dental Organization for Conscious Sedation, and the American Dental Society of Anesthesiology.

Dr. VanderMolen has been well-received as a national speaker to large audiences of dentists and dental teams on rapid practice growth while maintaining optimal patient care. He is known for his "straight talk" on success principles that everyone (not just dentists) needs to hear. Dr. VanderMolen is committed to helping as many people as he can inside and outside his practice. He offers free consultations in his office for most types of dental care including sedation dentistry, cosmetic dentistry, FastBraces™, dental implants, and cosmetic dentures. He is also available to speak to professional or business groups on success principles.

Please visit: www.SmileSpringfield.com

Or call: 217-546-3333 for more information.

CHAPTER 14

Creating A Compelling Culture

By Erin Skye Kelly

At the start of my career, I had some tumultuous times. Amazingly, I still have 80% of my team with me.

Someone pointed out that I have an extremely loyal team with low turnover, and that is when I started to examine some of the reasons we have such a strong culture.

I don't pretend to know it all. Most of the time I ask more questions than I have answers for. But it my goal to create healthy workplaces—where people are rewarded for their contributions and have a vested interest in the outcome...where they are rewarded for more than their time. I don't pay people for the hours they put in, I pay them for the results they get.

The face of business is changing. When you spend 160 hours per month with people, you need to be able to manage more than just their tasks. You need to give them a compelling reason to perform for 8 hours a day. You are competing with Facebook and texting to keep them engaged. Previously people may have had an easier time leaving their home-life challenges at home. Now they carry all their challenges with them, on their mobile devices.

My team almost always self-manages. If someone doesn't fit into our high-performance culture, they will usually weed themselves out as it is a lot of work to create the illusion that you look busy. They hold each other accountable. Not in a "HEY! YOU-SAID–YOU-WERE–GOING-TO-DO-THIS-THING" kind of way, but more in a "Hey! Just wondering how your thing went last week?" kind of way. It alleviates a lot of the managing I'd otherwise have to do as the leader. I believe that when you create a culture of achievers, you create a culture of success.

COMPASS

We share the company vision, and share it often. We remind people about the big picture.

When my team knows where the company is going, they can be autonomous, which people appreciate. The goal is to have all of our arrows aimed at the same target. When people know the end result, or the goals, I feel they are better able to make decisions that line up with the target. If something falls outside of what is going to get everyone to the goal, then they are empowered to realign their decisions with the vision. My goal has always been to have a culture of leaders, and people can't lead until they are invested in where we are going.

COMMUNICATE

Communication is a fine balance of telling people as much as they need to know to understand something fully, without so much information that you overwhelm them.

The communication should also be casual, yet professional. If I want my employees to read my emails, they must have catchy subject lines, and they must be friendly and to the point. They can contain private jokes, provided everyone on the team knows and understands the joke. I do not make private jokes with management that the rest of the group would not understand. The goal is to be inclusive so everyone reads every memo and understands it.

Words have power. It is critical that I use my words to breathe life into people with not only the words I choose, but how I use them. For example, a manager could say "this marketing proposal is stupid!" or they could ask "is there a better way we could word this marketing proposal?"

I think the word 'We' is powerful. It is inclusive, and represents teamwork. I want all my managers and employees to use 'We' when they are talking about the company or the business we do because it is really difficult to point fingers or cast blame if we use the word 'We'. For instance, I could say "Janice really messed up. She's in the shipping department and she should know better." Or I could communicate "we really messed up. We are now working to make sure our shipping protocols are improved."

The second one demonstrates a united front and has some strength behind it.

CARE

We consistently strive to demonstrate a caring attitude about what keeps our customers up at night. Because I often work in the finance industry, I have discovered that many of my clients are stressed about money.

According to the Wall Street Journal, 70% of North Americans are living paycheck to paycheck. Clearly, income is not the issue. Money management is! We will often have an expert come in and teach a course on paying down debt, investing, mortgages or planning for retirement. Dave Ramsey has an excellent course called Financial Peace University which we promote to all our staff and clients. I have found that when employees are not stressed about bills or money, they perform better on the job, and their attitude in the workplace is much better.

If someone loses a loved one, they receive a handwritten sympathy card. We also do birthday cards, anniversary cards, and "Way to Quit Smoking!" cards. More on that later. But taking a few minutes out of each day to acknowledge someone or express gratitude enhances our work culture. I always want to be able to recommend a great marriage course, a reputable mechanic, a wonderful book on parenting. As a leader, I need to be able to steer people towards solutions while demonstrating that I care.

I make sure I know the names of everyone on my team and have their numbers programmed into my phone. One thing I work at doing is being enthusiastic when I get a call from another team member. Rather than answer the call "Hello, Erin speaking" if I know it is one of my staff I can choose to energetically say "Hello Paula! How ARE you?!" as if I have been waiting for her call for years and am so happy she contacted me. It changes the tone of the communication from the start, and lets those key players know that I am always happy to hear from them, no matter what the reason for the call. It also opens the lines of communication because they will be less likely to hesitate if they have unfavorable news to share or action. But most importantly, I hire amazing people and it always a privilege to hear what is going on in their worlds.

CELEBRATE

Of course we celebrate people on their birthdays. Your company might have a policy for how this is handled already, but I like to send everyone a heartfelt personal card on their special day. Since I have a sales team, it is imperative that these skills are taught to that team so that they can participate in celebrating the lives of their clients. One of the girls on my team sends a bag of gumballs to our client's children on their birthdays. Another fellow in my organization sends a gift card for a free ice cream to his client's children on that child's birthday.

Here's the differentiator: we pay attention to the other small details. We train our managers to pay attention as well. It is important that if someone accomplishes a major milestone in life, quits smoking, runs a marathon, does something above average, that we recognize it. At the start of my career, I worked with an amazing woman named Karen Spelay who had been a smoker for many years. It was incredibly difficult for her to quit. On her 3 month smoke-free-anniversary, we had a surprise party for her in the lunchroom, complete with decorations and a cake. For years after I would send her a congratulations card on the anniversary of her quit date. She was so incredibly surprised and gracious. If we leave these things unnoticed, we leave people uncelebrated.

Celebrating personal growth reinforces the importance of accomplishment and goal setting. Personal success is built on a discipline that is carried over into the workplace. You don't typically find someone who has accomplished in their personal life slacking off to surf pinterest at work. A person either is, or isn't disciplined. The best way I've found to coach people into a disciplined lifestyle is with a healthy dose of positive peer pressure.

Celebrate enough successes in your workplace, and more successes are born.

CHARACTER

I try and be vulnerable when warranted. Nothing builds trust like vulnerability. When I mess up as at the leader, I strive to be transparent with my team. I want them to know that I am the first one to admit when I make a mistake so that I can work on the correction course. If I try to cover up or hide my mistakes, I create an atmosphere of mistrust, whether or not they find out. I also need to be able to laugh at myself and not take myself too seriously. Professionalism is always warranted, but when I clumsily spill coffee or walk into the glass doors accidentally, I earn a lot more respect by being that person who can laugh at the situation instead of pointing blame. (Who put that glass door there ANYWAY?)

I think it is easy for most of us to make good decisions when our teams are watching us. But it is more difficult to make good decisions if we think they won't notice. I've learned the hard way that it is better to just walk in integrity and make good decisions from the start so that integrity muscle is honed. I am not someone who naturally knows what the Right thing to do is. I always have to think about it. I have a girl who has been working for me for years named Celeste Wood who is the most principled person I know. She never has to think ,"I wonder what the right path here is?" She just knows. I wish I was wired that way, but often, I have to think about what the consequences might be before I decide. As an entrepreneur and business owner, my life is divided into Risk and Consequences, so I am constantly working on my character muscles so that I can live congruently with who I am, what I stand for, and what I believe. And I have to do that even when no one is looking.

CONFIDENTIALITY

NO GOSSIP. NO DRAMA.

We have a saying here that goes…if you are the type of person who has ever said, "Don't tell anyone I told you this, but…" then you aren't going to make it in our culture.

I watch out for brownnosers. Sometimes that employee that sucks up to me all the time is actually the cancer-causing agent in my organization. (*gasp!*)

Come on, you know who I am talking about! We all have encountered one of those do-gooders who knows her job so well, she can do it whilst simultaneously telling you who the dude in the mailroom was kissing, what he was wearing, and what his last Facebook status said.

If I have a culture with a ZERO TOLERANCE for gossip, I create a safe place for people to come to work. I create an environment that will lift people up instead of tearing them down.

We have implemented this so strongly that we do not have People magazines in our office. We replace US Weekly with Success Magazine. No surfing TMZ. No "did–you- hear–abouts…" or "I'm-not-supposed-to-mention-this–buts…".

It is also vital that my team knows they are responsible for their emotions. I do not tolerate outbursts. I do not put up with people who stir up drama. Though I do encourage appropriate friendships outside the office, I do not tolerate cliques. We are inclusive, supportive and we recognize and respect differences. It is something most of us have to work on as it does not always come naturally. But if the end result is a safe supportive workplace where people can grow to their full potential with little fear of judgment or rejection, then we are building a foundation of excellence.

COACHING

I put a lot of emphasis on personal development vs. job skills, in my organization. I believe that if I have the right person with the right attitude and the right passions, the job can be taught. But if I have someone with the right skills for the job, and they come with a negative attitude, or they aren't passionate about their work, I am going to have problems with them even if they know their tasks well.

I try and lead by example. I am someone who invests in new learning. I encourage great books. We share thoughts and ideas and encourage people to think outside their cubicles.

I always ask people what they are reading. "What is the best book on your nightstand right now?" It gets them thinking about how they'd like to answer. You don't want to be the gal in my organization that says "Twilight." Or "50 Shades." While I know a lot of the people who work with me might actually be reading about teenage vampires as a form of escape, they are all also investing in their growth and development because in a culture of achievement, no one wants to be left behind.

COMPLIMENT

I will brag about my team publicly. When they contribute to a result or a success, I will recognize it fiercely. I announce it on Facebook and tag them so their friends and family know. I put it in the company newsletter. I make sure other people hear how great someone on my team performed. This isn't about "kissing up" or "blowing smoke" as we say. This is about giving genuine compliments when due.

CHALLENGE

I challenge them to raise standards in the industry we are in. Give them a cause and a purpose to fight for. When people are participating in a movement, they behave from a place of passion and drive and camaraderie. I encourage them not to decide if something can be done, but rather HOW it can be done. We are not allowed to say "that's not my department" here. We take matters into our hands and fight for our clients and we are not allowed to throw team members under the bus to make ourselves look better. If one of us achieves, we all achieve. If one of us messes up, we all work for the solution rather than assign blame.

CONSISTENCY

I love the flight attendant analogy. When we hit turbulent air when flying, we often will look to the flight attendant. If she is FREAKING OUT and yelling "WE ARE ALL GONNA DIE!!!!!" then we are going to experience sheer panic. If she is smiling and calm, then I am less likely to panic and I will go back to my e-reader. As leaders, we are required to have unwavering tenacity and vision. We cannot "wing it" and let the day's circumstances dictate our plan. We must schedule and plan ahead. We must make purposeful decisions. In times of change, how I consistently behave will determine loyalty. I want people to say that working with Erin Skye Kelly is a predictably positive experience, and that will only happen if I am consistent every day.

CHARITY

We support a cause everyone can fight for. I will give my team time off to volunteer at an organization that impacts our community. We have a portion of proceeds of certain projects go to causes that resonate with my people. I strive to give them something bigger than themselves to work towards. We work as a group to make meaningful impact. But as always is the case when you are helping others, we are the ones who are meaningfully impacted.

About Erin

Erin Skye Kelly is an entrepreneur and radio personality in Calgary, Alberta, Canada. She is passionate about developing cash-flowing businesses and empowering women to run them.

She has two amazing boys, and in her spare time, she surfs, she runs, and she kicks Autism's *ss.

You can find her at ErinKelly.ca.
Or connect with her on Facebook at: fb.com/erinkellydotca

CHAPTER 15

The Secret Of Winning Big

By Siou-Foon Lee

In winning big, Asians use Chinese metaphysics as a tool for success. We take it seriously as we want serious results.

Fengshui and Chinese astrology are ancient traditions that we use to solve our modern day challenges.

OUR WAY OF LIFE

It is natural for us to seek top Fengshui advice to address business and personal concerns in health, relationship, productivity and managing finances. It is our way of life to make our living and working spaces harmonize with the energy flow of the environment by balancing the ying and yang aspects of the external and internal spaces.

According to our way of thinking, we accept that we are not masters of the universe, but we learn to master our inner universe. We realize we are not separate from Mother Earth but part of her universe.

We see our buildings as containers of qi. **Qi** is life force energy. Opening the container and placing an entry at the right location brings good energy flow inside. Opening the door at the wrong location impacts the circulation and vibrancy of earth energy of that given space.

In our way of life, we turn to Fengshui and Chinese astrology to 'win big' including business.

FENGSHUI

Choosing the right place to live according to Fengshui is using the right space. Buildings with the added benefit to accumulate positive cosmic energy for its residents are filled with earth luck. Spaces that have good earth energy channelled from the external into the internal spaces bring balance and harmony to our lives. Spaces with disruptive earth energy are disconnected from the energy fields of the immediate environment.

If we live and work in harmonious places we will lead lives in a deliberate way. Our action, skills and decisions are part of the factors that govern success. Our ancient sages teach this. Traditional Fengshui is a tool that opens doors to a greater capacity to achieve more when applied correctly. Its purpose is to enhance the capacity for bigger things that business owners and entrepreneurs wish to carry out.

On a personal level, it will subtly shift the energy in our homes when earth qi is harnessed—bringing us more earth luck and opportunities. We know that external and internal Fengshui application gives optimum results when best applied at the outset of a project. Many large corporations use Fengshui services in order to have a leading edge.

However, its ability to turn dwindling businesses around into success stories is a major draw card. Entrepreneurs recognize the profitable returns of their investments when traditional Fengshui is applied. Their priority is to enhance the capacity of their business potential and turn it into a realistic profitable enterprise.

We view Fengshui as a crucial and necessary component to winning big. With specific requests, Fengshui masters do create specific results within a specific time frame. The strategy is both practical and simple. The objectives are measureable and achievable. Our best approach to projects is to begin from scratch starting with consulting, selection of site, assessment, recommendations, implementation and review of project.

CHINESE PHILOSOPHY

Ambitious businessmen are familiar with the Chinese philosophy about taking appropriate action when time and space is appropriate. For the Chinese it is not about right or wrong. It is about being appropriate.

Every situation demands a different reaction. Rather than waiting for the right place and right time to do the right thing, we place ourselves in the right space at the right time to do the right thing in order to win big and grasp success.

Whatever luck we can garner helps to propel us in the right direction. However, we cannot attribute phenomenal success solely to earth luck. Going beyond luck it is necessary to have skills to build and grow enterprises as well as careers.

The Confucian way of thinking allows us to be quietly aggressive. We create the right connection, we use the acquired information, we are at the right place at the right time so as to do the right thing. We select the space to be in and connect with the right people. It is about maximizing the situation. Human actions and date selection count for much and it is the appropriate things we do and plan in a particular time that will make all the difference.

We want our Fengshui masters to investigate the capacity of land and space. In cracking the code for optimum health and well-being, wealth and success, our Fengshui experts ensure that there is a balanced and auspicious interaction between the external land and the internal occupied space. Placing ourselves well is vital to our ultimate success.

BAZI

Today, Fengshui has seen the rise and rise in its popularity. But not many new end users know that every Fengshui consult begins with BaZi (Chinese astrology) analysis. How will the Fengshui master do personal Fengshui for us if he/she does not "know" who we are?

Knowing our destiny is knowing our path in life. To know it, we use BaZi to decode our birth data. Knowing destiny does not amount to instant success. Success is governed by appropriate human action as well as living in the right space according to what the ancient sages teach.

A BaZi reading allows us to delve into the great mysteries of life. The interpretation of the eight characters within our natal chart, the information and insights gained help us in our journey through life. The purpose of this decoding is to help us make informed decisions and choices. The clarity and pre-knowledge is most beneficial. Should we go ahead with the decision or choice, we are informed about what we should do, what we should avoid and how we can have the upper hand.

Better strategies are formulated knowing our job functions, spouse and job compatibility and health conditions. Knowing what lies ahead prepares us. Knowing what we know about ourselves and taking appropriate action on what is known puts us in better positioning.

CORPORATE FENGSHUI

The evolving western corporate world can benefit from Fengshui as a tool to innovate significant change and to shift the focus to improve staff wellbeing to ensure maximum productivity. The mission is to design and provide businesses with Fengshui solutions to create balanced, harmonious and aesthetic working environments to support key decision makers and staff.

Right now there is a shift in consciousness and a definite capacity for change and renewal. Worldwide, people have grown to respect humanity and Mother Earth. People are recognising traditional knowledge in supporting community and the environment. As a group, people realise what is happening globally and go on to inspire each other. There is a trend where people are doing what they love, enjoy an incredible life and want to help others in need.

But can the big players step up in leadership, lead change and win big? Can they revisit the working space and create less stressful workspaces and work stations?

It is a win-win when caring more about mind, body and spirit of employees. It translates into progress and achievement. Creating harmonious spaces benefitting key decision makers and supporting staff is actually increasing the bottom line. Fengshui can be that tool to achieve that big win.

DIFFERENT APPROACHES

To win big is the ultimate goal in financial independence. To be really big on adding maximum value in learning to better our management approach towards financial freedom we turn to BaZi for validations.

In the analysis, we receive new information; we learn from our past experiences and gain new insights. Not only can our perspective on money and wealth be transformed, but our whole life-view as well. It can be a great, liberating and empowering experience. We learn how to make better decisions.

The real turning point in our life...can be when we learn about holding back from making rash decisions. When we know, we understand. When we understand and believe in our capacity to be high performers, we take appropriate action. Knowing destiny/heaven luck does not give us instant success. However, the most crucial factor for success is the timing and application of this heaven luck. We need to know what is appropriate to do, when to do it and how to do it better.

Space, time and action is the essence of 'winning big.' Failure to apply or take action with the given information indicates poor human luck. If we have constantly set goals only to see failure, we need to look for honest answers.

To say that a BaZi analysis is a life-changing experience just doesn't do it justice—fully satisfied clients have found it to be completely transformational.

'Winning big' can come in different forms. Informed decisions can be made leading to actions that have been known to completely change lives: resigning from jobs that were disliked, starting brand new businesses, selling and relocating to incredible new places or even going on health kicks.

When we discover the secret of 'winning big,' we can go from survival mode to becoming respected and successful entrepreneurs, leaders and visionaries.

TOP TEN TIPS

Here are 10 ways for you to get started on the secret of winning big:

1. The fastest way to get on the path of winning big is to have your destiny code deciphered. In today's economy you deserve to hear the truth 100 % of the time. Use BaZi analysis to make informed decisions.

2. Position yourself to be at the right place at the right time so as to do the right thing. Fengshui selects the space. You find ways to connect with the right people. It is about maximizing the situation.

3. Use BaZi to find out truthfully the ONE mistake that prevents you from winning big—and how to avoid it. Stop repeating this ONE mistake that is keeping you trapped where you are currently.

4. Get to know the core of what action unknowingly sabotages your own success—and how to stop letting your guard down. There is a path of least resistance available. Take it.

5. Take the SINGLE most important action to create massive results. To know how to do it better, use BaZi knowledge and Fengshui strategies to propel you towards winning big.

6. To gain authority and greater responsibilities, maximize your abilities to impress others of your potential. Good performance evaluations and praise can propel you up the ranks.

7. If the current time is wrong, plant the seeds of success for next year. Then prepare to charge ahead on a well-selected date. The appropriate action you plan and carry out in a particular time will make a difference. Not all 'thinking big' ends in 'winning big.' Timing is of the essence.

8. In the face of serious changes, BaZi advises on the best year to make long-term changes. Hold back on making major change when timing is wrong. Plan your strategies early in the year before the change. Activate Fengshui/earth luck to open opportunities to find new and unique paths to success.

9. Maintain courage under fire in the face of challenges. Changes for the better can be harnessed as a catalyst to make a breakthrough. To 'win big' you need to break through old patterns.

10. Exercise patience. Be quick-witted yet flexible when faced with abrupt changes. Self-pity or frustration will only aggravate the situation. Maintain the status quo. Take responsibility for your actions.

Here is a quote by Goethe: "Until one is committed, there is hesitancy, the chance to draw back…"

LIFE MANAGEMENT STRATEGIES

A destiny analysis is the missing piece of the puzzle - a powerful system that will ignite success, accelerate results and completely transforms lives.

BaZi and Fengshui are proven life management models that Asians have been using for generations to create success after success, systems that have been hidden from you, until now. It does not matter what your situation is, how bad or good it may seem, there is a lot to be learnt and BaZi/Fengshui can show you how. Take that leap of faith and just do it.

Believe in seeking benefactors who will assist in resolving problems, giving ideas, turning situations around even stepping in and providing protection.

To succeed big you need to have clear-cut goals. Infuse decisiveness. Be clear in thinking. Be strategic in planning. Use analytical abilities to achieve your goal in career advancement, a rise in power, an increase in authority and greater responsibilities. Go and achieve them.

There is no "magic push button" or real "secret sauce" if you want to win big in financial independence. Explore the finance sector of your BaZi—understand your mindset, attitudes and approaches to wealth creation. Challenge your beliefs and your actions in regards to money. Learn how to make better financial decisions. The decoding of your destiny will be a life-changing experience for you: not only will your perspective on money and wealth be transformed, but your whole life-view will as well.

BaZi takes you behind the scenes and explores hidden potentials with the exact systems that people use to go from survival mode to becoming respected and successful entrepreneur/professional.

BaZi cuts to the core of how to build creativity and performance; wealth and financial management; leadership and authority; knowledge and providing a comprehensive "GPS" that gives you the ability to pinpoint where you are and identify exactly where you want to go, detailing the quickest and easiest way to get the results you want.

With auspicious wealth stars in your natal chart, it is vital to know the timing when rewards and more rewards appear. Timing and action is of the essence. Implementing correct Fengshui strategies to 'win big' is just as important as windows of opportunity. When timing is right, you see gold nuggets while others just see a pile of dust. Some winners have found the missing piece of the puzzle - introducing them to the powerful systems that accelerated their results, ignited their success and completely transformed their lives.

CONCLUSION

Which path will you take to win? How about finding the right place with the big capacity for carrying out the projects you plan?

It is about finding the right place with the capacity for you to become a high-achieving performer. Your appropriate actions in the right space at the right time will activate good luck – bringing you favorable outcomes. Correct action in the correct space and time is the essence of this concept.

With auspicious wealth elements present in the natal chart, aiming for entrepreneurship can be achieved. If you strategize well, even if you work less you still earn more than usual, but if you are extra hardworking, you could really make it big. You have Lady Luck on your side.

Some people are cut out to succeed by digging for gold while others succeed better at selling shovels to the gold diggers. Some work hard working for money, while others work smart making money work for them.

A space with great capacity and potential to return Fengshui investments on it can enhance your efforts to 'win big.' Your decision and speed of implementation to commence any project at an ideal time is vital to success. According to ancient teachings, it is the right place that brings out human potential. It is the factors comprising the trinity of heaven, earth and human/man that governs success. The trinity is destiny reading, Fengshui and action/decisions.

Pay great heed to them if you want to win big. It pays!

About Siou-Foon Lee

It is about the journey, not the destination. In our anxiety to succeed, we think so much about the destination we forget to enjoy the journey.

When I first mastered Fengshui two decades ago, my first master told me to help people with my knowledge. I kept asking "Why me?" I was oblivious to the bigger plans lined up for me. After two years of indecision, I took time off to decide, but then a car accident changed my life. I recall my husband's words, "Your car has been taken off the road. What are you going to do now?" That was an 'aha' moment. I resigned and followed my passion. My new Fengshui/BaZi career opened so many doors that would have never been possible had I stayed fully employed. I was propelled into the limelight. It was as if this had been waiting for me all along. I have now learnt it is important not to question "Why Me?" but to accept it as "Why Not Me?"

I have come this far in my journey through life …

My niche is Fengshui and BaZi, which I pursued actively before going on a sabbatical. When I returned to resume business, I decided to keep my traditional practices alive by improving my practice. I collected a range of case studies paying attention to result-oriented practices and learnt from a respected master with a long lineage. In this second wave of study, my mentor gave me great grounding in well-tested principles. I feel blessed and thankful. Learning to be the trusted authority in my niche, I learnt it is important to have a clear message, share and make a difference in peoples' lives. I also looked at turning something outside my comfort zone into positive potential. Learning about Internet marketing opened up my mind and helped me reach a wider audience. For me, it is about being flexible.

What am I sharing?

I want to share that if you have a passion, unleash it. Take action. Do not stand at the fringes undecided about whether you have what it takes. If you want to leave a legacy of making a difference in people's lives, go ahead and do it. Never stop learning. It is the journey, not the destination. My legacy to my children and my grandchildren will be that I took the risk and trusted that my talents and passion will earn me a reputation that they can be proud of. The moral of my story is to honour your calling and pursue your passion. Until you read the signs, risk your comfort zone and trust that it is going to be alright, you will find yourself in limbo. It is about finally crossing the threshold of fear; pursuing my passion and heeding what my master said I should do – to help others – a decision that changed my life.

Master Siou-Foon Lee – master trainer, public speaker, co-author of *Cracking the Success Code*.

Website: http://www.fengshuiinnovations.com

CHAPTER 16

Living In The Question

By Mark Tosoni

Imagine life with a constant and steady flow of money; more than you would ever "need"—or how about abounding energy, vitality, and wellness in your body. What about relationships that are mutually supportive and conscious? How cool would all this be? Well these are things I've been considering for decades. I first began doing affirmations at 16 and decided that being rich would be cool. It's been quite a journey since those days in pursuit of "the secrets to winning big." Through my path, I've encountered all the great teachers of our time—like Brian Tracy, Tony Robbins, Robert Kiyosaki, etc., and have learned so much from these teachers. After I dropped out of college with a 1.8 GPA at nineteen (can you say entrepreneur), I had no money so I began selling cars—which led me to becoming a business owner, ...which led me to become a millionaire.

I've gone deep in many "self-development" strategies from goal setting to laws of attraction; and as great as they are, there's a dirty little secret in the world of personal growth and development. That secret is that much of what's taught doesn't work! Why? ...Because our backgrounds, traumas, and dramas affect us all differently. There are two kids from the same family—one becomes a criminal and the other saves the world. So are the techniques taught failing? Or are the people who apply the techniques coming up short?

For starters, very few actually discover and apply the techniques; and out of these who do, a handful succeed and "win big." But it all

changes here in this chapter, so please read with awareness. Friends, I struggled for years, broke, desperate, and almost hopeless. I've lived through divorce, health problems, and the suicide of my father. All the while reading "self-help" books voraciously, attending seminars, and actually working with the principles in the laboratory: my company and my 100% commission sales people. I've had it; lost it; got it all back, and then some. My conclusion about life, business; and winning big…
STAY OUT OF CONCLUSION!

We are indoctrinated in this reality to judge and conclude about everything. The bible is clear about this "judge not" thing; yet, …do we walk it? …demonstrate it? …live it? Or is it just another useless piece of ancient wisdom? The topic I teach is what I call "energetic influence" – which is designed to assist people in dumping their limitations and accessing their potential. The central strategy of "E.I." is to "live in the question." Why? Well you may have heard it said, "the mind is like a parachute, it works best when it is open." Yet how do you do this when life shows up? And life will show up if you haven't noticed! This reality in which we live I call "thinking 2.0", because it's all about figuring things out, judging, and concluding. Is there a time and place for it? Perhaps. That said, what if there was a more graceful way? If you're lucky enough to have ever experienced someone who was "judge-less" it is a tremendous gift, yet it's not too popular on our planet. Not in our politics; not in our churches; not in our schools, or our society. It seems it's all about good/bad/right/wrong/left/right, etc. It's the dual nature of the thinking 2.0 operating system and the limits of the mind. Does it work? Yeah. Might there be a better way? Let's see what else is possible?

The challenge with this way of operating is, it inadvertently puts you into "energetic resistance." So if things are good, we want more of them, and if they're bad we want them to go away. Then we find ourselves struggling in various areas and can't figure out why. We essentially become blockers of all that's bad. This presents a challenge – unseen to most. You see everything in our life is merely "energy," …your business, …your investments, …your bank accounts, …properties, etc. Science tells us everything is energy. If all these things were viewed under a high-powered microscope, you would discover they are all in motion and not solid, including the bed you sleep on every night. So it seems the game we play has more to do with energy than we might be aware of. Which would mean those really difficult people, like bosses, idiots, etc. that you're dealing with, were created energetically. Dis-ease in the body; lack of money showing up; they were all created energetically whether intentionally or not!

I used to cringe at the idea that I strongly influenced certain things to happen, but didn't know how to change them; so what I did was just toughed it out and worked through it; until one day I woke up with an adrenal problem; my body wasn't having it anymore, it was time to get to the core.

For years my mind and my body ran 110 miles per hour. In 2008, I discovered that my net worth was at an all time high; the economy was doing horrible, my economy was doing terrific, and my self-worth was at an all time low; in spite of all that I created. I told my girlfriend at the time (now my wife) that I couldn't shut it off. My life was like an engine that was revving near the red line. This over focus—figure it out living in my mind 2.0 way of being—resulted in depleted adrenals, and imbalanced thyroid, …and complete exhaustion. The bottom line: I call this "success with side effects." The recovery has been long and drawn out over a year and two months as of this writing.

Today things are very different. As of March 2011, I could no longer work like I once had; like an obsessed maniac; a missile (awareness). So all I could "do" were the bare essentials—coach my salespeople, a little recruiting, manage our admin, and get our people paid. All the while getting acupuncture, visiting various naturopathic doctors, having diet changes; supplements galore; using energetic strategies to help unwind; journaling; and meditating by the beautiful lake that I'm so blessed to live on. You could say I didn't listen to my body when this first began, and eventually I was hit by what I call a "universal 2x4," and I was knocked out. Of course, I had to be knocked out because I was simply too "dumb to quit (no disrespect)" even when my body was screaming for help. (Sometimes us human "doings" aren't too bright.) Upon awakening, I began to notice something interesting taking place; when I stopped going into the office to work; and was doing what I could from home, our sales and business began doing better; less effort and better results. Reluctantly I began to take notice.

We were doing better, our people were doing well; enjoyment began to increase along with our money, and not just in our business but our real estate investments began growing as well. My wife, family, and I were bonded tighter, and my health improved; ...and my mind began to get well. I couldn't ignore the growth of my life's garden; and I've always said, "you know the tree by its fruit" and it was fruitful.

THE BIRTH OF "LIVING IN THE QUESTION"

It was the gift of my condition to cause me to go even deeper into personal growth and development. I had to evaluate ways of being that simply no longer worked for me, and change my eating habits; and place my body at a higher priority level than my business. All the while, I had this thing called "question" coming into my awareness. I learned of one teacher who was teaching questions vs. affirmations. I began doing affirmations as a teen, did they work? Well, I accomplished a lot in business yet I compromised my body. So I went deeper; and began asking more questions, and went from missile mode to question mode. I was feeling curious about what it would take to get well! So I created a "CD" program with a bunch of questions set to really nice music, and began listening. I had one for health; one for six figures, seven figures; success, etc.

Not to be redundant, but this health challenge led me in a lot of directions, explaining and questioning things I had taken for granted: like "my point of view"; ...like my "resistant way of being." The lies that I was living, the energy of people in my life, the food we were ingesting, exercise, and the energy of our home. I was questioning everything that made up my life - My biggest question was, how do I turn off this mind? They say when the student's ready the teacher appears—Welcome to Bars™.

This is an energy technique I learned about that would release the electro-magnetic energy stored in our head (thought residue) from thinking too much; they told me at best it would feel like an incredible massage, at worst my whole life would change. And that's exactly what happened when I began practicing bars with myself and others. I didn't think as much. (Oh! what a relief it is.) I lightened up; joy began to emerge, my awareness soared and I have a new-found clarity as well as power tools to live life with—and would you believe one of the central tools taught by the founder of Bars; Gary Douglas- is "to live in the question." I was like "hala-frikken-luia." I can let go of figuring it out? Wow! Friends, our minds (and egos) are so limited, they only know what's been experienced in your life up to this point, it's very limiting. Although, I'm always trying to figure out everything in my life (living in my head), I never had peace, even when there was lots of money. Today we enjoy having peace of mind and money! What a concept; <u>what would it take to have peace of mind and lots of money?</u> Great question! Speaking of questions, that's a pretty good one.

You see in this thinking 2.0 version of reality, we are totally conditioned and trained to go into judgment and conclusion. This phenomenon of entrainment is similar to what happens to women when they live together; they begin their cycles together as well. This friends, is exactly what happens to us. We are highly sensitive to our surroundings; as the beings we are, we are massive receivers of energy, more than you could begin to imagine. Your parents' thoughts are energy; your siblings, your church leaders, teachers, the media, and here we are, sponging it all up. This my friends, is why we have challenges, because all this entrainment has been absorbed by us in the form of points of view, beliefs, perspective, etc. Many levels and layers—even if some are serving you they also limit possibility—for example, if you believe that "you will always earn six figures" that might be a good thing; yet it cuts you off from seven figures, or beyond. That's why beliefs are overlooked; questions are where the real power is. My point of view was "I'll get rich or die trying" and I almost succeeded at the dying part. Was getting rich that important? Now I choose life and abundance; and how I choose it is with questions, such as—for <u>"business"</u>—what would it take to generate _$xxx_ per week; or what would it take to generate _y_ sales per week profitably? For <u>health</u>—what would it take for my body to have vibrant health, energy and wellness? What would it take for me to be the ideal weight my body wants to be? For <u>relationship</u>— what would it take to have an abundance of depth full of relationships? What would it take for my relationships to be harmonious? These are the "what would it take" questions. Do not miss the brilliance to a simple question.

LET THE UNIVERSE DO HER WORK

Why do I call it a "her?" Just to mess with you, that's it! Actually, the "universe," "God," "source," "all that is," whatever you choose to call it —is the unequivocal gifting champion of life. That's why the good book says, "ask and you shall receive." Not ask and figure it out, or ask and force it into place (my favorite), or ask and get pissed off because it didn't show up as quick as a supersized order at a drive-thru window! <u>ASK AND YOU SHALL RECEIVE</u>; it is not ask, and you might receive; or you will receive if you're a good boy or girl (commonly taught here on planet earth). <u>NO</u>. It's ASK AND YOU SHALL RECEIVE! It's so clear and so simple we've over-thought it and complicated it with judgment and conclusion.

Let's say you can't stand your boss, chances are when you're out with your friends; it's like…"This guy/gal is an idiot"; "No, you don't understand, this one's a real jerk"; …and on and on vs. "What else is possible with my boss?" Or what would it take for this relationship to be harmonious? Or what would it take for me to love what I do, and whom I do it with? There is infinite possibility with questions; it takes a little practice at first; like 21 to 30 days! Habits do break; and know this, judgment and conclusion cut off energy; energy that the gifting universe might want to bestow upon you! One of my favorite questions I learned from Gary Douglas, founder of <u>Access Consciousness</u> is: "How does it get any better than this?" I taught this to my salespeople, we were up 20% for the first quarter of 2012: All I did was teach them a question, and reminded them to stay in the question when their mind tries taking them out—Like "what else is possible?" Isn't this fun? What if making money, making a difference, and doing business are easier than we make it? What if we have a point of view locking the difficult part in place? From my experience, friends; your life can expand in all areas if you so choose! So would you be willing to live in a question for 21 to 30 days and see what shows up? If you are, you'll be grateful you were—as you allow yourself to open to the infinite possibilities available to you. So get ready to win and win big…………..

With infinite love and gratitude,

Mark Tosoni

About Mark

Mark Tosoni started, built, and sold three million dollar companies by age 40. He is the author of two e-books titled *Sell Like Crazy without Going Insane* and *Fast Strategies for Maximum Influence*.

Mark is currently running strong in the Alarm systems business generating thousands of sales per year. Mark is also developing a system called "Energetic Influence" which will be an evolutionary program on how to influence ourselves and others. He is also the co-founder of: www.directsalespeopleonly.com which is an inbox magazine empowering sales people around the globe.

To learn more about Mark and to receive your free copy of *Fast Strategies For Maximum Influence* go to: www.marktosonitraining.com

CHAPTER 17

"DO" Sweat the Small Stuff

By Garrett Pierson

"But Mom!" I said. "It's July and almost 100 degrees outside. There's no way I am taking a coat." I can still remember my mom's sweet voice trying to reason with her unreasonable son who was, at the time, a 12-year-old scout.

I was preparing for summer scout camp at Camp Bartlett in Idaho and I don't think I had ever been this excited before in my life. Spending time with friends in the mountains, playing with fire, and more importantly, having fun. But my Mom was ruining it all, or so I thought. You see, to me, taking a coat to scout camp in the dead heat of the summer seemed like the most insane thing anyone could come up with. I thought my Mom was crazy.

I'll never know why she ended up letting me go without a coat. Maybe she wanted to teach me a lesson or maybe she was just sick and tired of trying to convince me that the "small" and simple act of taking a coat was important.

I arrived at scout camp and the weather was perfect. "My Mom is so silly." I thought to myself. "I can't wait to get home and tell her how warm it was up here." Later that day a storm approached the mountaintops. As the evening grew darker and colder, all I could think about was how easy it would have been to bring my coat. "I can't believe Mom was right." I said out loud. "Now who's the crazy one?"

For two days straight it got colder and colder. I have never been so miserable. When I got home, I was reluctant to tell my mom about what had happened. As I started telling her about the storms, she just smiled at me and began shaking her head up and down, demonstrating that she already knew, which made it more difficult to swallow. I learned a couple things that summer that I will never ever forget.

First, always listen to your Mom. (I love you Mom.)

Second, the "small stuff" does matter.

You see, I believe that our journey on earth is all about learning how to be happy. We all want to be successful, to be loved and to be the best we can be. But if happiness is what we strive for, why does it seem like we're in a constant battle to accomplish the things that we want or desire?

I've had the amazing opportunity to interview and work with some very successful people in my life. I guess you could say that I have been a life-long student of powerful people. The list is too long to mention all their names, but just trust me when I say that successful people have used and, more importantly, continue to use the same core skills to achieve their goals, find happiness, and obtain success. I uncovered a pattern as I studied these people, and have applied what I learned from their lives in my own life.

In this chapter I will focus on a powerful core principle. I believe it can be the key to your success and winning big in your life. I will share with you a few simple ideas and effective action steps that will create a life of abundance and joy for you.

Have you ever heard the saying "Don't Sweat the Small Stuff?" Well, it should be removed from our societal jargon. I have learned that successful people only sweat the small stuff.

Having said that, let me make an important clarification. In no way am I saying sit and worry about everything or get all stressed out about every little thing.

What I am saying is, if you carry out conscious, committed, consistent, forward-moving micro-decisions everyday of your life, then success is just around the corner.

Remember my earlier story about nearly freezing to death at scout camp? Think of how easy it would have been for me to grab my coat out of the closet and throw it in my bag. It would have only taken me seconds. It was a micro-decision. Had I made the correct decision, it would have made that weekend substantially more enjoyable.

You may have big, inspiring goals to change the world, lose weight, or even make a million dollars. Whatever your long-term goals may be, they are important to you, as they should be, because you are the one who created them. Regrettably, many of us seldom do more than start on the path to achieving the goal we desire. For those of us that do at least start, many get discouraged when we don't see immediate results. So, unfortunately, we give up.

Successful people achieve their goals because they have a steady approach to everything they do. They make important "small choices" every second, minute and hour of the day.

Let me bring this into prospective for you. Let's use the goal of weight loss as an example. Two separate people (who I will call Person A and Person B) desperately desire to lose 25 pounds. They feel that this will make them feel better about themselves and bring more energy and health to their life. They create individual but common goals, of losing 25 pounds in sixty days.

Person A creates a specific meal and workout plan, writes the goal down and commits himself to the goal (all small but powerful micro-decisions). He also takes time to build a healthy shopping list, then goes shopping and signs up for a gym membership right away. The first two days, he sticks to his plan and makes good decisions each day even when roadblocks get in the way. The third day, at his wife's birthday party, he eats small amounts of food and doesn't eat any cake (another small but important decision). The next two days he is offered ice cream and pizza and kindly declines. A week later Person A has lost 3 pounds and feels much better. He sticks to his plan for the next sixty days, making good decisions along the way and on day sixty, he has lost 27 pounds and is happier than ever.

Next, Person B goes on a binge diet, eating small amounts hoping and praying that he can lose the 25 pounds as fast as possible. The third day, at his wife's birthday party, he feels that he can just take one day off and eat as much as he wants, and it won't hurt. "I did so well the last two days," he thinks to himself. The next two days he justifies small things like eating ice cream and pizza. He soon finds himself at the exact same weight a week later and doesn't quite understand, so he gives up on his goal of losing 25 pounds; he tells his wife he'll try again later.

We make thousands of decisions each day of our lives; most are small, some are big. Person A understood the importance of "sweating the small stuff." Person B, however, decided to focus more on instant gratification and less on the goal and the happiness reaching the goal would bring. They both desired the same thing, and both were equally capable of accomplishing their goal. The difference came when one decided to make a powerful choice to make a plan and commit to it, a small decision that resulted in big rewards. This is just one simple example of how winning big requires our commitment to small and simple things.

I once read an interesting *Peanuts* cartoon by Schulz, a comic strip that I think will bring to light my point.

Charlie Brown seems to be having a tough time at a baseball game with his friends. He keeps striking out and sadly goes to the dugout burying his face in his palms and cries to Lucy, "I'll never be a Big-League Player! I just don't have it! All my life I've dreamed of playing in the Big-Leagues, but I know I'll never make it…"

Lucy looks at Charlie straight in the eyes and says, "You're thinking too far ahead, Charlie Brown…What you need to do is to set yourself more immediate goals."

"Immediate goals?" wonders Charlie.

"Yes," shouts Lucy. "Start with this next inning when you go out to pitch…See if you can walk out to the mound without falling down!"

As silly as this may seem, there is an important truth to what Lucy is saying. STOP thinking too far into the future and START focusing on today's decisions. You will never reach the goal of making a million dollars in a year if you don't make a decision to earn $2,739.73 today. What most people with this goal don't realize is that it takes $2,739.73 a day to equal 1 million dollars in a year or $1,369.86 a day to make a million dollars in two years. Most people just focus on the $1 million and not on the small amount they must earn today to get to $1 million.

Have you ever seen an anthill? How in the world does something so small make something so big? They do it by moving one small piece of sand at a time. If the ants focused on the big picture or the total number of pieces of sand they would all have to carry, they would give up long before they even started. It is no different for us. If we focus on the "BIG" instead of the "SMALL" we tend to fail. It's that simple.

We must think big but act small! The secret is consistent action. You aren't going to build a house, business, or fortune in a day. It's the small efficient steps and actions that lead to winning big.

Let's focus on another example to help illustrate the importance of micro-decisions.

I teach people how to write, finish, and sell books. I have learned from research that over 80 percent of people in the USA have a goal to write a book in their life. Now when you think of writing a book, more than likely you think of it being a herculean task similar to climbing Mt. Everest or running a marathon and you would be correct, it's not easy. But running a marathon, like writing a book, means running without stopping – one mile at a time. It's the small micro-decisions that create an author or marathoner.

I'll be more specific. For the average person to run a marathon here are some examples of some important micro-decisions that must be made before competing in the marathon:

• Get up tomorrow morning and run 3 miles
• Drink lots of water for the next three months of training
• Run 5 miles today at a good hard pace
• Today and everyday I need to eat quality food that will build stamina – like more protein and vegetables
• Take 15 seconds per minute off my regular running speed
• Do tempo runs today to help improve my strength
• Run 18 miles today because there is only 3½ weeks until the marathon
• Each day of training, increase either my speed or my distance

The list could go on and on and on. The bottom line is that in order to run a marathon, there are certain decisions and actions that need to occur in order to fulfill the goal of crossing the finish line. The same idea applies to writing a book. You must be conscious about the goal at hand and create a strategic plan that you commit to follow. Then you need to make micro-decisions every single day that will move you closer to your goal.

Here are some examples of some possible micro-decisions that a soon-to-be author chooses:

- I made a goal today to write for 1 hour, I am going to stop watching TV and start writing
- I need to take a break today and get a full 8 hours of sleep tonight
- I must find a copy editor to proofread and edit my book today by 11am
- It's time to write but I don't feel like it, I am going to do it anyway no matter what
- Today is the day that I write the final chapter of my book

Although the short-term goals I've shared are hypothetical, when small choices are acted upon, anyone can succeed at finishing a marathon, writing a book, or becoming a millionaire. Whatever your biggest desire happens to be, the same rules for success apply.

Today is the day you change habits, make better decisions and keep it small. If not today, then when?

Benjamin Franklin professed, "You may delay, but time will not."

It's time to "start sweating the small stuff" and move forward with happiness and success.

It's time to win big!

About Garrett

Garrett Pierson loves his amazing wife Lindsey and adores his two children - Gracie and Jack! Garrett is a family-centered entrepreneur that lives his passion each and every day, and it's his goal to help others do the same.

He coaches individuals and businesses in their quest to find what it takes to be successful by motivating them to create the life they deserve and the business they desire. His valuable, insightful tools and techniques make it easy for anyone with personal or business aspirations to reach the previously unattained.

Garrett currently runs an online software company with his business partner Scott Brandley. In 2010, Garrett and Scott successfully launched Shopper Approved, a fully-automated customer rating and review service that helps website owners create huge amounts of positive social proof which influence, educate, and motivate new customers to buy. They hit another home run in 2011 with the launch of Rhino Support, a web-based customer support management system for online businesses.

Garrett is author of the book *What Success Takes*, a print and audio book on "The Die Hard Principles of True Victory in Life, Business, and Soul." This book includes 30 interviews with successful people such as Raymond Aaron, Alex Mandossian, Carolyn Ellis, Noah St. John, Joel Comm, Russell Brunson and many more. He is also the co-author of *The Trust Factor* a print and e-book that teaches "7 Strategies To Convert Your Online Visitors Into Lifetime Customers."

Garrett has a passion for helping others. And, one of those passions is in helping others to write their first book and to do it fast. Nothing pleases Garrett more than seeing his students grow socially, psychologically and emotionally by writing and publishing their own books. His latest book and training system - *How To Write A Book ASAP* has been helping to create authors all around the world. It is his goal to create 500 authors in the next 5 years! To learn more about Garrett Pierson, visit: www.HowToWriteABookASAP.com

CHAPTER 18

Refine Your Skills, Handle Challenges And Set Goals To Win Big

By Marita Skårelid

Have you ever set a Goal, where you were really inspired to reach that Goal…but then you find yourself not taking action…even though deep inside you know you're capable of reaching that Goal ?

Or, you set a Goal, and go to work…but suddenly you can't even create results in areas that normally wouldn't be a big problem. You have a lot of knowledge in those areas, but still don't get results…or even worse, you move backwards, and the frustration gets bigger and bigger?

I will share some things that have been very useful for me, and hopefully you will find some pieces that may be blocking you from reaching your potential…

To be a good student of success, to be a good student in your field, to be an observer of successful people…

all those things are quite obvious if you want to succeed. But when things aren't working for you, you need to know specifically what to study…maybe it's not about putting a lot more knowledge into your head—it can be to get a better understanding of the things you already know.

Imagine you're putting a jigsaw puzzle together. You look at the picture, and pick up a piece… "H-m-m-m, that doesn't seem to fit in" at the first try…but then you realize "yes, it is the right piece," you just had to twist it a little to make it fit in. At other times it's not the right piece at that moment, but still, it's a piece of the puzzle so there's nothing wrong with the piece, it will fit in later. But it will not work to try to put it in place right now, even if you use force, it just have to wait until some other pieces are in place, and then it will fit in perfectly.

So how do you know if it's the right piece at the moment or not? The thing that really can change your results is to find a good mentor. Not just a teacher, or advisor…You need a mentor—someone in your field who has walked the path, and can guide you step by step.

The world is full of opinions and so many good suggestions, that it can be easy to fall into the trap of starting to 'walk in circles' instead of moving forward. Remember the jigsaw puzzle…When you start to put a puzzle together, everyone starts with "the end in mind"—they look at the picture on the cover.

Then some people start with the frame, some people start with sorting the colors, some people start from the corner, others start with different details in the puzzle and then find the pieces in between that glue it together. Which one is the best way to start? Maybe you have started with the frame…and then you read a book or get good advice that it's better to start sorting colors first…so you start all over again. Halfway through that process you get even better advice, to start building from the corner. So you start all over again.

Even the best advice can be distracting, so choose a mentor that you highly respect, one who can help you to keep focus and stick to the track you're on. It will make the process faster.

When I was teaching riding students, I learnt a good lesson that has also helped me in business. There are two areas that have to walk hand in hand…knowledge and skill. The learning curve looks like this :

You get some knowledge and you start to develop your skills…then you seem to reach a plateau. If you think you're on that plateau because you have stopped developing, it's easy to loose faith in your own potential…

Understanding that the plateau is just a place where the things you have already learnt need to get more fluent before you can move on to the next level in your learning process, can help you. You need to focus on specific details while practicing to get your "click"—it can be like twisting that piece of the puzzle to get it in place. When you're on a plateau, it's definitely not the best time to try something else. It's not the best time to put a lot more knowledge in, because if the gap between knowledge and skill becomes too big, you will very easily fall into a negative curve. Why? Because you know too much theoretically about HOW to do things compared to your ability to perform, which makes you tense and frustrated. Maybe you start to feel you don't have what it takes to perform at another level.

It's very easy to fall into this trap, because when things don't work out as you expected, the most natural thing to do is to think that you need more knowledge. But what you really need is a better understanding of the knowledge you already have, and very often you need to practice more of what you already know to get that "Aha" moment. When you get it, you realize there was another level of understanding.

With horses, you probably just need more hours in the saddle. Keep practicing the same thing over and over again until the penny drops. In business, maybe you need to keep making calls, keep making business presentations, keep setting goals and doing action plans…just keep twisting that piece of the puzzle until you get fluent at what to say, what to do.

Will there be frustration? Yes, of course. The best thing you can do is to learn how to turn frustration into something good.

When my son was sick, I learned to live by a "quote" I had heard many years ago:

"All the things I love will make me strong, all the things I hate will make me weak."

It doesn't sound like a very unique thing, when you first read it…but man, it's so powerful when you start to live by it…and I have also brought it with me into my business.

If you see it like a scale—where Hate is on one side and Love is on the other—in the middle is Neutral. There are different levels, different modes that will be on the same side as Hate…and different levels, different modes that will be on the same side as Love. For example ,"I hate that I'm such a bad closer." Hate is a very strong word, frustrated may be closer to the truth...if you're frustrated, you will be weak. How can you turn that frustration into something that would make you stronger, something on the Love side? Maybe you just need to focus on how much you love the things you offer, instead of being frustrated that they don't understand how good an offer it is...seems like a small change, but it can dramatically change your results. It's just like twisting that piece of the puzzle...same piece—different result.

Or maybe you need to go into a mode of fascination instead of getting stuck in frustration—fascinated about how people will respond if you make small changes. Remember that you are probably closer to those results than you think, we're just talking about twisting a piece, it's easy to try to change 3 or 4 pieces at the same time, but it normally will take longer...it will be a clutter.

Sometimes there will be situations you just can't find anything positive about, no matter how much you try. Then you can at least choose to not hate it. That's the situation I found myself in, when my son was diagnosed with Leukemia. As much as I tried to twist and turn it, there was nothing positive or fascinating about it. Maybe you think I could have loved that there are treatments, but it was just too hard to love those treatments. But I could choose to not hate it, so at least it didn't make me weak. I became very neutral and rational about the cancer. I saw the schedule as something we were going through. I put blinkers on and then I focused on other things that I loved.

Why do I bring this up, ...talking about Goal setting? ...Because I have experienced many times that when you set a goal, some kind of challenge will show up. It can be small challenges or big challenges, maybe in a relationship, or some financial challenges, or challenges to find the amount of time you would like for reaching your goal. It's easy to get frustrated about it, and then you will get weak...the challenge will rob your energy, and you stop. But when you learn to handle those challenges, twist and turn those pieces, and see if you can find anything fascinating about them, or at least treat them without negative feelings, it's easier to move forward towards your Goal.

For me, it is important to set a Goal big enough to get fascinated about it. I've been running for some years, and as long as I tried to run 5 km, it was a pain and it was boring…and I heard "No pain, no gain"…it will be easier. But I never got through that barrier, I really had to use a lot of self-discipline every time to put on my running shoes. I didn't study any technique, because 5 km doesn't need a lot of technique. Then I took a decision to run a marathon, it's a goal I haven't completed yet, but I will, and I can see the difference in my thinking and my actions.

You can't run 42 km without a good plan so I started to study technique, pulse, how to eat etc. And I got fascinated about what's happening in my body, amazing what you can do within just a few months that you never thought was possible—as long as you were just trying to survive a 5 km run. It was the same for me in business…a Big Enough goal brings more energy and excitement. Does your goal make you curious about how you can reach it, or is it just a 5 km goal?

If you still don't find yourself taking the action you need, maybe your deadline is the wrong one, not the wrong goal. Most people change the goal to a 5 km goal, because they lost belief in their potential. Try to change the deadline instead…and put it closer. Deadlines are our friends, they make us start and get things done. I'm sure some of you were like me in school; it didn't matter if I had 3 weeks to my next test, I started to study on the last day…so maybe you need to put a tight deadline that makes you start today.

A deadline doesn't have to be a pain, I once heard a speaker who said "A goal doesn't have to be like climbing Mount Everest, it can be like when you step outside in the early morning, take a deep breath and let the fresh air fill your body with energy, and you want to start running"… *I love that metaphor!*

During your journey to success, you will have many different tasks to handle—both in business and in family life. It can very often be hard to switch from one task to another, even though you have good skills in both of them. For example, you have taken care of the kids all day, or you have been sitting at a board meeting on your job and then it's time to make some phone calls to book appointments. Even though you have done calls like that thousands of times, you still have to start to think about what to say and get in the right mode to get results. This takes time, effort and energy…maybe you get tired just thinking about it… maybe you start to procrastinate.

I read in Brian Tracy's book "Maximum Achievement" about the power of making your own affirmation audios…and I thought maybe it would be a great idea to create my personal audios for different tasks as well. So instead of putting a lot of thinking about what to say or how to act every time, I can put on an audio and relax.

This is how I do it: I put on some relaxing music in the background and just use the voice memo on my phone to record, part one for relaxation, part two any subject I want to refresh, part three wake up full of energy. This means I can use part one and three over and over, and just record new subjects for part two, and then I put them in different play-lists.

So now I can relax and pick up energy while refreshing my mind about what the next task will need from me, what to say, etc. I can also use part two by itself, on the way to an appointment—to pick up what to focus on at the meeting. If you liked it, I recommend you read Maximum Achievement to get this idea to work for you.

Hope some of you already can see Goals and Deadlines as something that can be exciting and energizing for you, and not as something frustrating.

About Marita

I met my husband 30 years ago, and we have two lovely children, now teenagers. That's the biggest award in my life. And I believe my best gift to them is to show them how exciting life can be, … even when you pass the age of 25. I want them to expect that they can create a great future.

After school, I chose to follow my passion, horses. I became a good rider and educated myself to be a professional riding instructor. I have always strived for personal development, …as a rider of course, but also in creating a well-functioning organization and good economy at the Riding School where I worked. So after some years, I became the Manager for another big Riding School, then I started to work for the Swedish Equestrian Federation to develop the quality of the 600 Riding Schools in Sweden. I became the examiner for Riding Instructors, wrote a book for the Federation on how to run a Riding School, and was invited to be a speaker at their Business School education classes. I was voted to be the Chairman of the Branch Organization including trainers and breeders, so you can say I was at the top of my career in the horse industry – which is a very big industry in Sweden.

At this stage, our son was diagnosed with Leukemia, and I had to quit all my obligations and focus on his treatment, which was a very long journey. Now he's OK.

I had to find a new career, and I was really attracted by the idea of Network Marketing, to be able to build a business of my own, and at the same time have the opportunity to create successful teams together with other great business owners, and to leverage the results.

I realized I could use a lot of my earlier knowledge and experience in my new business, because success principles are the same whatever branch you're in. I've been invited to speak to share my experience using these principles at several Business Development Seminars. I love to help people see their own potential, and guide them on their journey to success.

CHAPTER 19

Transforming Your Destiny The Quantum Way

By Mimi Williams
"America's Destiny Transformation Expert"

"A QUANTUM METHOD FOR WINNING BIG IN LIFE"

Many years ago, I participated in a fire walk ritual as part of a weekend self-empowerment seminar. After many major setbacks in my personal and professional life, I was struggling to achieve several important goals. Those set-backs included two divorces before the age of 35, several major health issues, and two failed businesses, all of which created financial havoc. In addition, I moved across country to care for my aging parents while also paying college tuition for my son. You would think that fire-walking would be a cakewalk for me after some of the bitter pills I had swallowed. In my mind, it wasn't. It was a frightening idea that I was determined to conquer. I drove to Florida from Atlanta to participate in a 3-day event culminating with this exciting, yet still daunting challenge for me. Well, the goal for the weekend was to experience something that you totally believed you could not do, and then doing it easily and effortlessly. Yeah…right, I thought. Walking on fire was definitely something I thought was impossible for me to do, but if doing it would empower me to achieve my dreams and visions, then I was up for the challenge.

One of the things I noticed throughout the weekend was that the seminar leader never talked to us as if he expected anyone to back out and not walk on the hot coals. He talked as if it was a done deal for everyone there. He explained exactly what to do, step by step to make it successfully across, while making sure he reminded us of the dangers involved. Even though his explanation of the dangers scared everyone half to death, he continued as if he believed and expected everyone to go through the experience with confidence. He closed his eyes for a moment, and then he said, "I can see each one of you walking across the coals fearlessly and unharmed." The next four hours were spent practicing the art of visualization. We mentally rehearsed that fire-walk until it felt real.

Creative visualization is the process of using your imagination to create a particular outcome. It is the act of creating an idea or a mental picture of something that you wish to manifest. I really wanted to manifest this feat, so after being guided into a very relaxed state, I began the process of visualization. In the first few mental walk-throughs I saw myself saying things like, "Are you crazy or what" and "Don't do it you idiot, leave." My sweaty palms, along with the anxiety, and apprehension were all about to win. But after a few more mental walk-throughs or visualizations, I began to slowly feel as if I could really do this. I began to feel more relaxed. My visual images became so real to me that I actually saw myself walking over the coals a second time, as I couldn't believe that I had done it the first time.

After several confidence building exercises, meditations, visualizations, and a thorough step-by-step process to follow, it was finally time to take the walk. We followed our leader outside to the rows of brightly lit, burning coals. We formed several lines, preparing for the walk. The look of fear on the faces as everyone tried to NOT look fearful was almost amusing. OMG, I thought, what have I gotten myself into? The sweat was pouring again, the nerves were shot, and I kept going back to the end of the line. When it was finally my turn to walk, I began to immediately remember everything I had been visualizing on the floor of the auditorium. The leader looked at me and yelled WALK! I positioned myself as I was told earlier, I chanted the affirmation that I was given, calmed my mind, and proceeded to walk quickly over the coals. The whole thing happened so fast, I didn't believe what I had just done. You'll never guess what happened next! Because I was the last person in my line, I was able to walk all the way back over the coals again. Exactly like I had seen it in my earlier visualizations.

My life was never the same after that experience. My destiny had been transformed, I thought! I came back to Atlanta and for the first few months after the seminar, I was able to triple my income very quickly. Many of my personal and professional goals were achieved. For about a year I was on a roll. And then the bottom fell out again. After spending time reflecting, I realized that the many steps, processes, tools, and techniques that I used to walk successfully over the hot coals were the same tools that helped me to become successful in my business. But I stopped using them. I never really developed the habit of using those quantum success tools that are needed for massive wins in life. I realized then that I needed to hire a coach. I felt that having someone to help me maximize my strengths, and guide me to take inspired action would get me back on track. I was right. It didn't surprise me when my coach started out with an attitude of expectancy. It also didn't surprise me when my coach started instructing me to use visualization techniques to create the outcomes that I desired. However, she advised me that these tools and visualization techniques should become a part of my daily practice indefinitely. Because we are always creating our lives with our thoughts and feelings, I learned that the process of conscious visualization should be a lifetime commitment.

There are many important techniques, principles, and laws to follow in order to win big in life. I share these in my programs on and offline. I have found that using visualization consciously and in the correct manner is a vital key to winning big. I'd like to share the benefits of this wonderful process and then take you through a visualization exercise that you can practice repeatedly until it becomes a part of your winning strategy.

One of the most important benefits of creative visualization is that you will improve your self-image. When you impress images of yourself as successful, happy, and abundant onto your subconscious mind, it automatically improves your self-image. As a result you begin to feel happier, more capable, and more confident. Using visualization also helps you to develop a "prosperity consciousness." And who doesn't want that, huh? It just feels good to imagine, in vivid detail, yourself being rich and super successful, doesn't it? It feels wonderful to imagine yourself winning big in life. It's been said that "feeling good is your point of attraction." When you're feeling good and thinking about how rich you are, your subconscious mind begins to believe that you really are rich already. When that happens, you begin to automatically attract everything necessary to achieve the vision and goal of prosperity and success. Visualization is also good for the soul. Yes! When you visualize images of living your dream life, you begin to replace fear and doubt with possibility and desire. Visualizing yourself as you really want to be will cause you to become more relaxed and focused. All of these benefits are actually important keys and skills for winning in life.

Another name for visualization is "mental rehearsal." Mental rehearsal is a tool that is used by Olympic athletes, golfers, movie stars, top sales performers, elite business people, and basketball players. All winners have used visualization techniques in some way to improve their skills, maximize their performance, and ensure their ability to win. Even rappers love visualization. Kanye West in *The Good Life* says, "Before I had it, I closed my eyes…imagined…The Good Life!" That's visualization buddy!

In essence, visualization helps you to win big in life, and your mind and body is automatically set up to make this happen for you. When you vividly imagine achieving your dreams and goals, an entire series of subconscious processes are triggered to assist you. Visualization trains your brain to know what you want, which is an extremely critical step in winning big. When your brain knows what you want, you experience success almost like magic. Here's how that works! At the base of the brain stem there is a group of cells known as the reticular activating system or RAS. This system acts as a filtering device for incoming information. When your brain knows what you want, this system will begin to filter out all incoming information that is not pertinent to what you say you want, or to what you're actually paying attention. Attention is key here, so follow me. This non-pertinent or unimportant information is then sent to the subconscious mind. All pertinent information relative to what you're paying attention to (call it "your brain knows what you want" information) is now immediately sent to the conscious mind. Think about this, if you've ever had a car for a long time, let's say a silver Toyota, then you go out and purchase a red Ford Truck. All of a sudden, you begin to see red Ford Trucks all over the place. Where were all the red trucks before? They were there all the time, but that information was sent to the subconscious mind by your RAS, because it wasn't important to you at the time.

You may as well learn to use visualization correctly, because you are already doing it. Yes, you already "visualize"…without knowing it. You see, every time you worry about the future, or continue to think of how "bad" things are going in your life, you are actually visualizing. Your mind cannot think a thought without creating a mental picture. As you worry, you're creating pictures of negative circumstances of future events. I'll show you! Say the word 'chair' and see what pops up in your mind. A picture of a chair, right? That's the way the mind works. We actually live in a picture world and we're always visualizing, but mostly about the wrong things. When you begin to consciously visualize the things that you want to create in your life— as opposed to those things that you don't want, you will begin to take control over your experiences in a positive way. Your RAS will begin to work to your advantage. With consistent practice you'll see better and better results in your life. This one practice will bring you to a level of success that you've probably never dreamed possible.

When first learning to visualize effectively, I suggest starting with a simple goal. Choose something that is easy for you to believe in. Begin to create a mental picture of what that goal would look like once you've achieved it. Focus on this goal as often as you think about it, and bring the picture to mind. While you are focusing and picturing your goal as already achieved, begin to repeat positive affirmations to yourself relating to the achievement of your goal. Here is a short visualization that I have used with clients and students very successfully.

Close your eyes and get into a very comfortable position. Breathe slowly and deeply so that your body can continue to relax. Feel your mind releasing all thoughts and concerns of the day. Feel the wonderful relaxation as it flows through your body and mind, relaxing you even more. As you relax even deeper, visualize yourself feeling happy, prosperous, and full of joy. See yourself feeling vibrant, energetic, and full of vitality. Now think of your health, and see your body feeling healthy, perfect body weight, excellent vital signs. Get that image of yourself as healthy, trim, fit, and toned. Now think of your finances. Visualize your bank account filled with extra zeros. See your banker smiling each time you enter the bank. Visualize the beautiful home that you now live in. Visualize yourself driving the car of your dreams. Continue to visualize the positive and successful life that you know you deserve. Be sure to visualize these experiences as vividly as possible.

Think of all the details in each scenario, and then begin to feel what you would really feel like as all of these wonderful experiences are taking place in your life now. Now in your mind's eye, place these wonderful scenes on a giant movie screen and begin to amplify the visions. Watch this movie of your wonderful new life as often as you like. If your mind begins to wander, just gently bring your thoughts back to these beautiful ideas that you are creating for your big win.

Hiring a coach was such a gratifying and inspiring experience for me, I decided to become a coach and help others transform their destiny. We all could use someone to help us identify our purpose, and walk with us on the journey to self-improvement and fulfillment. I am now living the life of my dreams. I have created a very successful and profitable business helping heart-centered, professional women and smart men to transform their destiny using very unique processes that I have created over years of research and study in the human potential movement.

I sincerely hope that you get excited about the process of positive visualization and are inspired to get started right now. It's really an awesome tool, and certainly one that is highly recommended by winners.

About Mimi

Mimi Williams, "America's Destiny Transformation Expert" and founder of Mimi Williams International Consulting LLC, is a highly sought after inspirational speaker and ordained minister. As a specialist in life transformation, the "Law of Attraction," Hypnotherapy and Energy Psychology, Mimi has helped entrepreneurs and professionals alike to maximize their strengths and discover their hidden talents and sacred energy. She has studied and trained with experts in the Human Potential Movement for over 30 years and has a vast knowledge of both Energy Medicine and Energy Psychology, Universal Laws and Principles, NLP, and Subconscious Belief work.

Mimi's training and natural intuition are the driving forces behind her success as a consultant and coach to numerous professionals and entrepreneurs. Through online and personal workshops, seminars, private and group coaching, she is fulfilling her mission and purpose to teach people how to lead happy, fulfilling and successful lives in relationships, finances, and career. She resides in Atlanta, Georgia.

For more info: www.mimiwiliams.com

CHAPTER 20

The S-Factor For Success
—Speed Is The Name Of The Game!

By Donn S. Kabiraj

So you want to be a successful entrepreneur? I am sure you have come prepared to put in all the hard work, investment, determination and effort that it takes. Yet somewhere in your mind, there lurks that bit of uncertainty. How do you ensure that you are a success??

I have analyzed successful businesses from various domains and various sizes—small, medium and large. I have spent hours poring over their success stories and analyzing them to bits. What shone though was one special ingredient, an ingredient so powerful that it spelt the difference between success and failure! An ingredient that shines through like a powerful beacon in the stormy world of business! It is *Speed*—the **'S-Factor'**—as I have coined it.

Navigating the business world can be tricky! It takes a swift-mind to do it! This explosive chapter reveals how 'speed' is of foremost importance to win big and sustain your success!

HOW A BRAND BECAME REALLY BIG BY HARNESSING THE S-FACTOR

The best way to understand the *S-Factor* is to take a look at a real life situation. I had a client who was manufacturing filling and packaging

183

machineries for the beverage industry. They had quite a good brand image and were running a successful business in India. But their profit margins were falling due to heavy competition and erratic pricing from small time players. They were really very ambitious and wanted their brand to grow exponentially. They realized to do this they required a different approach. At this point, they consulted us. We analyzed all the data about their products and existing market. We applied our proprietary tool, the DNA-Compass™ that I had invented after years of research on the mystery factors behind the success stories of organizations of various denominations. This unique tool is a foolproof direction finder and allows an aspiring entrepreneur or business to relax, secure in the knowledge that they will now be able to move in the right direction with no doubts or fears.

Resorting to the proven **DNA-Compass™** tool, the following steps were recommended to the client by us:

- To consider an immediate market expansion and foray into potential foreign markets.

- To incorporate and highlight a few value-adds without significantly increasing the cost.

- To focus on product modification and brand repositioning to suit the new markets.

After considering several parameters, we figured out that Middle East and African countries were the best fit for an immediate Market Expansion.

Based on our suggestions, the client's top management swung into action quickly. Their Executive Director and the Vice President immediately flew to Dubai, the business hub of the Middle East and UAE. They even made cold calls across the length and breadth of the country and received feedback from various prospective customers. This enabled them to feel the pulse of the market even before they actually launched their local sales team into action.

After due analysis and a series of strategy sessions, we reconfirmed that it called for brand repositioning and the product needed some modifications in terms of quality control to meet the demands of the Middle East and African markets. Quick to seize the opportunity, they immediately added a few suitable features into their products—which translated into multiple advantages and benefits for the customers. Not only that, they also incorporated some value-added services for their new target customers.

The product was launched in the UAE, Africa and other Gulf countries. It went on to make history. Sales soared, demand grew and today, they are one of the well-established brands in the Middle East and Africa. Following this success story, the company is now confidently working towards their footprint in other countries as well. They have grown from $5-million USD to $97-million USD in turnover in a span of just 7 years.

The lesson we draw from this is that *fast* and *speedy action* will always bring excellent results.

1. GET THE RIGHT ATTITUDE!

No matter how many times you have heard this one, it's the first thing you need to have before you become a winner. *It's a positive attitude!* A positive attitude is what makes you give your all to your business and automatically brings the **S-Factor** into play.

You will actually be surprised at how having a positive attitude will keep you brimming with passion and energy—which will give your business the impetus it needs. Like a rocket that needs a great deal of force to take off, every business needs plenty of push, and after that it will move ahead of its own volition. A positive attitude also sustains you through the highs and lows that a business may go through and gives you that staying power.

2. BE THE FIRST MOVER

Speed counts; be the first-mover into any market! If you have researched your market well and find a demand-supply gap that you can fill, or if you have something innovative to offer, plunge into action immediately.

If you are in a market where there are existing players, make sure your product has that little bit of extra—maybe a feature or brand promise that others have not yet zeroed in on, which will give your business the 'magnetic pull' factor. Sometimes not all products or services have unique features. In that case what should you do? Take a look at your product or service once again. Find something you can highlight in a different way.

Being the pioneer in a market is a wonderful competitive advantage. Firstly, it establishes your business firmly in the customer's mind, and in the long-term can give you market dominance and higher-than-average profitability. One of the best examples of this is Amazon.com which was the first major online bookstore. It not only got a head start, but also continues to dominate since online book buying has become synonymous with it.

Another great advantage is that early entrants can file patents and prevent competitors who follow from copying it.

Buyer-switching costs are another area that first-movers make a killing in! When it's expensive or inconvenient for a customer to switch to a new brand, the first company to benefit will be the first-mover.

3. NETWORKING GETS YOU AHEAD FASTER!

Networking is an important part of achieving speedy growth in business and instantly creates awareness about your enterprise. This allows you to meet different kinds of people and gives you refreshing new perspectives on the way others think. This could open up a whole new world of business opportunities.

When you meet successful people, it automatically gives you a boost and induces a positive mindset. It motivates you to achieve more and keeps you happier. Meeting others in the same domain does help in knowledge gathering.

Networking can also play another role in helping you attract customers in a more subtle way and also increase your circle of influence. This is an effective way that helps you meet prospective customers in an informal environment. You will be able to exchange cards and information which could later lead to an increase in sales.

Social networking is a recent phenomenon that is very valuable to businesses. Social networking sites like Facebook, LinkedIn and others allow you to connect with like-minded people. You will also find professional groups dedicated to areas of your interest and can garner valuable information on them.

Social networking is also a cost-effective way to promote your business. It's a quick way to communicate the benefits of your product or service. Offering discounts or developing other promotions exclusively for users of that network will go a long way in bringing in traffic and more customers faster.

4. BUILD NEW SKILLS

As an entrepreneur, you must be ready to keep learning new skills. You may have to initially multi-task and even handle jobs at which you are not really proficient. For instance, you may be good at ideating or marketing but your knowledge of accounting may be negligible.

You must be open to learning new skills that will benefit your business, and in many cases are mission-critical to your success. Books, CDs and online programs are some of the resources you can draw upon to upgrade your knowledge. You can also learn from domain experts in the area in which you are weak. This will not only help you lead your business better, but as you improve your skills, you will also work faster.

5. BE PROACTIVE RATHER THAN REACTIVE

The business world changes by the second. A smart entrepreneur will not wait for the competitor's move, but will plan ahead to meet the evolving needs of the target. You keep a marketing plan that stays at least a few steps ahead of what competitors are doing.

Keeping tabs on your competitors and their progress is important to stay afloat in the turbulent world of business. Being proactive helps you to stay in charge and captain your business, rather than fall in step with the rest of the herd. This is a huge *speed-multiplier!*

6. THE PRICE YOU PAY FOR MISSING THE S-FACTOR

We had this client who was proficient in the software domain. He sought my advice for a real hot business idea that would really bring in the big bucks and catapult his company into the big league. I took a look at his strengths and came up with an innovative idea that he could easily implement—given the resources and technical expertise he had. I asked him to build a social network like Facebook for sharing only photos, videos and images.

He liked my idea and was thinking over it. I explained the strategy and also assured him that there was enough space in the market for him to step in and make a mark. Though he was happy with my idea, he never took action on it and instead spent time on repeated analysis, something I would simply call *'paralysis-by-analysis'*. In my experience, I have found many who suffer from it! Meanwhile the new social-media-network Pinterest was launched; it had the very same concept and went on to grow faster than Facebook. Had my client heeded the **S-Factor**, today he would have been heading to become a billionaire many times over!

7. AVOID PROCRASTINATION

Make speed a part of your everyday life, avoid procrastination like the plague. When we drill down and look at the reasons we procrastinate, here are a few. Fear is one of the biggest issues that keeps us from going ahead and accomplishing the task we set for ourselves. Fear brings down our level of self-confidence, and we end up with doubts that we might fail or that it will be too difficult.

Some of us procrastinate on certain tasks simply because we don't like them, but that should not be our attitude. Some things have to be done whether we like them or not, and the best way is to do them and move on to the next item. Expectations of others or from within ourselves also lead us to procrastination, as we are sometimes unsure whether we will be able to live up to them.

Procrastination can be a big problem when you are running your own business. It can not only affect productivity, it can also result in losses. The best way to get over procrastination is to analyze the root cause and then get rid of it. If it's fear that's pulling you back, assess the fear and move ahead. If it's a task you hate, see if you can outsource it or just quickly finish with it. To handle expectations, give yourself a shot of self-confidence and start on your task. Nothing tried, nothing gained.

8. RESPOND TO MARKET CHANGES

Markets change rapidly and speed is important to respond to market changes. For instance, if you entered a new market, initially you could be a monopoly, but soon competitors could develop or the trend could change. It's important to keep a hawk's eye on competitors and upcoming competitors. Businesses that do not track competitors could be in for a rude shock when 'the carpet is suddenly pulled out from under their feet.'

Invest in machinery, resources, technology or ideas that help you respond to change faster, this will prove to be a powerful competitive advantage.

If you find that your competitor has improved on your product, then try to 'value add' to yours as well. If you can't match the features of your competitor, then compete with offers, discounts, free gifts or other value-adds.

If you find the entire market has decreased due to external issues like say an economic downturn, this is a volatile scenario. Find innovative ways to promote your brand. Discounts could work well in such a situation. You can also try to look for greener pastures like other geographical areas where the economy is flourishing.

If yours is a domain where technology plays an important role, you just can't afford to stay behind. Constant R&D and technological improvements would be vital to keep your brand or service healthy and successful. Sometimes, if you don't watch out, your product or service could simply end up being obsolete. For instance, once cars were invented, the entire horse carriage industry went out of fashion and out of business.

Those who are quick to respond to change are winners. Do not look at change as a negative factor; instead, view it as one that can also flood you with wonderful new opportunities.

9. MISTAKES ARE LESSONS IN DISGUISE!

If you make a mistake, don't let it dishearten you. It's part of the learning curve and a natural process. Just make sure you put the mistake in the right perspective and learn from it. Get to the root of why it happened and be careful not to repeat it again. However, don't let it cut down the speed at which you are working at. Many entrepreneurs get bogged down when they make mistakes, but just pluck up your courage and move on quickly.

10. QUICK RESPONSE TO CUSTOMERS

Some of the most successful businesses are those that listen to the voice of the customer. Every time your customer buys your product or service, you can use this opportunity to get valuable feedback. This can be in the form of surveys or just a few casual questions.

If your customer has a complaint or query, the speed of your response will go a long way in preserving and improving customer retention and trust. It is actually an opportunity to demonstrate your *Rapid-Response-System* (RRS) which you could play up as your **USP** (Unique Selling Point) over your competitors! Reassure them that you take their complaints seriously and that you have put a plan in place to handle them. It could translate into repeat orders and even be a valuable source of referrals.

11. BE FAST TO THINK FUTURISTIC

Anticipate the future demand in your market and try to make sure your product or service has some futuristic features and advantages. This will help you stay a few steps ahead of any existing or potential competitors, and give you the required edge to maneuver faster when the time comes.

KEY TAKEAWAYS

The **7 factors** that add heavily to your *'S-Factor'*:

- Adopt the right attitude

- Be the first mover

- Avoid procrastination

- Be proactive rather than reactive

- Extend quick response to customers

- Exercise professional networking

- Respond to market changes quickly and be futuristic

About Donn

Donn S. Kabiraj, an astute Business Strategist and a Management Guru, is the Founder and CEO of Donn Corporation, which provides Business Strategy Planning and Business Facilitation Services around the globe. The company also helps in forming Strategic Alliances, acquiring Joint Venture partners, appointing suitable Franchisees, launching of Franchise Operations, Distribution Networks, etc. for various businesses and brands worldwide.

One of Donn's key achievements has been inventing the **DNA-Compass™**, a proprietary management tool that evolved after several years of management research. This *unique tool is a direction finder* and *it defines the natural agility* of any company! This strategic tool helps in guiding his clients to play on their strength – *whether it is to increase their turnover or to turnaround their company*!

Listed and named in ***America's Premier Experts*** as a Business Strategist, Donn S. Kabiraj is an alumnus of the Indian Institute of Management (IIM-Calcutta). Donn prefers to throw the rule book out and chart a course of his own. His fresh approach and bold strategies executed at lightning speed have always left competitors stunned and helped his clients reap rich rewards.

Donn is the recipient of the prestigious ***'Lifetime Achievement Award,'*** from UWA which was conferred on him by Dr. Rakesh Mohan, Global Adviser to McKinsey, and Professor of International Economics & Global Affairs in the Yale School of Management (USA). He was given this award for his excellence as an *"Outstanding Sales and Marketing professional."* He has also received special recognition from the *Chairman and CEO* of **PepsiCo** for his critical contribution towards the world debut of 'Aquafina' (bulk water).

His company, Donn Corporation, has won the most esteemed *'Udyogshree Award'*, in 2012 from the *'Council for Industrial & Trade Development'*, India, for achieving *'Excellence In Business Management & Strategy Planning.'* He has played major roles in not just setting up new businesses from scratch, but also in turning around myriad 'sick' ones, re-energizing them into profitable business enterprises.

Author of numerous articles on diverse subjects ranging from *'Women's Liberation'* to *'Cybernetics'*, this global marketing professional avers, *"Every business is in essence a marketing venture! Flexibility in approach is a must today to respond and maneuver in the present dynamic market conditions."*

To know more about Donn and how you could benefit from the **DNA-Compass™**, visit: www.donncorporation.com

CHAPTER 21

Power Of Preparation

By Joshua Awesome

Having a dream is important, taking action in the right direction is as important as the dream. So on January 1st 2011, I woke up with gusto, got dressed to exercise, and hiked approximately 5km on a day many woke up to celebrate the New Year, rejoice and enjoy every moment – because it was the dawn of a new day and a New Year.

I pace-walked on the treadmill, cycled, went on short and long walks daily, and over 60 days it became the routine of a young African from the most populous black nation on the continent—Nigeria. After going through so much pain daily over two months, March came, I flew out and touched down at Kilimanjaro International Airport, Tanzania, to take on Africa's tallest mountain "Kilimanjaro." Over six days, I slowly trekked from the base of the mountain via Umbwe Gate, and journeyed up Uhuru Peak where The Nigerian National Flag got hoisted for the very first time at 19,340 feet above sea level—Africa's highest point.

So based on what I learned, here are "8 Steps to The Peak":

1. **Preparation:** Preparation is defined in the English dictionary as a preliminary measure that serves to make ready for something; or state of having been made ready before hand. Tim Redmond asserts: "Proper preparation produces powerful performances." Taking time to prepare powerfully pours life into whatever dream you possess.

Preparation time is never wasted time as it becomes obvious only in time through the success journey. You and me, we all need to take time to prepare everyday, every way positively possible. Enjoy your preparation time and definitely you undoubtedly will look back with a broad smile on your face, and/or the face of your team, that the time invested in preparing wasn't wasted.

When I prepared for 60 days, it was an investment that turned out the harvest throughout the 6 days spent to climb Kilimanjaro. Only those who work at it will walk to success.

So in what area(s) of your personal or professional life will you commit time to preparing for that goal, dream or desire? Every amount of time invested in preparing gives us strength to perform much more than those that didn't take time to prepare. Every Olympic medalist takes time everyday in preparation to *'win big.'* Begin now.

2. **Positivity:** Defined as quality of being encouraging or promising of a successful outcome. Every day I wake up with h.o.p.e (having only positive expectations) even though challenges show up unannounced like it did on my way out of OR Tambo International Airport, Johannesburg. I got to the airport, as a frequent flyer who knows where to check-in for international flights, joined the queue only to find out I was in the wrong queue when it got to my turn.

So, I ran with my trolley that terrific Thursday. Upon getting to the right line it was late, the counter had been closed. The challenge didn't change my belief as I always say, "It's A Great Day!" Give positivity room in your heart to turn on the right energy, as a new day delivers some light that is proof- positive every day is trapped with hope, health, and possibilities.

Positive energy alone cannot generate electricity. An example of this is when a conductor, such as a copper coil, is moved through a magnetic field created by a magnet, the force from the flux lines of the magnet causes valence electrons to be dislodged from the copper atoms.

The direction that the electrons move through the wire (either positive to negative or negative to positive), is determined by the direction that the coil moves. Electricity that is produced by generators uses this method.

In other words, Positive energy is appreciated around negative energy. "Positive thinking and negative thinking are attitudes. They are points of view, and show the way people handle their affairs," Remez Sasson says. He asserts further, "You will be better off as a positive personality, since there's so much negative energy out there requiring positivity to create a balance."

Every individual in time becomes a V.I.P (Very Inspiring Person) or V.D.P (Very Draining Person) for good or bad. Deciding on a positivity path will hand you, as well as others, energy you can use. A school of thought concludes on positivity; "the power of positive thinking is like a car with a powerful engine that can take you to the summit of a mountain."

3. **People:** Defined as numerable individuals forming a group. Getting things done daily will require the help and support of people. As I found out at the base of Kilimanjaro, everyone on my team had one goal, "get this young African" to the summit of the mountain. My lead guide had actually done Kilimanjaro 177 times, so the excitement trapped within me on the morning the expedition began wasn't the same for him, even though he was simply delighted to lead someone up Uhuru Peak. There these words leapt out to me, *"People Enable People To Succeed"* ~ Joshua Awesome, as all humans succeed by simply helping someone else succeed. Daily success further up Kilimanjaro for me became possible, simply by the daily support the entire team gave me by carrying my bag, unpacking and packing the tents, cooking, cleaning, serving every day for six days. Supporting someone somewhere somehow will let you in some way summit successfully to the peak.

4. **Passion:** Defined as a strong affection or enthusiasm for an object or concept. Dr. John Maxwell puts it this way "A Great Leader's Courage to fulfill his vision comes from passion, not position." Nothing gets done well without passion.

I recall one morning halfway into my daily exercise schedule for the expedition up Kilimanjaro. My entire body was in pain; so painful I didn't feel like getting up from my bed that morning. However, I rose up and dressed to take on new day's schedule—which is why we need to take time to find or discover what we are passionate about—to make a success out of it.

This poetic craft by Mewlana Jalaluddin Rumi caps passion;
Passion makes the old medicine new:
Passion lops off the bough of weariness.
Passion is the elixir that renews:
How can there be weariness
When passion is present?
Oh, don't sigh heavily from fatigue:
Seek passion, seek passion, seek passion!

5. **Perseverance:** Defined as steady persistence in a course of action, a purpose, a state, especially in spite of difficulties, obstacles, or discouragement.

There are 25,000 persons who attempt to climb Kilimanjaro on an annual basis. Some 40% of that number never reach the summit of the mountain—which could be likened to our lives as humans. Seven billion people exist on planet earth, hundreds of thousands simply "exist," they don't live. Living includes stretching oneself, and finding something to die for as much as we want to live life to its full 'crush.'

I commenced to Kilimanjaro with a decision not just to start, but to finish. As John Wooden said; "It's not important who starts the game, but who finishes."

Some part of us dies the moment we fail to finish what we started, which has to require some form of perseverance. Everything we start doesn't always get finished which doesn't make one a failure. However, reaching for the peak requires starting, staying the course and finishing whatever we start. This is possibly the reason we are awarded the opportunity to begin a new day since we didn't finish what we began yesterday.

6. **Patience:** Patience is an ability or willingness to suppress restlessness or annoyance when confronted with delay. As I fly from my base to other cities and countries speaking, coaching, as compere/emcee at conferences and also consulting, one thing I notice every time I touch down as the plane's still taxi-ing down the runway to the parking bay, people get up from their seat, open the overhead lockers grab their bag or baggage and start walking towards the doors. Many times I have heard lead hostesses announcing that passengers should please return to their seats as the pilot has not switched off the seatbelt signs.

Sometimes when people don't take the advice or instruction of the lead hostess, the pilot gets on the loud speakers instructing all to take their seats until he switches off the seatbelt signs when we arrive at the parking bay.

Year 2011 was possibly my very first time aboard flights that this situation or experience I came in contact with year-in year-out, didn't happen in Tanzania, as I touched down at Kilimanjaro International airport

The Swahili phrase "Pole, Pole" means "slowly, slowly"—which is a part of their culture. 'Everyday spent around them taught me patience,' which we were told daily, aids successful summits up Uhuru Peak-Kilimanjaro.

Only the patient make it to the peak of Kilimanjaro. One vital lesson I learnt that keeps me on my seat till the plane arrives at its parking bay, bringing me to the point of discovering so much that many forget 'in-flight' from being 'in-flurry hurry.' It is said, "when one is in 'flurry hurry' you never have time for recovery." Your patience will pay off in time.

7. **Prayer:** Defined as communication with God, …making a fervent or earnest request. Someone said, "Prayer is the key that opens your day to every blessing. It also is a lock that closes the night to keep you safe while sleeping." So what you have to do is "use your key all the time."

These words were said several times on my way up Kilimanjaro, "By Your Grace, Gracious God, I will get to the Top." I am most delighted I arrived alive at the peak of Africa's tallest mountain and also descended safely.

You may call it a mantra, as long as it is done believing for the best outcome possible, expect the best. Take time to trust as you unlock your desire in prayers soon, and surely you will look up with gratitude as I did—atop 19,340 feet above sea level and also saw the sun rise.

8. **Purpose:** Defined as an anticipated outcome that is intended or that guides your planned actions. Several reasons governed my decision to climb Kilimanjaro. So from the very first day, my purpose was clear;

first to hoist the flag of Africa's most populous country—Nigeria—atop Kilimanjaro, which is the highest point in Africa, thereby meaning "Nigeria's On Top Of Africa." Secondly, over 200,000 children die every year in Africa's most populous country alone due to a lack of proper health care, so Sanford Health Foundation's castle-of- hope goal for Africa attracts the attention it deserves. The third reason was simply so as to be able to tell the world "there's no mountain too high."

Having a purpose on our way to the peak gives our lives meaning. Many mess up at the peak because of a lack of purpose—like a man I met at the summit of Kilimanjaro. He was so excited, like everyone who gets to the very peak, he screamed amidst the cold as I wondered what he was up to. The next thing I noticed he reached into his pocket, got a stick of weeds struck the match and smoked away his excitement.

Excitement that isn't channeled properly can 'cut shut' one's life. "The purpose of life is a life of purpose," asserts Robert Byrne.

Everyone on earth has a purpose for being here, regardless of where you are or want to be, there's a "Reason for Living" as Liam Francis' poem says:

A purpose we all have on this earth

Something hidden inside even before our birth

Gift and abilities we all possess

But getting them out is our greatest test.

Wherever you go

Whoever you meet

Whatever you do

There is a reason.

There is a task on this earth for us to complete

And it starts on the day you and your mum first meet.

– continued on next page

Some know their purpose early

Some know their purpose late.

Whatever it is that you have to do

I'm sure that you will make it through.

Our lives that we live is a testimony

And it's called the reason for living.

Give these 8 lessons I learnt on my way up the peak-Kilimanjaro attention as you journey in life everyday, and soon you will find yourself at the peak of purpose.

To Your Summit – Success.

About Joshua

Joshua O.AWESOME is a high performance consultant, coach, columnist, *compere* and adventurer that has been on Africa's biggest TV network (NTA) for over half-a-decade every week as Anchor, Monday Morning Motivation and The Continent's Business Newspaper currently published with the Financial Times Of London (Business Day) read by over 50,000 decision makers in Sub-Saharan Africa.

Joshua has been seen around the entire African continent on Good Morning Africa (Africa's biggest breakfast show), broadcast on DSTV, Channel E (E-news) over 45 satellite stations globally, Guardian, Vanguard, Sun, Thisday, and Businessday amongst others.

Over 100,000 persons and professionals have heard him. Multinationals like GlaxoSmithKline, MTN and Africa's Airline of Pride, South African Airways, have hired him to enhance professional performance. "Enabling everyone to earn like sports stars is impossible" in the eyes of those that think impossibility, but Joshua Awesome knows impossibility is in the mind – where everything gets shaped.

Driven daily by a life mission to: inspire and inform individuals so they can get involved in life are what govern his "Awesome Mind."

A product of South Africa's Prestigious University Of Cape Town Graduate School Of Business; Professional Member, Professional Speakers Association Of Southern Africa(Psasa); Member, International Association Of Coaches, USA and Founder, Motivational Speakers Network(MSN)Nigeria and Flag Bearer Of Africa's Most Populous Country Flag(Nigeria) atop Kilimanjaro on his way to the seven Summits.

Should you want to hire "The Awesome Coach," contact him via Email: awesomecoach@gmail.com

Or call: +2348164799445/ +27738255557

His web address: www.awesomeadventurer.com

His blog:www.awesomecoach.blogspot.com

Twitter:@awesomecoach

CHAPTER 22

The Business Trifecta: The Secret Formula For Media Success

By Nick Nanton, J W Dicks, & Lindsay Dicks

"Success is simple. Do what's right, the right way, at the right time."
~ Arnold H. Glasgow

Imagine a new movie studio starting up with modest means. Anxious to get off on the right foot, they put every dollar into making the most amazing feature film anyone has ever seen.

Note two critical words in that last sentence: "every dollar." Because when the studio finishes this amazing movie, they have no money left to market it. They can't get anyone to see it because they don't have any funds to tell anyone about it.

Anxious not to repeat that mistake, they raise more money and put a bundle into hiring the best movie marketing company in the country to sell their next very-modestly budgeted film. The marketing company delivers to them an amazing film trailer and TV commercials.

Except, again, they've spent everything. Now they have no money to do the PR (Public Relations) to do the all-important press junket and get the stars on the late night talk shows.

The moral of this story? You can't properly grow your company without the right "business trifecta"—the perfect combination of media, marketing and PR. Over-emphasizing one or the other leads to an imbalance, just as if you tried to sit on a stool with two legs.

First let's walk through all three of the elements we're talking about here, so you can better understand why each is important. We'll start with...

MEDIA

Entrepreneurs and professionals create media to sell an aspect of their businesses—it could simply be an image-booster, useful information or more of a hard-sell pitch. Media can be in the form of a brochure, a video, an audio CD, a book, etc.

This kind of media is usually not a client's main business, even though media can be sold just like any informational product. For instance, a tax specialist could write a book on tax secrets. That book could then be sold on Amazon, even though the specialist's main business is, obviously, helping his or her own clients with their tax issues. The book serves as an indirect advertisement for the specialist.

Of course, it's sometimes more worthwhile to give the media away for free to generate leads, establish expertise and grab contact info for future marketing. Downloadable information on company websites that require an email entry for access to that kind of media is a prime example of that.

When producing media, it's really important to look at your target market and your distribution method, to make sure that your media is produced in a fashion that will be in-line with the distribution method and target audience. Note here we're not saying that it all has to look like it came out of a Hollywood studio, because, even *with* a Hollywood studio, sometimes you want it to look "home brewed" (think "The Blair Witch Project").

Whatever your creative approach, the presentation of the media and the packaging can be the first step in establishing the critical elements of credibility and trust. But again, no matter how good your media is, you still need...

MARKETING

How do you let your target group and/or customer base know that your media, which is probably of great interest to them, is out there and available? Well, that's where marketing comes into play.

Marketing can involve everything from low-cost viral videos to highly-polished TV spots, from free emails to expensive direct mail campaigns, from simple robo-calls to sophisticated referral programs. Marketing is how you get prospects to either buy what you're selling or, at the very least, get them to take a good look at you.

The purpose of your marketing, of course, can be multi-faceted. You may want to drive people to your website…and then, have your website convince them to leave their contact info…and then generate an email sequence designed to get them to buy. Or you may want a simple, targeted campaign with just one end result in mind—a simple sales letter designed to get people to buy your product, for example.

But either way, once you've done that, it's time to employ…

PR - PUBLIC RELATIONS

PR, or Public Relations, is all about creating *awareness*. You know the age-old question: if a tree falls in a forest and nobody's around, does it make a sound? Well, PR doesn't really care about the answer to that question—it just wants to make sure somebody is around to hear when that tree hits the ground.

That awareness comes primarily from press releases and media appearances. When your business has sold its one millionth widget (or whatever it is you sell), that's impressive to people—so you want them to know about it, because it boosts the image of your company. That's why you want to put out a special press release about that special widget, both online and offline.

If that press release hits at the right time, it could land you a story in the newspaper, in a magazine, on the radio, TV or online. It can also get you invited on radio and TV interview shows to talk about that special millionth widget. Or, if it's an online press release, it could just drive more traffic to your website—which, if you've got your ducks in a row, could end up being far more profitable than any media appearance you could get!

(By the way, that's why we mostly concentrate on the online press release, rather than the old-school offline variety. Online press releases boost your internet presence and, since they're written in the third person, also act as powerful online testimonials to anyone Googling you or your business - and its ROI is pretty much guaranteed.)

Should you nab those special media appearances, stories, and the traffic to your website, the great thing is you got it all *totally free*. Your main cost might come from hiring a PR company to help you make all of that happen. But, unless you have a legitimate story that really does stand out, that PR firm might be hard-pressed to get you much of an afterlife beyond that initial press release.

As a matter of fact, that's one of the biggest mistakes I see companies make—hiring PR firms when they don't have the marketing or media to back it up. When you try to get PR and you don't really have a story to tell…well, let's get back to that tree-falling-in- the-forest fable. In this case, there are people around to hear it—but nobody really bothers to listen.

Which is why we came up with….

THE SECRET FORMULA

How you put all three of these elements together—media, marketing and PR—is critically important. If you don't allocate enough money and resources to each one of them - and/or if you don't use each of them in the right way—you'll end up spending a lot of money without much to show for your efforts.

What we'd like to do is walk you through our "secret formula" for using all three in an orchestrated and effective system for our CelebrityPress™ authors. We're not doing this to toot our own horn, but, quite honestly, it's one of the few all-in-one campaigns that we know of.

First of all, as we noted before, we produce a great high-quality hardcover book that's got an attractive eye-catching cover, powerful overall theme and the participation of a lot of great authors. Those authors usually only have to worry about contributing a chapter rather than generating an entire book—making it much easier on their end. They still get credit for authoring the book, however, and can order special customized copies of the book with their picture on the cover. That takes care of the **media** portion of the program—because our client now has a terrific product around which he or she can build the marketing and PR.

Next, comes the **marketing**. We've created a targeted marketing system that guarantees each one of our books becomes a best-seller on Amazon. The other half of that marketing formula is that we give our authors *over 30 ways* to use their new best-seller to market their business. Having a book is a great attention-getter, but having a *best-selling* book is impressive on a whole different level. So, again, we're handling the marketing to make the book a Best-Seller, which will get it lots of attention, and at the same time, our authors are using more than 30 of our marketing strategies simultaneously to market the book to their own audiences to create a far greater impact.

And that carries over to the **PR**. Remember when I said you needed to have a real story to tell when you put out press releases (another way to think about it is "you've got to *find* the news in what you're doing)? Well, a best-selling book gives you that story. Our PR starts by putting out a press release that says so-and-so has signed a publishing deal with CelebrityPress™ - and then, after publication, the all-important follow-up press release that proclaims our author's book has achieved best-selling status. Those press releases spur media outlets to pursue any one of our authors for stories and interviews about their new book and, of course, their business.

Everything feeds into each other—but all of it springs from the fact that we have created a *real* media product as well as a *real* story about that media product. Which brings us to the magic ingredient of our special formula….

MELDING MEDIA

What we left out of our discussion of media earlier in this chapter is the fact that there are *two kinds of media.*

Mass media is the type most people know about. We're talking about commercial TV networks, national magazines, radio stations, etc. that are operated specifically to bring in consumers of all stripes. Mass media is about numbers—they want to attract the most users, so they can't really mess around; they *must* produce content that's genuine and interesting to the most people or they lose money.

All of us put the "mass" into mass media—we seek it out every day by watching our favorite shows, reading our favorite newspapers, listening to our favorite music and so forth. And because it has no other visible agenda than to entertain and inform the most people, mass media automatically brings two things to the table—awareness and credibility. If there's a story about you on CNN, people (1) see it and (2) think more of you because of it (unless, of course, you just murdered somebody or something…but we won't get into that here!).

This is why people hire PR companies - to get them on mass media outlets. The problem is, you can't "eat" awareness and credibility— in other words, if there isn't a direct solicitation involved with a mass media appearance, it's not really a big revenue generator. You're a story for a day and then it disappears (another reason we prefer online PR—it pretty much stays online forever!).

Now, let's talk about the second kind of media, known as "direct media." This is more of a targeted informational sales tool that takes the form of a CD, DVD, newsletter, direct mail piece, website copy, etc. The business distributes this direct media to an audience it selects (or in most cases the audience has identified itself by "opting in" on the website), with the sole purpose of selling to that audience—and it's created by that business for that specific purpose.

The problem? *Direct media lacks credibility.* There's a reason direct mail campaigns only have an average response rate of between 2 and 3 percent. Whenever anyone knows that a business is directly trying to sell to them, they immediately put up their guard and get suspicious. They don't know if what the sales piece is telling them is true because they know that the company is mainly interested in their money.

One way around this credibility gap is to use testimonials and product reviews, and other third party verification that appears objective. But there's still another way around it that takes the cake…

…and that's melding *both* kinds of media—mass media and direct media—into one.

For example, when you talk about having a best-selling book (mass media) in your direct media, that gives you an awesome level of credibility you wouldn't otherwise have. We also often place our clients on shows that appear on NBC, CBS, ABC, FOX and other national outlets. They can then talk about those mass media appearances in their direct media. If someone sees those network logos on your direct mail piece or your website, again, you're suddenly elevated in their eyes to a national expert (which you may already be—but would have a hard time convincing a stranger of that fact otherwise).

But any business person can do the same thing. For example, you use PR to get on mass media—television, radio, newspapers/magazines—the fastest and easiest way you possibly can. Then you take your direct media, stuff you can easily control the cost and distribution of, and put your mass media credibility in the direct media.

In other words, say you managed to get a spot on CNBC talking about your business. You trumpet that fact on your website, your newsletter, your e-zine, whatever direct media piece you create. That mass media "stamp of approval" can mean the world to a potential customer and can mean the difference between them paying attention instead of throwing it in the trash—and we all know the ROI on the trash can!

Even better is if you post a copy of that mass media appearance on your website, or put a copy of your newspaper article into a direct mail piece. We even hang ours up on our office walls—and our clients will invariably comment on them, which inevitably leads to us telling those clients how they can get the same coverage for themselves.

So ask yourself - don't you think that kind of mass media "stamp of approval" will get you taken a little bit more seriously? We can tell you, based on literally hundreds of case studies, it absolutely will get people to pay closer attention to you and what you have to offer.

So get yourself some mass media credibility—and insert it into your direct media. Don't spend all your time and money trying to get on TV or in the paper without having a plan for using that mass media exposure —in conjunction with direct media for your marketing.

When you successfully combine media, marketing and PR, you're guaranteed business growth and increased revenues. Correctly using the business trifecta raises your enterprise to the next level—and trust us, you'll enjoy the view from up there!

About Nick

An Emmy Award Winning Director and Producer, Nick Nanton, Esq., is known as the Top Agent to Celebrity Experts around the world for his role in developing and marketing business and professional experts, through personal branding, media, marketing and PR to help

them gain credibility and recognition for their accomplishments. Nick is recognized as the nation's leading expert on personal branding as Fast Company Magazine's Expert Blogger on the subject and lectures regularly on the topic at major universities around the world. His book *Celebrity Branding You®* has also been used as the textbook on personal branding for University students.

The CEO of The Dicks + Nanton Celebrity Branding Agency, an international agency with more than 1000 clients in 26 countries, Nick is an award winning director, producer and songwriter who has worked on everything from large scale events to television shows with the likes of Bill Cosby, President George H.W. Bush, Brian Tracy, Michael Gerber and many more.

Nick is recognized as one of the top thought-leaders in the business world and has co-authored 16 best-selling books alongside Brian Tracy, Jack Canfield (creator of the Chicken Soup for the soul Series), Dan Kennedy, Robert Allen, Dr. Ivan Misner (Founder of BNI), Jay Conrad Levinson (Author of the Guerilla Marketing Series), Leigh Steinberg and many others, including the breakthrough hit Celebrity Branding You!®.

Nick has led the marketing and PR campaigns that have driven more than 600 authors to Best-Seller status. Nick has been seen in *USA Today, The Wall St. Journal, Newsweek, Inc. Magazine, The New York Times, Entrepreneur® Magazine, FastCompany.com.* and has appeared on ABC, NBC, CBS, and FOX television affiliates around the country, as well as on FOX News, CNN, CNBC and MSNBC speaking on subjects ranging from branding, marketing and law, to American Idol.

Nick is a member of the Florida Bar, holds a JD from the University of Florida Levin College of Law, as well as a BSBA in Finance from the University of Florida's Warrington College of Business. Nick is a voting member of The National Academy of Recording Arts & Sciences (NARAS, Home to The GRAMMYs), a member of The National Academy of Television Arts & Sciences (Home to the Emmy Awards) co-founder of the National Academy of Best- Selling Authors, an 11-time Telly Award winner, and spends his spare time working with Young Life and Downtown Credo Orlando and rooting for the Florida Gators with his wife Kristina and their three children, Brock, Bowen and Addison.

About JW

JW Dicks, Esq. is America's foremost authority on using personal branding for business development. He has created some of the most successful brand and marketing campaigns for business and professional clients to make them the Credible Celebrity Expert in their field and build multi-million dollar businesses using their recognized status.

JW Dicks has started, bought, built, and sold a large number of businesses over his 39-year career and developed a loyal international following as a business attorney, author, speaker, consultant, and business expert's coach. He not only practices what he preaches by using his strategies to build his own businesses, he also applies those same concepts to help clients grow their business or professional practice the ways he does.

JW has been extensively quoted in such national media as *USA Today, The Wall Street Journal, Newsweek, Inc. Magazine*, Forbes.com, CNBC.Com, and Fortune Small business. His television appearances include ABC, NBC, CBS and FOX affiliate stations around the country. He is the resident branding expert for Fast Company's internationally syndicated blog and is the publisher of Celebrity Expert Insider, a monthly newsletter targeting business and brand building strategies.

JW has written over 22 books, including numerous best sellers, and has been inducted into the National Academy of Best Selling Authors. JW is married to Linda, his wife of 39 years and they have two daughters, two grand- daughters and two Yorkies. JW is a 6th generation Floridian and splits time between his home in Orlando and beach house on the Florida west coast.

About Lindsay

Lindsay Dicks helps her clients tell their stories in the online world. Being brought up around a family of marketers, but a product of Generation Y, Lindsay naturally gravitated to the new world of online marketing. Lindsay began freelance writing in 2000 and soon after launched her own PR firm that thrived by offering an in-your-face "Guaranteed PR" that was one of the first of its type in the nation.

Lindsay's new media career is centered on her philosophy that "people buy people." Her goal is to help her clients build a relationship with their prospects and customers. Once that relationship is built and they learn to trust them as the expert in their field, then they will do business with them. Lindsay also built a patent-pending process that utilizes social media marketing, content marketing and search engine optimization to create online "buzz" for her clients that helps them to convey their business and personal story. Lindsay's clientele span the entire business map and range from doctors and small business owners to Inc 500 CEOs.

Lindsay is a graduate of the University of Florida. She is the CEO of Celebrity-Sites™, an online marketing company specializing in social media and online personal branding. Lindsay is also a multi-best-selling author including the best-selling book *"Power Principles for Success"* which she co-authored with Brian Tracy. She was also selected as one of America's PremierExperts™ and has been quoted in *Newsweek, the Wall Street Journal, USA Today, Inc. Magazine* as well as featured on NBC, ABC, and CBS television affiliates speaking on social media, search engine optimization and making more money online. Lindsay was also recently brought on FOX 35 News as their Online Marketing Expert.

Lindsay, a national speaker, has shared the stage with some of the top speakers in the world such as Brian Tracy, Lee Milteer, Ron LeGrand, Arielle Ford, David Bullock, Brian Horn, Peter Shankman and many others. Lindsay was also a Producer on the Emmy-nominated film Jacob's Turn.

You can connect with Lindsay at: Lindsay@CelebritySites.com www.twitter.com/LindsayMDicks

www.facebook.com/LindsayDicks

CHAPTER 23

Striking Balance: The Way of Martial Wellness™

By Ken Marchtaler

When one door closes, another door opens ~Alexander Graham Bell

My dad was a wonderful man. He was a dedicated worker, a loving husband, and a great father. Not unlike the many "family men" of his era. He had his own business, and he worked extremely long hours trying to keep customers, employees and suppliers happy. A former semi-professional football player, after his athletic career his health became secondary, and he had succumbed to some fairly poor health habits. He was a heavy smoker, and probably could have eaten a little better.

Unfortunately, like many people on a similar life path, my dad never lived to enjoy the fruit of all his efforts. At the age of 50, he suffered a major stroke. He was hospitalized and told that he had a high-cholesterol count, high blood pressure and the arteries of an 80 year old. At that point, he was able to adjust his diet a bit, get some good medications that helped control his blood pressure and squeezed a few more years out of his life. At age 65, my dad had a massive heart attack and was dead in minutes.

When I think about the secret to winning big, first and foremost would have to be in discovering the path that leads you to optimal health. Because if you do not make this one of your main life goals, you are not going to be able to fight off illness, degenerative disease, and more importantly, enjoy the fruit of all your efforts. And like my dad, you will constantly be running around putting out fires including the ones inside your body. In today's fast-paced lifestyles, it is getting harder and harder to achieve that. But it is there, one only needs to know how to get to it.

As a teacher of martial arts, I have often asked myself, what exactly is it that I do? I am teaching Okinawa Karate, a martial art, yet I am helping all my students to make drastic changes to their mental and physical health and overall well-being. The self-defence techniques I had worked so hard to develop were only secondary to the benefits and impact I was having on their everyday lives. So in 2005, I started to question what I was doing and looking further back to the roots of what I do. At that time the word "Wellness" was just starting to get thrown around. And I thought—why not Martial Wellness™? It was then that I began to develop a model for success in life. Here is only one account of many:

"Four years ago I began having back pain; three years ago it was determined that I needed surgery. Just over two years ago, after a few visits to a good chiropractor, I happened to see Ken-sensei's picture on the cover of *Senior Living* magazine. Sensei called it Martial Wellness in the article, and went on to explain how training is useful and valuable at any age. The changes in my physical well-being have been profound. The stretching we do at the start of each class combined with the physical exertion has helped to lower my blood pressure back into normal range, has built greater strength and endurance, has given me more energy and has motivated me to get back into the kind of daily morning walk that builds up a sweat. The best news was when I went for my pre-surgery evaluation. I told my doctor about going back into training and how the pain was almost all gone. He checked my mobility range again and was happily surprised. Surgery was no longer necessary, he said. What a relief!" *Solveig Norwall, age 65, Artist.*

At the age of 54, I have achieved many things in life including raising two beautiful daughters, acquiring two grandsons and a son-in-law, marrying the woman of my dreams, earning a living from what I enjoy doing the most, winning two Gold Medals in world competition, and being awarded a Gold Level health assessment by the Canada Life Assurance Company. Even so, I have had my own challenges in my journey through life. Dysfunctional relationships, a degenerative knee that will eventually require replacement, and one thing that I have really struggled with a lot - coming to grips with the need for financial success.

It wasn't until I built the Martial Wellness™ Model that I understood why.

Most of us base our own, or other people's success, on financial achievements. As a martial arts teacher, I can tell you that at one time, the furthest goal on my list was financial freedom. Martial Arts has been a way of life for me. It has taught me to be patient, to learn how to connect with other people easier, it has given me the confidence to stand up for myself when I have needed to, and also to be able to do it in a way that makes the other person feel like they are not losing. It has helped me through a divorce and the death of my father, and given me the ability to travel around the world. What you have to understand is that I love what I do, and so it is difficult to put a price tag on sharing that.

As I started to study the concept of Martial Wellness™ more, I realized that people who were very successful at one thing were not necessarily happy, nor were they achievers in everything. And as I looked further, I started to understand that balance was the most significant piece that was missing from people's lives. Whether it was a wealthy individual with health problems, or an elite athlete without money, people will generally place themselves in the middle of something and rarely get out of it. I refer to this as the 7 challenges of life, Mind, Body, Spirit, Relationships, Finances, Happiness and Time. They are all intertwined, and all dependant on each other.

1. MIND

"In the beginner's mind, there are many possibilities. In the expert's mind, there are very few." Shunryu Suzuki

When I think of the mind and its potential, I think of two very interesting Japanese words: Mushin - empty mind, and Shoshin - beginner's mind. The reason that they are so important is because it is really the difference between being able to center oneself and learn, or not being able to center oneself or learn.

Mushin is pretty much absent from Western culture. We have let our daily activities meld together and in turn they affect each and everything we do. For example, stress in our personal lives leads to absence at work or to degenerative health. Past history or future fears often prevent us from taking advantage of opportunities that present themselves and achieving all that life has to offer—as will worrying about what the future holds. Emotions can direct our lives. Mushin is simply a frame of mind that allows us to overcome emotions and give full attention to what is in front of us. It is achieved through breathing.

Shoshin on the other hand, is something we need to have—to allow our minds to grow. Too often we are caught up in our own belief systems and we forget that others may have new or better methods. Why do children learn so quickly? It is because they are open to whatever is in front of them, and they just let their inner mind accept, reject or modify whatever is center on the mind.

The way to a healthy mind is to take time each day to listen to others, to separate our activities and learn how to breathe again.

2. BODY

Some people say that a healthy body is a healthy mind, but why do we often neglect that premise? What has happened to our internal health care system? Why have we shifted to dependence on others for our health and well-being?

If I had all the answers, the world would already be saved. But one thing I do know is that a number of things have changed. The pace of our lives keeps getting faster. We are in a rush to get from point A to point B. We believe we have less time to look after the important things in life like regular exercise. Food has been modified and mass produced. Both exercise and food intake has become a quick-fix rather than a way to long-term health.

The key to a healthy body is in the practice of regular exercise, proper nutrition and in the way you live your life.

3. SPIRIT

So much in the world keeps us apart from one another. Yet there is very little that separates us. There is a common thread that connects all of us to each and every living thing. That much we know for sure.

In the aftermath of 9/11, I watched television with amazement one night as religious leaders from various beliefs came together to share in some common understandings. The result was proof that regardless of what people believe, there is still a set of universal principles that connect us all. It was inspirational for me to see this.

Developing spirit is not about religion, although one can certainly apply it to religion. It is about understanding the laws of nature and how we can connect with them. For example, if we are willing to respect other people's points of view, they are more likely to respect ours. If we help other people, we are more likely to receive help when we need it. When we treat people with kindness, they in turn will treat us with kindness. When we want to accomplish something, the world will generally rally around us as long as we include the world in the plan.

A colleague of mine, Dr. Allison Rees, once reminded me that there is a difference between acting nice and being nice. People can see and feel who you really are. So when developing spirit, make sure you are not just creating a camouflage. Spirit is the heart that we put into everything. It is what keeps us motivated and what allows us to achieve.

In whatever you do, always allow your true spirit to shine through.

4. RELATIONSHIPS

Of all the things that we need to nurture the most, it has to be relationships. That is because it involves other people and the aligning of our internal values and goals. Ignore someone for a period of time and you will need to take great steps to re-connect. That is why many marriages fail. Two people brought together in time, working together to become one unit while drifting apart emotionally. Too often we get too focused on one of life's other challenges to take notice.

Regular communication is the only way to keep relationships on par.

5. FINANCE

I could live in the penthouse of a downtown high-rise, or in a log cabin deep in the woods. I can enjoy the finest things in life but can also find satisfaction in having nothing. But one thing I have come to realize. Everything is better if you do not have to worry about money. It is not so much how much money you have as how much you need to do the things you want to do, or for the people you care about.

For many years I led the simple life of existence. But over the last few years, I have realized that I have people I love who depend on me to be the best that I can be. The more finances I apply to my Mind, Body, Spirit & Relationships, the faster and better the results have been.

Find your motivation for living and then fuel it with the capital it needs.

6. HAPPINESS

A few years ago I learned of the Kingdom of Bhutan. What interested me most about this this tiny gem in our world community was their government's measurement for success. Unlike the rest of the developed world, the government of Bhutan does not measure their success by Gross National Product. They measure their success by "Gross National Happiness." And their people as a whole are quite happy.

Our own happiness can only be complete if we are balanced. Giving each area of our life the right amount of attention it needs will cause our happiness to flourish.

Remember that success can also be measured by Gross Happiness!

7. TIME

"Everything happens to everybody sooner or later, if there is time enough", *George Bernard Shaw*

In order to achieve balance and happiness in in each area of your life we must come to grips with the laws of time. Time is a commodity, and no one understands that more than someone who is dying.

We have created a world that lets us steal from tomorrow in hopes that we can outrun what life holds in store for us. As in George Bernard Shaw's quote, "Everything happens sooner or later. But nothing happens if we do not apply ourselves".

If you do not have the time, make the time!

BALANCE THROUGH MARTIAL WELLNESS™

In order to balance our lives, we need to constantly nurture the 7 major challenges of life:

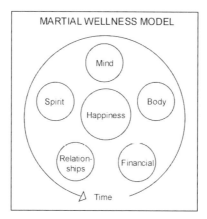

Take the time to look at this model before you begin each day. How can you nurture each of the areas to make sure you are putting big dollars into the Jar of Happiness? If you only have a certain amount of time, what are the things that you need to do that will ultimately result in the best return on your investment? Happiness is the key. It is all up to you.

When my father died, I could have followed in his footsteps. But I chose a different path instead. Finding balance was my passion, and my passion has become my work. Martial Arts is the path I chose to help me achieve my life goals. Martial Wellness™ is the method I use to achieve them. And the fact that I am internally happy most of the time must mean that I am winning the battle!

One door has closed but another has been opened in the process.

About Ken

Ken Marchtaler was born in Vancouver, Canada. He has studied and taught martial arts for more than 20 years. He holds a 4th Degree Black Belt in Okinawa Shorin-Ryu Shorinkan Karate. On his trophy shelf are two Gold Medals he won at the 2005 World Martial Games, and a number of lifetime achievement awards. His group of companies, Marchtaler Group includes a martial arts studio in Victoria, Canada as well as several programs developed for the martial arts community. These include EMPOWERED™ for Children, POW-R-GIRLS™, EMPOWERED™ for Women, Little Warriors®, 30 Minute Warrior® and the concept of Martial Wellness™.

Ken draws his ability to design and instruct programs from his experience in various senior banking positions. He has served as officer/director on a number of non-profit boards, including Chairman of the World Martial Arts Games Committee (WMAGC) and President of the Canadian National Martial Arts Association (CNMAA). He is a regular guest speaker and has made several appearances on radio, international news and television. He has also been featured on the cover of Senior Living Magazine.

When not immersed in other activities, he enjoys writing. As an accomplished writer, Ken's articles have appeared in newspapers and magazines around the world. Ken is also the author of the 'up and coming' book *Little Warriors: The Book of One.*

To learn more about Ken, Martial Wellness™ and how you can access his products, please visit the Marchtaler Group at: www.marchtalergroup.com.

CHAPTER 24

Innovate And Differentiate

By Hatem El Ghamry

This chapter revolves around the orbit of - Differentiation and Innovation- two sides of one token to this era's excellence and success for entrepreneurs and individuals. Nowadays, people, companies, and even Governments, are changing to cope with this New Era's dynamics and fast pace, and reformulate their strategies to innovate and differentiate themselves from their competition or other individuals.

Differentiation strategy was introduced by Porter—eminent strategy professor and guru—for corporate use and still it could be used by organizations, entrepreneurs and mainly products seeking distinction to stand out among others.

Hereunder, the figure shows Porter Generic Strategies.

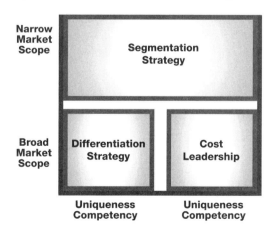

Differentiation - in my opinion - is an umbrella that could embrace any strategy including the cost leadership and segmentations strategies; that could be techniques for achieving differentiation. Hence the focus would be on how to differentiate.

While there are different means of differentiation that you could think of; I would sum up all the alternatives in a single term to avoid exuberance, and would say differentiate using **Innovation**.

WHAT IS INNOVATION?

It is simply the process by which an idea is translated into a good or service of which people will pay for, or gain something that results from this process. To be called an innovation, Entrepreneurs must develop replicable ideas at an economical cost that necessarily satisfy a specific need. Innovation involves deliberate application of information, imagination, initiative in deriving greater or different value from resources and encompasses all processes by which new ideas are generated and converted into useful products or outcomes.

From a business perspective: Innovation often results from the application of a scientific or technical idea in reducing the gap between the needs or expectations of the customers and the performance of a company's products.

Innovations are divided into two broad categories:

1. Evolutionary innovations. These are brought about by numerous incremental advances in technology or processes and are of two types:

   (i) - Continuous evolutionary innovations. These result in an alteration in product characteristics instead of a new product, and do not require any user-learning or change in his or her routine, e.g., the multi-blade shaving razor.

   (ii) - Dynamic continuous evolutionary innovations. Require some user-learning but do not disrupt his or her routine, e.g., handheld computers.

2. Revolutionary innovations (also called discontinuous innovations) require a good deal of user-learning, often disrupt users' routine, and may require new behavior patterns. Examples are photocopier (xerography) machines, personal computers, and the Internet.

Innovation is synonymous risk-taking and organizations/entrepreneurs that introduce revolutionary products or technologies take on the greatest risk having to create *new markets*. A less risky innovation strategy is that of the imitator who starts with a new product (usually created by a revolutionary-innovator), having a large and growing demand. The imitator then proceeds to satisfy that demand better with a more effective approach. Examples are IBM with its PC against Apple Computer, Compaq with its cheaper PCs against IBM, and Dell with its still-cheaper clones (sold directly to the customer) against Compaq. Although many innovations are created from inventions, it is possible to innovate without inventing, and to invent without innovating.

From a personal perspective: Innovation is a tool for entrepreneurs and individuals who finds out an idea, put their hearts on it and never lose a chance to utilize any opportunity to earn cash, success and growth by fulfilling people's needs and wants. Personal/Entrepreneurial Innovation is about self and environmental awareness.

One of the most important factors of success for entrepreneurs and innovation is their opportunity-hunting skills. Like the business opportunity hunting and close attention to human needs and wants; entrepreneurs and individuals need to show interest in themselves and their capabilities without substituting the environment around them.

SELF-AWARENESS AND INNOVATION

Self-awareness is a key and a means to success. Personal goals are determined based on self- awareness, which in turn determines its own capability, passion and strength, followed by applying this to opportunities available to hunt. That requires a reasonable understanding of yourself and what opportunities exist in the environment to reason the need for innovation.

Referring to the previous page where the section of Innovation type – Revolutionary Innovation- applies to products as well as to Individuals.

We usually tend to think about innovation in terms of changing something in the world around us. How about innovating ourselves? Wouldn't that be an interesting thought? Sometimes we are stuck by looking at something in a set way. It can be the way we go about a particular task or problem. It becomes a 'fact' so that we unquestionably assume it's just the way things are. A fresh new perspective can give us a whole new meaning, and to our own amazement we realize there is a better way of dealing with ourselves and our lives—in a way we never imagined possible before.

Possibly, women can be more receptive to this. The reason is that women tend to have more self-motivation to go through regular 'makeovers' like changing their hairstyle and general look, and re-design other things in their immediate physical and social environment. On the other hand, men tend to go through such 'makeovers' as frequent as celestial alignments of an intergalactic scale. Though change in appearance is not taken as genuine innovation, yet it could be a start nonetheless.

INSPIRATION

Whether it's been in my personal or professional life, taking the time to reflect on the person I aspire to be and assess whether I'm really on track to be that person—including making major shifts in my behaviors, job and relationships—has proven to be a key factor in my life journey.

These moments of self-reflection don't necessarily have to be in a life-threatening moment, they can happen at any time in life and you can even bring the moment about yourself. I don't believe that we can move forward with our jobs, in our relationships, or in our lives in general – without stopping at points along the way and asking ourselves a series of fundamental questions:

- What am I doing?
- Am I truly following my passion?
- Am I moving in the direction of the vision of who I want to be?
- How am I perceived by others?
- How am I responding to the changes around me?
- Do I need to take any further actions?
- What could these actions be? …etc.

I would even say that it is our responsibility to be the ones that spark those changes, to innovate ourselves and inspire others to do the same.

In my personal journey of innovation, which started after digging deep into myself to identify my strengths and capabilities to realize how can I take myself to another level and reach my potential, I aspired to rediscover myself, not wanting to match the success of any other. I aimed to be different and stand out from everybody else.

"I am, indeed, a king, because I know how to rule myself."
~Pietro Aretino
(Italian author, playwright, poet and satirist, 1492–1556)

I initiated the self-discovery journey to identify what other talents, gifts and passions I possess that might be still unleashed and towards what. I realized that Development ***passion*** was my winning horse; once I acknowledged the passion, I started to seek opportunities to test water for fulfilling this passion.

I went on to pursue work and find jobs in my area of passion – managing putting my heart and soul into what I do. Sometimes it was challenging, yet some unexpected energy and enthusiasm ignited in my heart towards more risky and courageous decisions in order to take tougher challenges.

"The person who risks nothing, does nothing, has nothing, is nothing,
and becomes nothing. He may avoid suffering and sorrow, but he
simply cannot learn and feel and change and grow and love and live".
~Leo F. Buscaglia
(American guru, tireless advocate of the power of love, 1924-1998)

In the first many years of my career, despite the diverse experience, achievements, development and success I achieved, still I had a belief that my potential was higher than what I accomplished. Where I worked I had reached the ceiling. I experienced success in different jobs within different corporate structures. Though I was growing, developing and succeeding, I still did not excel like I believed I should or aimed at. I then realized that I reached a ceiling but not my full potential.

My personal innovation journey was inaugurated by self-awareness, stretching my comfort zone, readiness to take risks, and most importantly, the willingness to change and innovate. Eagerness to utilize my talents and skills lit the path to new directions and careers to pursue. That was the corner stone to directing the innovation strategy. Taking advantage of my network while capitalizing on existing skills, qualification and competencies were my initial steps in the thousand-mile journey.

The moment I started doing what I am passionate about did not take much time to show results. Very shortly, results and achievement showed an unprecedented upscale—professionally, socially and financially. It was merely a satisfaction that exceeded expectations. That was tangible evidence being on the right path and taking the right innovation strategy towards fulfilling the passion.

CONCLUSION

The personal innovation strategy benefit is not limited to the change experienced; it is about the self-awareness, fulfillment and satisfaction; it is about the benefits of finding opportunities for development and growth through discovered skills and competencies, and best utilizing them. Doing this opened new horizons and re-energized the batteries for accomplishments and contribution.

Accordingly, I decided to shift my career and work to a totally different field where I found myself passionate. The self-discovery and innovation journey plays a vital role in opening new skies of critical development on both personal and professional levels. Hence, my innovation was in shifting careers with courage to satisfy my passion where I started experiencing even more success than ever achieved in my earlier career initiatives—which I still consider successful—and that lead to more satisfaction, higher self-esteem, better personal and professional results.

Differentiation in this case was from innovation from within; after having a proper self-awareness and reaching down to the passion lying within. Innovation on an individual level is simply utilizing the existing experience to support the available talents and skills to unleash inner power and reach maximum potential whether personally or professionally.

RECOMMENDATIONS

• Differentiate - Be yourself. Always remember that what it takes to make it in this life is to be you. You don't have to copy any other. All you have to do is use what is naturally yours. Know what you are good at, what your skills and talents are; bring them out and use them to define yourself as unique. No one else has your assets, when you are yourself, you instantly become un-replicable, as there is only one of you!

- Use your heart, your mind and your talents to "Innovate" your own career or path. Once you start on this new path, once you understand what you must do for yourself; the road to success will become clear. Be aware of your assets and ask yourself if you have taken the time to rediscover yourself. Just because many skills and talents come naturally, you are not aware of them, so beware of what you have and let your brilliance shine.

- Believe in yourself - The first quality of an entrepreneur or a successful person is to believe in themselves, in their success and have self confidence. When they have a problem, people turn to those who know what they can do and are sure about their success, so find the confidence in yourself so those around you believe in you as well.

- Show your passion - you are successful because you love success, because you have so much to give to others and you want to achieve as many wins as possible. Bring your passion to light and let everyone see your drive.

- Let your true self shine. Utilize your talent in new ways or even new careers or jobs. Unleash the power of hidden talents, strengths and passion in everything you do and soon you'll realize that your success starts from within... yourself.

- Finally, never give up and have a nice differentiating innovation.

About Hatem

Through a diversity of exposures to private and multinational corporations in USA, Canada and Egypt; Hatem's extensive Management experience stems from both corporate management positions and academia. His formal education includes B.Sc. Hotel Management and Masters of Business Administration. Hatem's experience includes positions in Strategic Initiatives, Marketing Management, Decision making and Customer Relations.

Hatem's consulting experience focused on assessing organizations and personnel, hence helping them amending or developing strategic directions, setting goals, developing functions or processes as applicable and develop action plans to pursue their ultimate goals with excellence.

Hatem, the usually known as "The Catalyst" utilized his practical experience and people development skills in transferring harmonized professional applications and theoretical knowledge to learners and participants while co-lecturing, tutoring and instructing at University of Toronto, Edinburgh Business School's, The American University in Cairo, Arab Academy and other institutions on both under and post graduate levels.

Hatem is the founder of the management and training company "Differentiation". His activities involved management and talent development and coaching for major multinational corporations and executives.

As a certified trainer and coach Hatem managed and conducted more than 4000+ hours of training. Within several years "The Catalyst" has coached at least 110+ managers and life coached 300+ individuals to achieve their goals. His commitment is to be " The Catalyst" to companies, executives or individuals he works with.

As for awards, Hatem is named one of Forty under Forty top executives of Egypt by *Business Today* magazine.

To learn more about Hatem; The Catalyst, visit his company website:
www.differentiation.ca.
You can contact him at hatem@differentiation.ca or at either of his work numbers:
+1-905-783-3350   +2-0100-142-0102

CHAPTER 25

Success Is No Accident

By Peter A. Howley

As a kid in high school, I didn't have a lot of self-confidence. My dad and I, one hot summer day at home in New Jersey, were sitting on the front porch. Suddenly, my father made a surprising forecast leaving me dumbfounded. "Pete," he said, "someday you will be president of your own company. Do you know why? Because you don't follow the crowd; you're your own man." Wow! I was shocked. But, that statement changed my life and self image. It was perfect for me and showed a huge understanding of this then-shy kid. I loved it. It became my major goal in life; it gave me direction, motivation and was tremendously uplifting. President of my own company, now that would be "winning big."

So twenty-five years later, when I arrived in San Francisco, it was to take over an exciting new disruptive startup company as President and CEO. I was clearly on my way to "winning big." But life has its surprises.

In taking the required physical exam to comply with this company's medical insurance coverage, I was shocked when they notified me that I had extremely high cholesterol. This level gave me a 600% greater chance of dying from a heart attack than if it had been normal. That got my attention! Following one of my secrets to success, I thoroughly researched the subject, asked around and soon discovered from one of my coworkers a wonderful book that fully explained high cholesterol, its causes and provided a concrete course of action to correct it back to normal levels. Being focused on my goal and highly disciplined, I did more than follow the guidance provided. I prepared a two-page "cheat sheet" and followed it religiously. Religiously. If it said chicken once a week was "okay" but not great for you, I totally eliminated chicken. Within less than one year, my cholesterol dropped from a high of 312 to below 150, an astounding positive result. Even the doctors wanted to know my secret.

In chasing your dream, you are bound to run into obstacles. Aggressively addressing mine allowed me to continue to pursue my dream of not only being the president of my own company, but also "winning big" in a way that would make a positive impact in my life.

I then led that company, Centex Telemanagement Inc., through a very successful Initial Public Offering until its even more successful acquisition some nine years from my arrival. It became, according to *Inc. Magazine*, *the fastest-growing service company in America, and the fourth fastest-growing company of any type in America.* The early investors received a 20 times return on their investment within the first three years.

Its later successful acquisition price was a quarter billion dollars, a "big winner" for me, my Centex Associates and our investors. The company and I were written up in *Business Week, Forbes, The Wall Street Journal* and many other publications. We were on the cover of *Equities Magazine* and written up by them as one of only a few companies to grow our revenues and earnings during both good and bad economies. The Wall Street Journal called us "the darling of Wall Street." More importantly, it had created an almost cult-like following among the six hundred highly-dedicated Associates that made those results possible. Many of those young Associates have since gone on to great success in their own rights. This is truly "winning big" on many fronts.

Later, I served as a key Senior Advisor and Director of Exodus Communications, which grew within four years from a start-up to being valued at thirty-seven billion dollars. It was a big win, professionally and financially, for me. Its young founder was valued at over a billion dollars. That founder has since gone on to further success with another Internet technology company recently written up in a national magazine as #4 in its field, beating out a number of industry giants. That's a "big winner."

GOAL SETTING

So what is the secret to winning big? ***It starts with determining what it is you want to accomplish. What is your "winning big" goal?*** How important is it to you? In my case, my father helped make it clear: I wanted to make a big mark in life through business, making an impact that would make me exceptional, perhaps even make a positive difference in people's lives. If I made some money in the process, great, but money was not my goal. Perhaps I'd even be written up and long remembered. One such early model and mentor to me was Bill McGowan, the legendary founder of MCI, who opened the telephone/telecommunications world to competition.

I discovered that success is no accident. But first we have to define success as it applies to us individually. Is it money, fame, health, happiness, or maybe climbing Mount Everest before you die? Success can be defined as truly world changing, a la Steve Jobs, or more modestly, as perhaps being the best doctor, teacher or mother in town. It could include being the best runner in your age group or the tennis champ at your country club. Or getting a pilot's license or taking up sky diving, two wild things I did in my youth. The answer will differ for each of us.

And sometimes the success you start out pursuing is not the one that you end up making the number one priority in your life. However, I cannot over emphasize the motivation, excitement, enthusiasm, *and satisfaction*—that extra zest in your life—that determining and setting a 'winning big' goal in life can have - everyday. Even, if ultimately, you fail to achieve all of it.

Regardless of where we are in life, I believe all of us should have grand goals, defined by us, that give us direction and purpose, while motivating us to enjoy every day. Put another way: "What do you want on your tombstone?" Our human nature is stimulated and motivated by grand goals, which if successful are truly winning big. Aiming high, giving it your best and even ultimately falling short of your goal can still be extremely rewarding and satisfying. In other words, do you just want to muddle along in life, as so many of us do, or do you want to genuinely try to make a difference, make a mark, and perhaps be fondly remembered years after your passing? That has certainly been my philosophy in life.

THE SECRETS TO WINNING BIG

I. Clearly & Carefully ESTABLISH YOUR GOAL
- Put it in writing.

- Break that goal into concrete milestones, with specific time frames, 1 through 5 years plus long term.

- Aim high.

- Follow your own path. Dare to be different.

II. Courage, Drive and Attitude
- Have courage – fortune favors the brave.

- Be positive. "I can do it, I can do it; yes I can, yes, I will."

- Always be working toward that goal. Always.

- Be almost obsessively focused on accomplishing that goal.

III. Execution and Learning
- Always be learning, overcoming fears and acquiring skills helpful to succeed.

- Never, never, never give up - as long as the goal still makes sense.

- Only take jobs that move you in the direction of your goal.

- Setbacks and failures are learning opportunities. Take advantage of them.

- Create and gather the support needed – advisors, a team, etc., then excite and motivate them to reach your goal.

IV. Luck
- When it happens, take advantage of serendipity. Luck counts.

THE KEY STEPS

Success is no accident. And "winning big" certainly requires even more focus, determination, and smarts than just creating success. Winning big, as mentioned, can be in business, health, happiness, and other spaces.

So start by clearly determining what is truly your long-term goal, your passion, and how you will measure success. Early in my career, a good friend published an article about goal setting. I took advantage of that information, setting goals for one to five years, as well as later. Success back then included earning double your age in salary. Those milestones were invaluable to my ultimate success. It kept me on track and focused, not letting me even momentarily forget where I was heading.

DANGER

Winning big does require being brutally honest with yourself. Are you really willing to commit to earn that reward? Are you being honest about the facts supporting your goal? Commitment is different from daydreaming!

COURAGE, DRIVE & ATTITUDE

I encourage being brave and positive about your goal, no matter what others may say, as long as you're not kidding yourself. You have to be committed to following your own path. Everybody isn't motivated to win big. Take full advantage when you can find similar and supportive souls. In fact, seek them out. But realize that by aiming high you may find you're largely on your own, particularly in the early days of your quest. I am an independent person, as dad pointed out, so I've never had a problem with that. On my leave time while in the military, I traveled throughout the Pacific and Asia, South America, and Europe, frequently by myself. While it's nice to have companionship, I realized early on that I might frequently be traveling my own path alone.

As a youth, I certainly lacked the cocky confidence that so many of my peers seemed to possess. Public speaking was intimidating and yet I knew it was critical to my long-term goal of successfully running my own company. Taking positive action after college, I joined Toastmasters, which was an invaluable learning opportunity. Learning, improving and getting ahead go hand in hand. Don't let your fears stop you. Today, I am a sought-after speaker and enjoy this activity immensely!

I am still highly driven to succeed, to continue winning big. I also like to run foot races, play tennis, sail around beautiful San Francisco Bay, ski and travel to discover new places. I try to squeeze these in, but if you are setting a high goal, it's impossible in my view to do that and live what is emphasized today as a "balanced life." Fortunately, I thoroughly enjoy what I do. I have never found the long hours, challenging work assignments, and travel that comes with it to be a chore. Plus I hate failure, not necessarily a bad trait. As legendary Intel CEO Andy Grove wrote, "Only the paranoid survive."

EXECUTION AND LEARNING

I recently saw a very insightful quote: "A leader doesn't always need to know the right answer, but they need to know how to find that answer." I cannot overemphasize how critically important that wisdom is for success and 'winning big'. All the distinguished and legendary CEOs with whom I've worked clearly knew how to collect information, synthesize it and make good timely decisions. Information may come from many sources. These include the people around you every day: bosses, peers, subordinates, board members, advisors and consultants; as well as from: Google searches, taking a related college course or reading relevant books and articles. The key is to be always learning, acquiring knowledge and skills.

Don't fall into the fallacy that books are no longer relevant. Books, printed or digital, are an amazingly source of knowledge, information and valuable experience. They're a great way to master a topic or issue; you can even learn from the masters of industry, Henry Kaiser to Steve Jobs, during your morning commute.

Books give me very helpful tools not only for my own use, but also for leading and motivating those around me. Teams need to work together, relentlessly, to successfully reach goals. Many of my earliest book heroes are still relevant today: management guru Peter Drucker, Robert Kotler of Harvard Business School and motivational folks like Zig Ziglar and Napoleon Hill. Great books are being published every day. Use them.

Job decisions can be pivotal to your success. After I found myself in the exciting telecommunications field, I carefully reviewed new opportunities based on their value in helping me reach my long-term goal. I turned down job offers, some at substantial salary increases, that didn't take me in the right direction. That's not easy to do. However, having clearly established my winning big goal, I knew what was right for me.

LUCK

Luck can frequently play a part. In the U. S. Air Force, I was responsible for maintaining long-range B-47 jet bombers. When I completed my active duty, I applied to the leading airlines, Pan Am, Eastern Airlines and TWA. I was disappointed when none responded. However, staying focused on my goal of becoming president of my own company, I quickly accepted AT&T's offer of a management development position. At that time the telephone world consisted of staid monopolies, a poor "fit" for hard working outspoken me. Then suddenly, Bill McGowan's MCI opened the door to aggressive worldwide competition and I was —purely by luck—positioned to join his disruptive industry "upstart" in one of the most dynamic exciting fields imaginable. My phenomenal climb to winning big was launched.

During the seven years that I worked at AT&T, despite not liking the big company bureaucracy, I worked very hard at learning everything I could. I even completed an NYU Masters of Business degree at night. My goal was clear; I wanted to win big and never stopped working and learning toward that challenging goal. Thomas Jefferson said it so well, "I'm a great believer in luck, and I find the harder I work, the more I have of it."

CONCLUSION

Carefully set your goal for 'winning big,' creating a detailed roadmap and then go for it. It's exciting and can be tremendously motivating and rewarding. To miss this aspect of life - winning big - is to miss a rich slice of life.

About Peter

Peter A. Howley is a bestselling author and serial entrepreneur with unprecedented experience in successfully building high-growth disruptive technology and service companies. As Chairman of The Howley Management Group he works closely with CEO's, Boards and Entrepreneurs internationally to accelerate companies into industry leaders.

In addition to founding five companies, Howley has also advised, served on boards and as interim CEO in numerous companies looking to accelerate their success. He has the distinction of leading his first venture-backed company through IPO and acquisition into the pages of American business history as CEO of Centex Telemanagement. It was recognized as one of the fastest growing, best managed, most profitable companies in America. It retains a cult status in the service industry.

Howley joined the founders of Exodus Communications, a Global Web Hosting Company, at its inception as senior advisor and director. He served on the post-IPO Board until June 2000. Exodus still holds a NASDAQ record for consecutive quarters of greater than 40% revenue growth. As the CEO and co-founder of IPWireless, Inc., Howley raised more than $120 million in venture capital. His leadership was instrumental in the company's successful acquisition by Nextwave.

He routinely publishes articles and books. Howley speaks frequently to a wide array of audiences on industry topics, and has been quoted extensively in publications including *USA Today, the Wall Street Journal* and *Fortune Magazine*. Recently Howley co-authored a bestselling book, *Trendsetters: The World's Leading Experts Reveal Top Trends To Help You Achieve Greater Health, Wealth and Success* and received both the *Golden Quill* and *Editors Choice* awards from The National Academy of Best-Selling Authors™. Howley is currently completing his forthcoming book, *The Good CEO*.

Updates and newsletters can be found at: www.HowleyManagementGroup.com

CHAPTER 26

Getting Over The Hump
—Life Isn't About The Cards You're Dealt, But How You Play Them.

By Russ Jalbert

It's something that happens almost every day.

Just like a phone call, letter in the mail, or visit from a friend, a knock on the door in the 1960s was usually one of the most harmless events. It was something that you almost never thought twice about, and something you never expect to be an introduction to a life-changing moment.

Five fingers coming together to form a powerful, compacted fist, which pounds against reinforced wood and chipped paint.

It was a Wednesday. There was a knock on the door, as my mother and I were coming home from a water skiing event. It was a good day - Aug. 19, 1960. Just family fun, the kind you only see on TV, while my father was away, as he always had been.

He would leave on Sundays and come home Fridays.

The pounding on the door continued. With no hesitation, I jumped to answer the door and saw a familiar face standing on the other side of the entrance. Not my father, but his best friend.

I will never forget the horrid look painted across his face. My excitement from the day quickly deflated, like a balloon losing helium after being pricked with a razor-fine needle.

"Something's wrong, isn't it?" I asked.

"Yes," he plainly responded.

"My father's dead, isn't he?" I followed up, expecting the worst.

"Yes," he answered. One word, three letters, yet so sharp a word that it could cut like a stainless steel blade.

He calmly ushered me into my home, his footsteps light, gentle, and slowly gliding across the floor. He had a generous demeanor, as he approached to tell my mother the ghastly news. I was 16 years old at the time, and the scars from that moment still feel as fresh and deep as a crater.

My father's plane was ripped apart in mid-air. He didn't have to explain further.

Instinctively, my father's confidant asked if we had anything to drink in the house. We didn't. So, I hustled over next-door looking for some kind of liquid "medication" to ease the pain.

"Do you have a bottle of whiskey?" I asked my neighbor, who only knew me as the bright boy next door, ahead of his class, and heading into his senior year. He could see the urgency on my face, so he kindly obliged.

It was right after that simple, yet excruciating task that I realized as the only son, it was now on me to care for the family. I walked back into my home, put on a brave face for my mother, and accepted my new responsibility.

I've never told my story, but as painful as it might be, this is something I hope will help others. I am a positive person, driven by religion and helping people. I want this story to be one of hope and inspiration.

My story is not one that begins with privilege, but a story of falling down and picking myself up. You too can pick yourself up. No matter what happens, the hump is never anything we all can't get over.

Parts of my tale are a lot like many of yours, high school and college were fun. I joke that college was the best six years of my life. My sophomore year was my best two years. I overcame this phase of my life by learning.

Nowhere were the basic tenants of life passed on to me. It was up to me to learn, after a past of loneliness and abuse, mainly originating from my hurtful, yet impressionable father.

I've stumbled, I've fallen, but I've always had a goal. Goals are what help me pick myself up, dust myself off, and get back to life. I came from what looked like a perfect family—the "Ozzie and Harriet" of my time. But inside my home's walls, terror reigned supreme. Two children, myself included, were subjected to rage and alcohol.

While my father's passing marked the end of this gauntlet of terror, it marked another set of trials and tribulations. Our family's financial situation was about to come crashing down.

We lost the house within a year. We went from being in a country club, our home in the suburbs, to my mother tenaciously working in a department store. College was an unknown, as I didn't know if I would have any money for school.

I would have to work, and take on any job that could help foster an education.

I cleaned crew bathrooms of a Great Lakes ship. I saved money, used government loans and went on to school. I was a party guy, trying to escape my checkered family past, and I got through it in six years.

WHAT DROVE ME

You can't escape your past, even in forgiveness—for the airtight cage of fear my father trapped me in growing up, I still aimed to show this man I could be more successful than he ever imagined. Even six feet under the ground's surface, lying in a seemingly secure pine box, this man drove me in death.

It's funny how the intangible can often haunt you much more than what's actually present in your world. "My father would be proud, my father would be proud," was a common line which I would tell myself during each and every milestone climbing the ladder of success.

But success isn't always what it's cracked up to be, something I found out years later.

A RISE TO GREATNESS

After college, I went into the insurance industry. And from that moment on, I learned **Six** vital lessons that I would love to bestow upon you. This is my gift. This is my legacy.

My success has been a blessing, and my goal from this very instant is to touch as many lives as possible. I would love to pass on these vital tenets, because my father was never able to do that for me.

1 – Risk The Relationship
Nothing worth its weight in gold is worth anything if there is a security blanket attached. What I mean by this is if you are going to be in sales, you need to risk the relationship. Push the product, if it's for the client's best interest! Don't put the friendship first.

My father had a ton of friends, but none risked this relationship to force him to do what was right, and he died without enough life insurance to help my family survive.

We can't always be in business to make friends, but do a job and do it well. Someone will respect you much more if you place the job first. A lasting relationship will follow in the form of respect.

You're there to convince them of what they don't have, but they need. That's sales in a nutshell. You have a service that they not only want, but that will make their lives better. Risk the relationship. They will thank you later, I promise.

Like in "Behold The Turtle," a turtle may cross the beach, but he only makes progress by sticking his neck out.

2 – Perception Is Reality
The saying goes, "Don't dress for the job you have, dress for the job you want." Never did a saying succeed in so many ways.

You need to become the part in your chosen profession. Don't just kind of, sort of, try. This is your career, and you need to become it. A boss, a co-worker, or anyone can read right through you if you're only acting.

How you show up is how others will see you. You might not be feeling good one day, but don't let it affect your work or your demeanor. It sounds like common sense, but hold your head high and exude confidence. This confidence will translate into respect.

3 – Always Invest In Yourself
Knowledge really is power, and investing in your education is the "smartest" thing you can do. I always invested in my education, including materials for marketing. I presented myself as a special individual.

In 1978, I became a Certified Financial Planner. From that very moment, I knew I had found my calling. I always invested in myself to get the message across, "I'm the right planner for you!"

I was, in fact, the right planner; I just needed others to know it too.

Instead of the boring business card, which gets buried under pile upon pile of other cards in the desk drawer, I handed out audio cassettes. Potential clients could play them in their cars on the way to work.

The goal was to get them thinking about me on the commute to work, and wrap their heads around not having to make that drive, because I would help them retire early!

Before it was the thing to do, I went as far as to hire a public relations firm to get me in the newspaper and on radio. I wanted to show up in a different, more distinguished light than all the other cookie cutter advisors.

I always tried, and still try, to stay ahead of the popular trends.

4 – Develop Trust
The only type of trust that can last a lifetime is built through visible success. With the innovations just mentioned like the cassette business card and my continuing education, I wanted my client to be thinking just one thing.

"I can trust this person with my life," is what should be running through anyone's mind when they sit across my desk.

Exceeding expectations and always doing just a bit more than promised is another avenue to gain trust.

I was never satisfied with doing just what I told the client I would accomplish. You want a 5% return; I would shoot for 6%. It may not always happen, but overproducing is a goal you should always shoot for in any industry.

You want to do more! You need to do more! Keep pushing the envelope. If you reach a benchmark, don't get complacent. Set new goals.

5 – Believe In Yourself And Your Work

If you don't truly believe in what you do, you might need to look for a new line of work. It's passion and drive that will make you successful in any industry.

When 9/11 occurred and the two planes hit the Twin Towers, it caused me to take a look at my business very seriously. Could I do in the future what I had done in the past?

Through my hard work and dedication to my clients, I had become one of the elite financial planners in all of the country, but I had a hard decision that needed to be made. Do I stay the course as a planner and keep doing what I had previously done, or walk the road less traveled away from traditional thinking, looking for a better way.

Naturally, the market took a huge hit around 9/11, along with the tragic loss of life our country will never forget. I will never forget.

I had been investing money for seniors, a demographic that couldn't afford market hits. They just didn't have enough time to regrow their savings after a recession. Following 9/11, I asked if this could happen again and if it did, what would happen to my clients?

I felt compelled to think outside the box, and look beyond my traditional menu of products and techniques for other, safer options. As a Certified Financial Planner, I wanted something with principal guarantees. Isn't that a novel concept? I wanted to make sure my clients didn't lose their money.

I wanted the best of both worlds, and I found hybrid annuities. These beautiful financial vehicles were a major part of why when the market plummeted in 2008, my clients didn't lose a penny!

With hybrid annuities, if the market goes up, an option is exercised and returns of 5% to 7% are common. If the market goes down, the option expires and goes away - no principle is used!

I believe in this product. It has also helped my clients to believe in me.

6 – Let Faith Fill You Up

I'm not a preacher, but I am evidence of how faith can change your life.

Aug. 3, 2003 - that was the date I gave my life to Jesus Christ. I let go, and I let God take over.

During my journey to prove to my father that I could stand on my own two feet, this hollow pilgrimage destroyed two marriages, got me into alcohol, and forced me to neglect what was important – family.

The healing process of Jesus took me in a new direction – a journey where I would do things God's way, for the right reasons, and see what comes from living a purer life.

I look at the past differently now, learning to let go of things I cannot change, and only stay focused on the tasks ahead. This change of perspective let me believe in a better tomorrow. I now welcome the future.

Thanks to God, I have faith that anything I want or set my sights on will come through perseverance. After all that time thinking success was the only way, I let Jesus lead my life. I have never been more fulfilled. Everyone whom I touch can clearly tell I'm on a better, more positive path.

> *"You can always count on Americans to do the right thing – after they've tried everything else" ~Winston Churchill.*

I had done everything else my way, and after trying everything else, I tried Jesus. It is the single most important decision for any current success I may be enjoying.

Being driven by a man who died when I was 16 wasn't the way. Jesus Christ was the way, and he brought me the peace I needed. He centered me. He helped me let go. Today, I live for him, not my father, and everything has fallen into place.

A PERSONAL NOTE - MY MOTHER THE HERO

What can I say about this amazing woman?

At age 46, she didn't let my father's death ruin her. She didn't buckle under the pressure of having to finish raising two kids on her own. After his plane's accident, we never found his body or saw his face again, and he died with very little life insurance.

Just $50,000 is nothing when raising two children, but that is what my mother did. There was no hesitation, as she was forced to work long hours to keep us fed and clothed. Saying my mother is my hero doesn't do justice to what she endured.

"Character cannot be developed in ease and quiet. Only through experience of trial and suffering can the soul be strengthened, vision cleared, ambition inspired, and success achieved." ~Helen Keller.

My mother is my muse, and Jesus is my compass. I love what I do, how I help people, and I am truly blessed. <u>It's not the circumstances you are dealt, but the choices you make that define who you become.</u>

It is only through my mother's inspiration, that today I can make sure my clients live in peace and prosperity.

About Russ

Russ Jalbert, CFP, has been a top financial planner for nearly four decades. During that time, he played an active role in the Reagan Administration and amassed a list of accolades that boggles the mind.

The Michigan-based Jalbert Financial Group provides clients with safe and proven products designed to make sure money lasts through retirement. That's Jalbert's current recipe for success. It was around 9/11, when the Twin Towers were hit, where Jalbert began his crusade against the risks of Wall Street.

America's 'Dean of Financial Planning,' Jalbert now points his clients toward much safer products and approaches, and his record speaks for itself. When the market began its ascent in 2003, Jalbert's clients were enjoying returns of 5% to 7%, growing steadily. When the market plummeted in 2008, Jalbert's clients didn't lose a penny!

In fact, as of the printing of his most recent book, "Rescue Your Retirement," his clients still stand an impressive 40 percent ahead of the market. Jalbert's current success is nothing new. The Ferris State University Graduate made a name for himself from the onset. He co-founded the National Financial Counseling Board in 1975 and was named an Outstanding Young Businessman of America on two occasions.

"The business of helping people manage money is the only business I have ever been in and the only business I have ever wanted to be in," he says.

Russ Jalbert's most recent book is an in-depth look at the insurance system of retirement and how it differs from the market for long-term financial health. Fixed Indexed Annuity products are an example of a much safer vehicle that Jalbert now advocates. This product is a hybrid that combines the best aspects of the two dominant types of annuities: fixed and variable.

The difference of the new hybrid is how the interest is applied. Instead of paying to the individual, the interest is put into an index like the S&P 500, and call options are purchased. If the market goes up, the option is exercised, where returns of 5% to 7% are common. If the market goes down, the option expires and goes away - no principle was used!

As if all of these accomplishments were not enough, Jalbert is also an accomplished radio personality. The Jalbert Financial Forum airs on WMUZ 103.5 Saturdays from 2-3 p.m. and on WJR 760am on Sundays from 2-3 p.m. The goal of the show is to provide the public with the most straightforward, non-biased fiscal information possible.

To learn more about the Jalbert Financial Group, visit:
www.jalbertfinancial.com
Or call 877-807-SAFE (7233).

CHAPTER 27

The Kingdom or The Empire?

By Jeff Gunther

"He likes to build little empires." I wasn't quite sure whether this was intended as a compliment or a criticism – but it was absolutely true!

In my early twenties, I'd achieved enviable success in the field of ski resort management. I knew how to form fiercely loyal staff. I knew how to control costs and increase revenues. I knew how to innovate and constantly create new profit centres. What I didn't know was how to win BIG.

All of my achievements, no matter how impressive I made them out to be, were admittedly small. In my effort to make a name for myself, I had inadvertently limited my potential and risked relationships. And here's the problem: the empire I was building was built around me.

As it turns out, I'm not the only one who suffers from this problem. As humans, our natural tendency is to put ourselves first. We all want to be the centre of our own little universe. When we do this, pride crowds out humility and we end up exchanging our rightful place in eternity for something shorter, smaller and significantly less exciting. And as long as we do, we can never win BIG.

Deep inside, I longed for more than my little empire. I flirted with success and empty victories as I struggled to discover what seemed like an elusive secret. And like so many secrets, when I finally found it, it was surprisingly simple: *Rather than struggling to build my little empire, I could join an infinite God in building his Kingdom!*

Yes, simple – but not easy!

I immediately released control of my empire, and put my future in the hands of a trustworthy God. Then I set about the daunting work of discipleship—seeking to find practical truth in his Word. As I began putting principles into practice, I came to realize that freedom is the ultimate reward of discipline. By trading my little empire for his Kingdom, I was no longer limited by self-imposed boundaries.

We live, however, in an imperfect world. While I now consider the Holy Bible to be the single greatest success manual ever written, I confess that I am constantly challenged by what it seems to be saying.

Although I am no longer involved in the ski industry, I still love to spend a day on the slopes followed by an evening with friends around a fireplace. On one such ski trip several years ago, I was invited by a group of young adults to share something from Scripture. I opened my Bible, turned to the New Testament book of Acts, chapter 4, and simply read:

> [32] All the believers were one in heart and mind. No one claimed that any of their possessions was their own, but they shared everything they had. [33] With great power the apostles continued to testify to the resurrection of the Lord Jesus. And God's grace was so powerfully at work in them all [34] that there were no needy persons among them. For from time to time those who owned land or houses sold them, brought the money from the sales [35] and put it at the apostles' feet, and it was distributed to anyone who had need.

I was older than the others and, at this point in life, enjoyed a level of success in both business and real estate investment that easily set me apart from them. I paused, and then said: "As much as anybody in this room, I truly want to be obedient to the Word of God… but I'm having great difficulty with this passage. Can anybody tell me why?"

Silence…

And then the response came – in a soft, but steadfast voice: "You don't trust us."

That's exactly what I was thinking! Give up my possessions? Share everything I have? Sell my land and houses? Give it to you? I don't think so! Where will you be when I need you?

And I think I'm right. But as long as we live in a culture that cannot trust, we will continually be pushed back into our own limited little empires.

Were you hoping that the secret to winning BIG would be easy or instant? I'm sorry to say that it's not, but neither is it out of reach. The moment we put our trust in an eternally-reigning King, and join him in building his Kingdom on earth, we've already won—but there will be work.

We can have faith in what we do not yet see, but faith without work is worthless. In life we all have setbacks, but that is never cause to give up. As cliché as it sounds, we learn far more from our mistakes than we ever do from our success. It is often in weakness that we discover strength.

For me, it was following a disappointing business failure that I found myself in the midst of an opportunity to win BIG by choosing the Kingdom over my faltering empire. Financially and emotionally exhausted, I was forced to take inventory of what I stood for, and what I had left to offer. I sought assistance from others in areas where I was lacking, allowed myself to be guided by gratitude rather than greed, and became accountable by placing the interests of others above my own.

For you, the secret to winning BIG will also be found in choosing the Kingdom over the empire. Here are *Seven Keys to Kingdom Building* that you can begin using right now:

KEY #1: KNOW YOUR VALUES

We all have a set of values that governs the way we live our lives. However, until we have stopped to identify with crystal clarity what they are, we can easily be distracted—to our own detriment—by the world around us. When I work with business owners I tell them that, while I'm interested in *what* they do and *where* they're going, I'm far more interested in *how* they will get there. *How* you choose to live your life – your values – has greater impact on your results in life than anything else you will ever do.

Take a moment right now to write down some of the values that define you. You can always come back and refine your values later, but you can't win if you don't start!

KEY #2: BECOME AN EXPERT

We have all been given unique gifts and abilities that set us apart. However, until we identify them and determine to become an absolute expert in a specific area, we can never expect to win BIG because we simply don't have enough to offer.

What do you have to offer? Examine yourself right now. Write down two or three areas in which you have sufficient interest, experience, or passion to create tremendous value for others. Then narrow your list to one, and decide to become an expert in that area. Do it now!

KEY #3: SEEK WISE COUNSEL

There is no such thing as a self-made success. Learn to leverage the knowledge and wisdom of others—especially as it pertains to your area of expertise. Every author in this book has the potential to help you win. You likely already know others in your field whom you hold in high regard. Reach out to the very best.

Take a moment right now and write down the names of at least three people you will seek out for wise counsel. Next, make a plan to contact them, and do it!

KEY #4: ENGAGE OTHERS

It's not enough to become an expert. We all have gaps in our ability or resources. If we want to win, we need to actively engage the assistance of others. Think of yourself as part of a body. We need the other parts of the body in order to survive and thrive. What are you missing? Chances are great that the person with *that* is missing *you*. Find a partner, partners, or suppliers with values highly-aligned to yours. It's okay to have some overlap in contribution, but it's pointless to partner with someone exactly like you. It is not a sign of weakness to need others; needing others is absolutely essential to winning BIG.

What do you need and who has that? Begin engaging others to join you in building the Kingdom.

KEY #5: BE GENEROUS

The Dead Sea is dead, not because there's nothing flowing into it, but because there's nothing flowing out of it. Don't be like the Dead Sea; learn to hold your treasures lightly. We must be good stewards of our talents, but we must also remember that their highest and best use is in building the Kingdom. People known to be genuinely generous with time, treasure, and talent more easily attract others to engage with them in winning BIG.

Many people mistakenly believe that they are more important if they are a big part of something small, than if they are a small part of something big. Read the illustration at the end of this chapter and invest a few moments in considering how much more you might have to give when you choose the Kingdom.

KEY #6: BE ACCOUNTABLE

We are all susceptible to temptation. Kingdom builders learn to count on others and be held accountable by others. Part of the secret to winning BIG is the ability to stay the course and finish well. This includes both what we do, and what we don't do.

What systems can you put in place to ensure that you always do what you say you will do? Find a person, or small group of people, with whom you can be completely transparent, and insist that they hold you accountable.

KEY #7: PUT RELATIONSHIPS FIRST

It may seem somewhat odd that our last *Key to Kingdom Building* is about putting something first, but I saved this for last because it's probably the most important. I won't argue with you if you tell me that religion tends to complicate things. I will, however, point out that Jesus makes them remarkably clear. Once, when asked which of all the commandments is most important, he simply responded: Love God and love your neighbour. The story of the Kingdom is all about reconnecting people to God, and people to people. The secret to winning BIG is found in being connected to the Kingdom.

Never allow 'winning' to stand in the way of relationships. Resolve now to be quick to forgive, and to seek forgiveness. Partner with people whose interests you willingly place above your own.

I recall a breakfast meeting some time ago with a man I highly respect. He honoured me throughout our conversation and, as our time was coming to a close, looked me straight in the eye and asked: "How can I serve you?" I was caught by surprise, but only because his behaviour so closely resembled that of the believers described in that challenging passage of Acts, chapter 4—challenging me to choose the Kingdom.

I love to lead live workshops. When I do, I frequently invite people to physically participate in the presentation by joining me onstage.

First, I invite one person to stand in front of the audience and make a circle by holding their arms in front of them. Then I'll invite a few others up to do the same. For fun, I'll sometimes challenge one of them to make their circle a little bigger by somehow stretching their arms or releasing the clasp of the fingers just a little bit. Of course, it's very hard to make the circle any bigger. This, I suppose, is the secret to winning small. And this is what most of us do most of the time. We go through life building our little empires. If we're feeling generous, we'll occasionally give out of our little empire, and then we must work hard to replace what we've lost.

Next I ask my volunteers to hold hands and form one big circle. Then I ask the audience: Which is bigger—one small circle; the sum of the small circles; or the product of the big circle? The answer is obvious. (The geometry is only slightly more difficult.)

When we recognize that we are small and God is big, we begin to get a glimpse of what it means to win BIG. Rather than struggling to build our own little empires, we can choose instead to build his Kingdom.

And that, my friends, is the secret to winning BIG!

About Jeff

Jeff Gunther is a gifted entrepreneurial leader and strategist. He has demonstrated proven results through bottom line accountability in restaurants, hotels, ski areas, investment real estate, sales and management training, dental centre development, professional practice management, financial services, franchising, international development, and business advisory services.

Jeff co-founded *Associated Dental Care* – a system of large customer-oriented, multi-disciplinary group dental centres in Ottawa – where he served as Managing Director from 1991 to 2002. This was one of Canada's largest and most successful dental enterprises.

As a practical philanthropist, Jeff serves boards of non-profit organizations, counsels young people in the integration of faith and work, and seeks out virtuous business opportunities. Jeff believes that freedom is the reward of discipline and that simple questions often lead to profound answers. He finds great joy in the privilege of walking with others as they discover their own true value.

Jeff earned an MBA at the University of Ottawa and an MCS at Regent College. Both academic degrees have revealed that he still has much to learn, and have helped him appreciate and model the genius in clear explanations of complicated concepts.

As an inspirational speaker, Jeff delights in disrupting the status-quo. As a business advisor, he adds value by collaborating on the creation and implementation of great ideas. Jeff also welcomes inquiries from financial partners interested in the acquisition and amplification of solution-oriented real estate projects.

To learn more about Jeff Gunther…

www.jeffgunther.ca I www.kingdombusiness.ca I www.secrethomes.ca

jeff@jeffgunther.ca

780-244-8001 Edmonton, Alberta I 778-388-5775 Vancouver, British Columbia

CHAPTER 28

No Excuses Customer Service

By Carmen Stine

I was recently in the market for a new car. I had narrowed my potential purchase to three major models all within the same price range, so price was not a factor as I started the search for my shiny new black car.

I visited the three respective dealers in reverse pecking order of what I believed would be my ultimate choice, believing that if I started my test drives in this way I might ultimately get to love either choice #2 or #3 more than #1. Just maybe.

So off I went one bright Saturday morning for my test drives. It was quite an education in customer service, mostly on what not to do when hiring people to represent your business.

As I entered the doors of dealership #1, with three salespeople sitting around chatting with each other, not one acknowledged my presence. They just went on chatting as if I wasn't even there. After about 2-3 minutes, one managed to pull himself away from the group to ask if he could help me. Well, yeah! I thought. I explained I was interested in test driving car X. He stepped away, grabbed the car keys, and handed them to me, mumbling something about the car had plates so I was good. Up to this point, he never introduced himself to me, nor did he ask my name or any relevant information about myself. He just handed me the keys, said I could take as long as I needed as long as I didn't take the car on the highway. OK, I thought. Odd behavior, especially for a dealership, where in my previous experience the salesperson would go along for the test drive if for nothing more than to make sure I wasn't leaving town with the car.

Having spun the car around for about 20 minutes or so, I returned to hand the keys over, and left. There was no conversation between us about my impression of the car or my interest in it. "I'm out of here, you're not getting my business" is where my thoughts were. Needless to say, I never returned.

At dealership #2, with several people of various ages viewing the cars in the lot, I thought it odd that with all these potential buyers, there was not one salesperson with or near any of these people. As I walked inside, where two salespeople sat at their computers while one other walked around aimlessly looking out the showcase window, again no one acknowledged my presence and clearly all were oblivious to the people in their lot looking at various models. As I approached the gazer at the window, he appeared very distracted but managed to introduce himself half-heartedly to me, asking if he could help me. I expressed my desire to test drive car X and off he went to get keys. This time I was accompanied on the test drive, but at no time during that 20 minutes did he engage with me to either give me information about his product, to ask when I would be buying, or if I had a trade-in—all information that I know salespeople generally ask whenever I've bought a car in the past. Not a good start once again. And just as at the previous dealership, this salesperson never asked my name or contact information for follow-up. When we returned from the test drive, I politely thanked him for his time and left. And once again, I was never to return. I loved both cars but neither one of these establishments was getting my business!

Feeling irritated and incredulous, my experience at dealership #3 was an amazing and exceptional one. What a breath of fresh air! I was barely out of my car when a delightfully friendly and very polite young man approached me. Extending his hand as he introduced himself as Eric and welcomed me to his dealership, immediately inviting me inside where I could sit comfortably and quietly with him to discuss what I was looking for. He asked my name and contact information and wrote it down. He maintained eye contact while asking probing questions as to what model I was most interested in. Questions followed of how soon I would need to purchase and whether I had a trade-in. We discussed the differences and similarities of the two most popular models and which one would suit my needs best considering the amount of driving I did. Eric offered detailed information about the new features of each model and how these features would make my driving experience more pleasurable as well as safer. Throughout his conversation with me, this young man referred to me respectfully by my surname. He listened attentively to my questions and answered all with great precision. When I was ready for the test drive, he graciously handed me the keys and said he would await my return and we could discuss my impressions. It merits mention here that at no time was I feeling pressured to make a decision until I had all the information I needed.

No contest as to which dealership got my business. Hands down, this young man and the owner of this dealership understand the meaning of *no excuses customer service*.

In tough and competitive economic environments, to maintain and grow our business we need to do more than just have the best price in town. We need to assure that every customer is made a customer for life. Loyal customers will keep coming back no matter the price. Loyal customers are our best advertisements. And loyal customers ensure the ultimate strength and growth of our business. Having said that, we need to have a commitment to excellence that far exceeds anyone else's in our industry. A standard for excellent customer service will assure that no matter what else happens, our customers will be loyal to our product or service. And to build loyalty for the long term, we must develop and practice what I call a *no excuses customer service* mentality that will permeate our business from the top down.

How can you create this commitment to having loyal customers for life? Here are a few of my favorite tips whether you're in a brick-and-mortar store, professional service provider, or in a trade. Follow these and you're on your way to building a very long-term customer base:

TOP 7 TIPS FOR PROVIDING EXCEPTIONAL CUSTOMER SERVICE AND CREATING LOYAL CUSTOMERS:

1. Make sure you know what your customer wants:
Develop a relationship with your customer from the very beginning, at the point of your first encounter. Learn who your customer is, where they live, what their interests are, the names of their spouse and children, the kind of pet they have and don't forget the pet's name as well. Ask them for their respective birthdays and special anniversary. Create a database with this information. Find out what other product or service similar or related they use and prefer. Ask them what their biggest

challenge is that directly relates to your product or service, then meet that need. Personalizing your customer's buying experience makes you stand out from the pack. People love it when we can make them special and will tell their friends and family.

2. Make sure your product or service does what it says it does:
Customers keep coming back when they know your product or service stands the test of time. Constant breakdown headaches are annoying and time-wasters for your customers and create the impression of poor quality and service. Knowing your product or service is reliable is crucial to customer loyalty. As you expand your product line or service, your customers will know that you deliver what you promise every time and will buy more from you.

3. Hire and train the proper people to bring the product or service to the customer:
Hiring skilled, knowledgeable, caring, compassionate, and engaging people is vital to the long-term success of your business. Customers want to deal with sales or service people that are knowledgeable and skilled and make them feel like family. Customers want to feel that your sales people are in it because they really care about them. Likewise, customers want to interact and engage with the same people over time. If your staff is constantly turning over, your customers perceive that very negatively. People buy from people they know, trust, and like.

4. Develop a system for correcting what may go wrong before it happens:
While we all know that that nothing is foolproof, having a plan of correction in place in the event the inevitable does happen is crucial. When customers know upfront that you stand behind your product or service no matter what happens, they are more likely to keep coming back over and over again. Along with this, have something extra to give to your customer for their trouble. Customers love getting free stuff that adds value and solves a problem for them.

5. Ask your customers for feedback:
Create customer satisfaction surveys to monitor what's working and what needs improvement. Ask your customers for honest feedback after every transaction or interaction. Review all surveys and use this information to create customer service initiatives for continued staff train-

ing. Share this information with the customer that gave the unfavorable feedback. Making personal contact with a dissatisfied customer assures them you are addressing the issue of dissatisfaction and care about their overall satisfaction. Often an acknowledged dissatisfied customer becomes one of your most loyal because you took the time to care about them.

6. Deliver your service or product in a timely manner:
Customers want to know that your service or product will be available for their use immediately or at least when promised. Avoid delays as much as possible. If an inevitable delay occurs, inform your customer immediately. Make sure they agree with the new delivery date. Unless your customer's purchase is a custom-made item, offer them the option to cancel their order. Informing your customer of an unexpected delay promptly and getting their approval is generally enough to keep them with you.

7. Develop a customer follow-up system after the sale:
Designate either the same salesperson or an administrative assistant to make a follow-up call to the customer within 5 days, 14 days, and again at 30 days to ensure your customer is enjoying his new purchase and is using it as intended without a problem. This is crucial for nipping potential problems in the bud early on and keeping your customer happy. If the customer has a problem, no matter how minor, offer to fix it for them. Going the extra mile with follow-up will be remembered and talked about by your customer for a very long time. A happy customer is a long-term loyal customer and one of your best referral sources.

And now for a final word:

Making a commitment to giving each customer a unique purchasing experience before, during, and after their purchase is the best legacy your business can live by. You will be known to potential future customers as the "go-to" business because of your exceptional customer service. Through economic downturns, slowdowns, or price increases, your business will thrive for many years and decades, after many others have come and gone.

About Carmen

Carmen Stine is the owner of No Excuses Customer Service LLC in Smyrna, DE, a company she formed as a result of her own frustration and dissatisfaction with many service providers.

Carmen works with small and medium-sized business owners to increase their business by developing exceptional customer service programs that increase customer loyalty.

Carmen has worked with car dealerships, restaurants, graphic designers, salons/spas, medical practices, dentists, event planners, personal injury attorneys, and home care agencies in the NYC, NJ, MD, and PA areas. She is a highly sought-after think-out-of-the-box trainer and speaker. She is also the owner of CS Legal Nurse Consultants and Sola Mia Jewelry.

Carmen holds a Bachelor's degree in Nursing and a Master's degree in Management.

She can be reached at: 201.920.6781 or at: Carmen@www.noexcusescustomerservice.com

CHAPTER 29

Pentad of Success

By Dr. Rick Kattouf II

Having personally coached thousands of individuals all around the world, I have been very fortunate to have the opportunity to assist these individuals in making their goals and dreams in life, fitness and sport become a reality. Watching these individuals turn fantasy into reality and achieving goals beyond their wildest dreams is as good as it gets for me as their coach.

Let's take the 30-year-old mother of two who could not lose weight and believed that she was overweight because her family members were overweight. Despite eating healthy and doing a lot of cardiovascular exercise, she just could not lose any weight. What was it that finally allowed her to drop 50+ pounds, get mind-blowing results and a very lean physique that she could have only once dreamed of?

How about the extremely busy surgeon who continued to watch his body weight increase? With a very busy lifestyle and successful medical practice, this doctor struggled with fitness and nutrition. What changed and allowed this successful physician to find mega-success in fitness and sport? He went on to shed 50 pounds and add a 2:55 marathon to his resume.

Or, what about the 40+ year-old female who believed her weight gain was due to her age, despite doing a very high amount of cardiovascular exercise and eating healthy. What changed allowing this woman to shed 30 pounds, get lean and put together great performances in triathlon and running?

What about the gentleman in his 20's that was already an accomplished Ironman triathlete. What was it that allowed this athlete to shave a whopping 1 hour and 15 minutes off of his Ironman time on his way to a personal best of 8:50?

Or, what about the gentleman and his young son who were both morbidly obese. What was it that allowed these two individuals to develop amazingly lean physiques (the father drops over 120 pounds) and both go on to be accomplished triathletes and runners?

So, what is it that these and all of the other TeamKattouf success stories have in common? Each of these individuals embraced and followed the Pentad of Success. Let's examine the 5 stages of the Pentad of Success.

I. THE MIND

"We must change the belief in order to change the result"

The mind can either be our biggest asset or our biggest limiter. Always remember, whatever we believe to be true, we will continue to reaffirm that belief to be true...good or bad. It is the limiting beliefs that individuals develop about themselves that are holding them back from success in life, fitness and sport. It is limiting beliefs such as, "I can never lose weight no matter how hard I try!" "This must be my set-point for weight because I can never get under this." "I'm not a good swimmer." "I can run on a flat ground, but I am terrible at running hills." "I am big-boned and that is why I cannot lose weight." "I just have a slow metabolism." "I am terrible at climbing hills on my bike." "My mother and father are overweight and that is why I have the body that I do." "I do not lift weights because I will get bulky."

I want to help you make your mind your biggest asset and not your biggest limiter. In order to accomplish this, you first have to identify any limiting beliefs that may be holding you back from success. Keep in mind, if you believe that you are big-boned and that is why you cannot lose weight, then you are right. If you believe that you have a slow metabolism, then you are right. If you believe that you are a poor swimmer, then you are right. We must change the belief in order to change the result.

This was the very first step that allowed the individuals above to achieve such amazing results. When the mind is right the body will follow.

When you identify your limiting beliefs, write these down, as this will help you to become even more aware of how your mind is holding you back. Immediately begin to catch yourself as these limiting beliefs enter your mind. And when they do, pause for a moment, and quickly turn the limiting belief into a positive belief. When you hear that voice tell you, "I am not a good swimmer", change this to, "I am a good swimmer and with the proper beliefs, work and effort, I can and will become an even better swimmer."

You are now taking full control of your life and the results you desire are within your grasp. It is all up to you; you have a clean slate, what are you going to do with it? If you believe you are a good swimmer, then you are right. If you believe you are a great businessperson, then you are right. If you believe you can become lighter, leaner and have an amazing physique, then you are right.

Let's start each day with a very powerful and positive mindset. Each morning, before you get up and before your feet hit the ground, do a simple countdown in your head, 3-2-1; and then say to yourself, "Today will be a great day!" At this point, begin to repeat to yourself your positive thoughts and beliefs. Always remember, whether you think you can or whether you think you cannot, you are right…Simply change the belief in order to change the result.

II. STRENGTH TRAINING

As I mentioned earlier, when the mind is right, the body will follow. Once you start to change the belief in order to change the result, now comes time to implement the physical components that will allow your goals and dreams to become a reality. Do you remember the all-too-common limiting belief above regarding strength training? "I do not lift weights because I will get bulky." If this is your limiting belief, we first have to put the brakes on and change this belief in order to get the results from strength training.

Whether you are looking to get lighter, get leaner, have an amazing physique, become a great athlete, etc., strength training will be one of your secret weapons. It is the proper strength training that will build lean muscle. As you continue to build lean muscle, you will increase your metabolism and increase your body's ability to burn fat.

If you are looking to lose weight and lose body fat, strength training will not get you bulky and hinder your results. If you have the thoughts and belief that "my hips, butt and legs are already big enough; strength training will only make them bigger"; this is not true, let's change this belief immediately. If you are a runner, cyclist, swimmer, triathlete or duathlete, strength training will not at all hinder your performance as an endurance athlete. Actually, it will greatly improve your performance and recovery. On all of the above success stories, prior to implementing the Pentad of Success, strength training was the missing and ignored element in these individuals lifestyle.

I highly recommend strength training at least two days per week; focusing on both the upper and lower body. When it comes to proper strength training, it is all about quality over quantity. You will be amazed at what a quality strength training workout you can get in a very short period of time, 15-30 minutes.

During each strength training session, I want you to have laser-like focus, moving quickly from one exercise to the next, as this will minimize rest and increase quality. I want you to focus on muscular endurance (15+ repetitions) and muscular strength (5-8 repetitions). Choose the maximum amount of weight that allows you to successfully complete the prescribed repetitions. You can choose to alternate each week or even each strength-training day in terms of muscular strength and muscular endurance.

If you are ready to develop the most amazing physique you have ever dreamed of, lose body fat, lose body weight and perform at your very best…incorporate strength training into your workout regimen.

III. HEART RATE TRAINING

When it comes to fitness and exercise, cardiovascular exercise is the most common type of workout that individuals gravitate towards especially when they want to lose weight. Cardiovascular exercise, no doubt, is a very important piece of the puzzle for success in life, fitness and sport. But, if your belief is that cardiovascular exercise is the key to weight loss and body composition change, refer to the above section "strength training." Always keep in mind; we must change the belief in order to change the result.

Whether your cardiovascular workouts are for general health and fitness or sport-specific training, proper heart rate training is critical for success. All too often, individuals engaging in an exercise program tend to workout at too high of a heart rate. I am not at all advocating easy training, I am simply advocating training smart and within the right heart rate zones for maximum results.

Determining proper heart rate zones is very detailed and specific for each individual. So, for our general purposes here, we can use a basic formula. The first step is to determine your current fitness level;

(a) beginner – you have not worked out consistently, 2-3 days per week, for the past 6 months.

(b) intermediate – you have worked out at least 3 days per week, every week, for at least the past 6 months or

(c) advanced – you have worked out a minimum of 4-6 days per week, every week, for at least the past 12 months.

In order to determine your heart rate zones, use the following formula, 220 - age. For example, at 40 years old, 220-40 equals 180. Then, 180 x .65 = 117bpm; next, 180 x .85 = 153bpm.

The above gives you a heart rate range of 117-153 bpm. If you are a beginner, I recommend using this range. If you are an intermediate, add 5 bpm (122-158 bpm). If you are an advanced, add 10 bpm, 127-163 bpm).

Maintaining these heart rate zones during exercise will help to facilitate fat as your primary fuel source, improve efficiency and teach your body to go longer, harder, faster at the same or lower heart rates. As a competitive athlete, I recommend much more vigorous testing in order to determine your heart rate zones.

It is time to take total control of your cardiovascular training, obliterate the mindset of "more/harder is better" and embrace training smarter.

IV. NUTRITION

"Don't just eat healthy... Eat right!"

All too often, individuals form three limiting beliefs about nutrition; "It is all about calories in versus calories out." "Eating healthy is the key to success." "I'll just work out longer and harder tomorrow to work off the extra calories I ate tonight." (As I discuss in my 3-DVD set, *Rx Nutrition*, "If it were as easy as calories in versus calories out... It would be that easy!")

Eating right is not a diet; it is a lifestyle. Diets/food fads are disastrous and do not work. Before you begin any nutrition program, ask yourself one simple question, "Can I eat this way every single day, every single meal/snack for the rest of my life?" Look back at every diet you have ever been on and I can guarantee you that the answer to this question is a resounding "no." Hence, diets/food fads do not work... Ever!

In order to eat right (not just healthy) and get the biggest return possible on your nutrition, let's start to implement the following 4 components:

1. The proper eating frequency: in order to "stoke the fire" within your body, you want to eat early and often; a minimum of 5-6 times per day.

2. The proper nutrient timing: begin to fuel your body immediately upon awakening and every 2.5-3.5 hours thereafter. Remember, we must stoke the fire within your body.

3. The proper macronutrient combination: at every meal and snack, we want to have the proper balance of all three macronutrients... Carbohydrates, protein and fat. For example, while a bowl of oatmeal is healthy, it is not right because protein and fat are missing. So, in order to make this meal right, add a side of ¼ cup egg whites/substitutes (protein) and add approximately 100 calories almonds (fat) to the oatmeal.

4. The proper total calories: there are potentially 4 areas throughout a day where we can burn calories; BMR (basal metabolic rate), ADLs (activities of daily living), workouts and TEF (thermic effect of food/digestion).

Eating right will help to to stabilize your blood sugar, insulin and serotonin levels. This will lead to high and steady energy levels all throughout the day as well as significantly diminished (if not totally eliminated) food cravings.

V. REPAIR, REST AND RECOVERY

All too often, we have the limiting belief that "more is better." As important as the proper mindset is, the proper heart rate and strength training and the proper nutrition, repair/rest/recovery is vital for the Pentad of Success.

Be sure to give your body at least one complete day of rest each week. In addition, I want you to put a big focus on sleep. I realize you are all very busy, but, in order to maximize your success each day, the proper amount of sleep is critical. Focus on getting 7-8 hours of sleep each night. In the nutrition section, I had mentioned a neurotransmitter called serotonin. Serotonin affccts our mood and appetite. If we do not get the proper sleep, this can lead to low serotonin levels. When our serotonin levels are low, the body wants to increase them quickly. This is where your food cravings begin.

When you begin to have food cravings, what are you craving? I'll bet that your answer is chocolate, sweets, sugary snacks, salty snacks, etc. Am I right? Can you start to see the vicious cycle that is beginning when you do not get the proper sleep? All of a sudden, when the food cravings begin, a feeding-frenzy follows. If the proper sleep has not been a big focus for you, I'll bet that after reading this, sleep just moved up your list of priorities.

THE PENTAD OF SUCCESS

The Pentad of Success is the secret to winning big and it all starts with the mind becoming your biggest asset. You are in total control of how you want your results to turn out; you simply have to believe this to be true. Keep in mind; you must change the belief in order to change the result. I want you to focus all of your energy only towards the things that you can control. There are far too many things outside of your control that will zap your energy if you choose to focus on them. Have laser-like focus on those things that you are in complete control of – your beliefs, strength and heart rate training, eating right and rest.

Let the Pentad of Success assist you in bridging the gap between where you are and where you want to be!

About Rick

Dr. Rick has personally coached thousands of individuals around the world, assisting them in enhancing their lives and achieving their goals through proper fitness and nutrition. Rick is one of the most sought after fitness, sport-specific and nutrition coaches in the world. Dr. Rick Kattouf II has been named as one of America's PremierExperts® and has been seen on ABC, NBC, CBS and Fox affiliates as well as in *Livestrong.com, Florida Cycling Magazine, Go Magazine, Chicago Athlete* and *New O.D.* Rick is well known for assisting individuals in making mind-body changes and enabling them to completely change their body composition. Dr. Rick has also helped produce multiple national champion and world champion athletes, both amateur and professional.

Rick is the CEO/Founder of TeamKattouf, Inc. and TeamKattouf Nutrition, LLC. Dr. Kattouf is the author of *Forever Fit*, the host of the 3-DVD set *Rx Nutrition*, the author of *9Round Nutrition*, the creator of TeamKattouf Nutrition Supplements and the creator of 5-Round Fury Fitness workout app. In 2005, Rick was a panelist on the *Inside Triathlon Magazine-Science of Speed* seminar. He is an accomplished athlete himself having won three Duathlon Age Group National Championships. It is Rick's passion for fitness and nutrition that continues to drive him and his desire to assist as many individuals as possible around the world to become the champion they want to be. In addition, Rick has been named a World Fitness Elite™ Trainer of the Year.

If you are looking to get the biggest return possible on your investment of time with nutrition, fitness or sport specific training, let Dr. Rick Kattouf II assist you in bridging the gap between where you are and where you want to be.

To learn more about Rick and how your goals and dreams can become a reality, visit: www.teamkattouf.com and www.5roundfury.com.

Dr. Rick can be reached at rick@rickkattouf.com or call toll-free 1-866-966-1422.

www.teamkattouf.com

www.5roundfury.com

CHAPTER 30

Partnerships

By Eveline Pierre

PARTNERSHIP—AN ARRANGEMENT WHERE PARTIES AGREE TO ADVANCE THEIR MUTUAL INTERESTS (Wikipedia).

On my journey of success in creating the museum, forming the right partnerships is one of the ingredients that is key. Just like when you are baking a cake, your cake will not rise without baking soda—which is a key ingredient. You can try to bake without it and you will get something, but it will not be what you had set out to get; a well-fluffed and round delicious cake. This is also true in getting the right partnership. Without one ingredient, it can be difficult to succeed. You may have some kind of interim success but it might not be long standing. You will also feel like it is a challenge to acquire even minimal success without the right partnerships.

When I first got the idea of creating the museum, I went to a few people who really did not believe in or understand the vision until I approached Serge Rodriguez. I was blessed, because he instantly said that "this is a million dollar idea and he would like to be a part of it." Serge's skills were completely opposite from my skill set—which was perfect from the standpoint of accomplishing the development of the museum. His weaknesses are my strengths and my weaknesses are his strengths. As a result, we complement each other very well. Serge has a background in construction and architecture, two areas in which I have no understanding. Both industries are literally foreign to me. I remember once we had to submit the proposed rendering for the museum after finding out the night before that it was a requirement for the museum's first public presentation. Serge was able to do it without a hitch. Honestly, I would not have been able to provide it because it would cost thousands of dollars to produce, which was not in the budget.

In another example, I remember when we moved into our very first space and had to do the interior remodeling. I'm not sure who the previous tenant was, but the entire space was painted in battleship grey, including the hardwood floors and ceilings. After getting three contractor quotes to retrofit the space, I was in shock that the least expensive quote was roughly twenty five thousand dollars.

Serge reviewed the quotes and declared that we were not paying those prices for the work. He stated, "I am going to contact some of my construction friends and we will go from there." Well, we got some assistance with demolition and hauling from Serge's friends in the construction industry and the rest of the work was performed by Serge and one of our employees. The complete scope of work to retrofit the space came in under five thousand dollars, because Serge had the tenacity to go the extra mile.

Again, having the right partner with the right skill sets will save you time, energy and money, which is extremely important at the beginning of your journey. This is also relevant as you continue on throughout the course of your journey. Many times when situations got very challenging and I wasn't sure that I wanted to continue on my journey, Serge was able to encourage me to keep on because we were on the right path. If he was not there to encourage me, on many occasions I do not think I would have made it through to see the fulfillment of our success.

The statement "No man is an island" is so true. You might not be able to get to your highest level of success if you do not have sound partnerships with the right people. As you build your team, the wrong people can undermine what you've worked so hard to build. However, having the right partnership will catapult you to your highest capacity. We will always need people to help us along the way, but the right people will keep us on the right path to success.

The two things you should do in order to have sound partnership are:

    1. Find someone who understands and believes in your vision.

2. Find someone who complements your weaknesses and vice versa.

"If you do not seek out allies and helpers then you will be isolated and weak" ~Sun Tzu

STRATEGIC PARTNERSHIP: A "WIN/WIN" ALLIANCE AND COMMITMENT BETWEEN TWO ORGANIZATIONS FOR THE PURPOSE OF ACHIEVING SPECIFIC BUSINESS OBJECTIVES.

Having strategic partnerships is also very important for your success. I understood early on that our growth would be fast tracked by having the right collaborators. When we started the organization, no one knew who we were. Therefore, it was key to collaborate with the right organizations to do sound programming and events that got the word out about the museum and its mission. We looked to organizations and companies that had a good understanding of our mission, a great track record, who are already established and who wanted to support our new endeavor.

Some of the strategic partners were sometimes able to facilitate space for our events and even provide financial support to help us with expenses early on. One bank in particular was able to facilitate space for us to hang up paintings in the section of the bank that their most wealthy clients frequented. This gave us lots of exposure and which drew interest from their wealthy clients to donate financially to the museum. These types of partnerships are truly a "win/win" because they are willing to facilitate you with resources that you need. I have been very fortunate that about 90 percent of the strategic partners that I have worked with during the past eight years still continue to work with the museum today.

The top two things one must identify in order to have great strategic partners are:

1. Find an organization/business with resources that you need.

2. Find an organization/business with a great track record who is already established.

Ecclesiastes 4:9 Two are better than one, because they have a good return for their labor. (Bible NIV)

About Eveline

Eveline Pierre – also known as the "Campaigner of Empowerment" – is an author of forthcoming book entitled, *The 7 Pillars to Success: How We created the 1st Haitian Heritage Museum*, and a speaker that is highly sought after by the media for her expertise in the Cultural Arts and Entertainment.

Ms. Pierre has been seen on NBC 6 South Florida, CNN affiliates, Comcast Media Makers and on WLRN Caribbean Current. Notably, Ms. Pierre is on the advisory boards of Art Basel Miami Beach and Brickell Avenue Literary Society. In 2011, Ms. Pierre was awarded ICABA Most Accomplished Executive, and appeared in Miami Today 2011, on the front cover of the Achiever 2011, and the In the Company of Woman – Arts and Entertainment Women of the Year 2011.

In 2004, she founded the first Haitian Heritage Museum in the world outside of Haiti to create a legacy for future generations. The museum has been critically acclaimed as Miami Best Museum 2010 by Miami New Times. Ms. Pierre has also received a proclamation from Miami Dade County Public Schools for the children's book collaboration with local Museum partners entitled "Through the eyes of my Haitian Friend."

Ms. Pierre uses cultural Arts and Entertainment to empower others and believes creativity is the doorway to success. Ms. Pierre is a graduate from Howard University and resides in Miami, Florida.

To learn more about Eveline Pierre go to: www.evelinepierre.com or www.haitianheritagemuseum.org

CHAPTER 31

It's All About The People

By Allison Higgins

You picked up this book because you are an achiever and you are ready to take your success to the next level and WIN BIG! Congratulations for stepping up to the plate and taking the responsibility to do what it takes to get there. I have had the opportunity to win big in several areas of my life and am thankful to be able to pass along to you one of my most powerful secrets to winning big…you must master the art of people. Every big win I have had in my life has required the help of others, and the best way to get help from others is to form strong connections, build solid relationships, and help others as much as you can.

I know you are likely saying to yourself that you have heard all this 'people stuff' before.

- Be a better communicator.

- Develop your interpersonal skills.

- Improve your emotional intelligence.

Yes, yes, and yes. BUT there is more…so much more. To really master the art of people and upgrade your success to win big you must go deeper and become a people expert. Notice I did not say you should master the *science* of people. Let's not think of people as a science. Let's think of them as amazing miracles of individual expression that cannot be reflected in a metric, a formula or an equation. Each person is a piece of wonderful art that speaks to you in a way that no other person on earth can or ever will. It is up to you to develop the awareness and skill set to really connect with each one you come in contact with.

I have had the opportunity to study and learn from some of the most successful people over the past 25 years. Each and every one of them would agree that their big wins in life were not only a direct result of their personal efforts, BUT were very much influenced by the people in their lives—and would not have been accomplished without their help and support. You must change your mindset to understand and know that if you want to accomplish anything big in your life, you must do it with others. Once you understand and internalize the truth of this fundamental principle of winning big, then you will make yourself more aware of your connections and begin to develop your skills to improve how you connect with others. Remember, it's all about the people.

Now, it is going to take some time and effort to really become a master at the art of people. I have understood this principle of winning big for many, many years and I still forget and struggle at times when dealing with others. Remember, we are people, too.☺

To help you win big, here are seven secrets to mastering the art of people that you can practice each and every day with every person you come in contact with:

THE 7 SECRETS TO MASTERING THE ART OF PEOPLE

Secret #1: Relax And Know Your Value
The very first secret to mastering the art of people has nothing to do with others and everything to do with you. You have to be comfortable in who you are before you can truly connect. I know this is easier said than done. How many times have we questioned ourselves when we approach someone or attempt to make a connection and wonder if they want to connect with us? Well, stop those types of questions and know deep down in your soul that you are going to help this person in some way and this person needs your connection. You have a tremendous amount to offer this person even though it may not appear that way on the immediate surface. Know this fact and internalize it. I know it for you already.

Secret #2: Be The Other Person
This secret probably sounds a little weird, but you have to learn to be

the other person. This is more than just putting yourself in their shoes. Really take some time to be the person you are interacting with. This is obviously easier with the people that you know a little bit about, but it can also be done with someone you have just met by studying the person and watching how others interact with him/her. Ask yourself a number of inquisitive questions such as:

- "Why is this person here?"

- "What is this person looking for?"

- "What are his/her goals?"

- "What is this person worried about?"

- "What would set this person at ease?" (…if he/she appears nervous or upset.)

- "How can I help this person get what he/she wants?", etc.

Learning how to be the other person will help you connect with him/her by understanding who that person really is, what he/she wants, what he/she fears, how he/she feels most comfortable communicating, etc.

I certainly understand that no amount of skill will enable you to really 'become the other person.' However, you must start to work at that as much as you can. This is key to your ability to win big in your life. By truly understanding the other person you are connecting with, you will forge a stronger connection, build more trust, be able to help that person reach his/her goals and move yourself closer to your goals.

Secret #3: Listen, Observe, Engage, And Adjust

We have all heard the rules of listening first and listening most, but you must become a fanatic at really listening to others. Do not let other thoughts get into your head while the other person is talking. It just cannot happen. You must be totally focused on the person you are connecting with. Additionally, you must deeply observe the person as they are talking. What are their non-verbal queues telling you? What is the tone of their speech? How fast/slow are they talking? Ask yourself these kinds of questions as you interact.

While you are listening and observing, you must also indicate to the other person that you are engaged. The other person needs to know that you are hearing them and acknowledging what they are saying or sharing with you. You can do this unobtrusively by nodding your head, making consistent eye contact, giving an occasional verbal response, etc. This type of engagement is essential.

Finally, you have to adjust your actions as the conversation or interaction moves forward. Be prepared to slow down or speed up your side of things as you listen, observe and engage. Be ready, willing and able to move as the other person moves through the conversation. Develop the skills to spot subtle queues from your counterpart that the conversation needs to end or that he/she is starting to get uncomfortable. Be in control of the connection, but in a submissive way.

Secret #4: Maximize
Your job is to make people feel special. One of the best ways to do that is to recognize what people are good at, acknowledge those skills/traits and figure out how to stimulate that person to utilize their strongest skills/traits to reach their goals. Become a 'maximizer'.

As a maximizer, when you are working to connect with a person, be sure to note what that person is good at and complement them on that skill or trait. Certainly you must be genuine in your compliment but that is typically easy to do when you are thinking like a maximizer. Over the course of your relationship building, be sure to continue to acknowledge a person's strengths, and even begin to suggest ways that person could benefit by utilizing those strengths more often or even in a different way or situation. Learn to be a mini-cheerleader for everyone you meet and want to connect with.

Secret #5: Be The One
Many people move through life with worries and struggles that they just cannot seem to move past. Additionally, groups and organizations that you become involved with have problems and issues that they need to solve. As a strong connector and a master at the art of people, you will begin to notice this more and more. You have got to be the one to step up and help.

Now, I certainly understand that you cannot and should not go through life solving everyone's problems and taking on all the issues of the world. That is just unrealistic and unhealthy. But I am saying that when and where and to your capacity, without harming yourself or your loved ones, you need to be prepared to step up and fix what you can fix, help where you can help and solve what you can solve.

So many people walk through life with blinders on and pretend not to notice so they do not have to invest their time and energy in others. This is not the way of a people master or the way of someone who wins really big! Even something as small as offering a bit of encouragement or advice to someone who is struggling, or offering to drive the soccer practice car pool on your off night to help a time-strapped mom could really make a huge difference in someone's life. Recognize those opportunities and be the one to do something.

Secret #6: Smile All The Time

This is one of my favorite secrets to becoming a master at the art of people. Everyone needs a smile and you can be the one to offer it up on a consistent basis. This small facial gesture can do so many wonderful things for so many people. This is a very simple secret and does not need much explanation. Smile at everyone you meet and the world will smile back at you.

Secret #7: Be Nice

Another powerful, yet simple secret to mastering the art of people is to be nice. It really is that simple. People are attracted to nice people. Now, this does not mean you have to be a push over, but there is no reason not to be nice to everyone you meet. By being genuinely nice, you will be known as someone that can be trusted, someone that others can turn to for encouragement, someone that has a big heart and someone that others would drop everything to help out should that ever be needed.

In summary, in order to win big, you must become a master at the art of people. Utilize the 7 secrets listed above and you will be well on your way. Remember that this is a process that will take time, personal investment and practice to master. But once you can build strong connections and solid relationships you will not only be working for the betterment of others, you will be creating a support team that will be more than eager to support you in your goals as well.

IN CONCLUSION

Take this material on the Seven Secrets and keep it in front of you every day—so you remember to work on your connection skills every chance you get. Mastering the art of people will take practice and lots of it. Start with the next person you encounter and see how you do. Be purposeful and genuine and you cannot go wrong. You will start to develop connection-building habits, and creating solid relationships will become second nature for you.

Here is one last point to remember…We are all human. There will be times when you just do not want to connect or work to build any kind of relationship. If you are not in the mood then do not force it. It will happen to each of us and probably more often than we would like to admit. Gracefully remove yourself from the connection and try again later. If working on this 'people thing' is just not your cup of tea, start with baby steps. Do not rush. Take your time. Look for the fun in meeting new people and see this process as a way to help others and yourself.

As you begin to see the power of mastering the art of people, remember that these secrets are just as effective in the online world as they are in the offline world. You can and should work to build strong networks, connections and relationships online as well. While the techniques might be slightly different, the core principles are certainly the same.

Now get out there and win big! I am cheering for you and know you will do it. Give me a call or shoot me a friend request on Facebook so we can connect, help each other win big and make this world an even more amazing place.

Wishing you amazing success and many big wins!

About Allison

Allison Higgins is a motivator, encourager and lover of life. She has worked in the corporate world for over 15 years and is also an Author, Speaker and Success Coach.

Allison founded SuccessBookCase (www.SuccessBookCase.com) to share her passion for personal growth and business success books. She recently launched the 'Your Big Success' coaching workshop to help others reach their big goals, and she founded 'The Side Biz Women's Network' (www.SideBizWomen.com) to provide a place for women to build businesses, share their passions and together make a difference in our world.

You can find out more about Allison at: www.YourBigSuccess.com

And she invites you to connect with her at: www.Facebook.com/AllisonDHiggins

CHAPTER 32

Success: It's an Inside Job!

By Sunil Tulsiani, aka "The Wealthy Cop"

It all begins with your mind.

In Tibet, one of the biggest honors a person can achieve is to become a Monk. You are seen as a spiritual leader; others look up to you to set the direction for the entire society because of your wisdom.

Monks constantly give without expecting anything in return. If someone needs help, they are there to do what they can. They believe that when you give, you will get more back—it just might come from a completely different person or situation. That, of course, is what the concept of Karma is all about.

What's interesting is how you earn this exalted position. You must begin as an assistant to a Monk and successfully perform your work with a consistent effort. Obviously, you must study and learn to meditate at an advanced level.

How advanced?

One of the meditation techniques you must master is known as *Tum-mo*. Tum-mo allows you to actually *raise your body heat* despite the fact that the temperature might be freezing. The final test happens on one of the high mountain areas at night. One of the head Monks will sit you down by an icy mountain stream as you sit naked and cross-legged on the cold ground.

The monk will then dip a sheet into the freezing waters and drape that sheet around your neck. Using Tum-mo, you must dry the sheet with your body. As fast as you dry it, it is removed and immediately replaced with another cold wet sheet. This goes on until daybreak.

Now, if you think this is merely a fairy tale, you should know that Dr. Herbert Benson and Dr. John Lehmann from the Harvard Medical School studied this phenomenon themselves back in February of 1981, and verified that the Monks were *actually physically raising their skin temperature* through the power of meditation.

THE SEEDS OF SUCCESS

How do those Monks do that, you might wonder? After all, *you* can't just sit down and dry clothes on your back. You'd save a few pennies on electricity by not using your dryer if you could!

They do it through the power of *visualization*. They prepare for a long time before they can actually do it, of course. They must *see* themselves sitting there, not feeling the cold and, instead, making themselves warmer and *being able* to dry that wet and almost-frozen cloth.

The Monks aren't a different species than us. We all have that power - but few of us actually tap into it. We get distracted by our everyday lives and lurch from one crisis to another - when, in reality, if we were just able to apply the same kind of focus to our own personal goals, we would achieve them.

Or even out-achieve them.

For example, I was a Police Officer for about 15 years when I finally made a decision to do something different due to family reasons. At that time, I went through my own personal development process where I ended up doing 77 real estate deals in 12 months.

I don't say that to brag - but to prove that you can achieve everything you want and more, if you commit your mind and your spirit to those outcomes. In this chapter, I'd like to share my proven step-by-step secrets for winning big.

STEP #1: Think It And Write It!
What do you really, really want?

Go back to being a child who is about 8 years old and ask for what you want. And you must keep it simple and start with few goals. Then *write them down*. Place them where you will see them regularly.

When I left the police department, my main goal was to make a million dollars. At the time, having no real estate experience, this was a pretty crazy dream. But…and this is very important…*it was just crazy enough.*

Here's what I mean by that. Most people create tiny goals - "I want to lose 10 pounds in three months, "I want to save $3,000 by the end of the year," "I want to buy one more property," "I want to improve my relationship with my spouse," things like that.

Don't get me wrong, these are important objectives, but they're very manageable, small-pain-for-small-payoff propositions. You might get a little thinner, a little richer and have a little less stress in your marriage, but these are not dreams that are *life-changing*.

You have to think…in the next few years…what do you really want? It needs to be big. Just like my dream of making a million dollars…it was huge for me. And the interesting point is, I didn't really know HOW I would make that million, but I knew it could be done.

Now, I may have wanted that million dollars by the next day, but I didn't set that kind of timetable. That's TOO crazy. And I didn't set my goal as a billion dollars in a year. At that point, I couldn't comprehend what having a billion dollars would be like.

During my mentoring sessions, some of my students have a hard time defining their big goals. And if you are in the same boat…here is my suggestion for you.

Find out what is "normal" to you and multiply it by ten. For example, if you make $50,000 per year and you wanted a life-changing goal, you may write down, "I want to make $500,000 per year by December, 2014." Do this, even if you think this is impossible…*especially* if you think this is impossible.

Remember, your dream of becoming financially-free is not as crazy as risking your life like those Monks who are trying to dry clothes around their necks in freezing temperatures!

STEP #2: Say It!

In Step 1, I said, you should create dreams that were simple. There are important reasons for that. These are the easiest to focus, meditate and plant into your subconscious. That last part is very critical, because:

"Rewiring" your subconscious mind is the most important thing you have to do to get what you want."

If you think of yourself as a computer, then the subconscious is your "Operating System." Whether you're a Windows or a Mac person, you know what that means; you can try to install all the software you want, but if your OS doesn't like it, your computer crashes or freezes.

Your dreams are like that add-on software. You "install" a dream to lose weight. But if your "O.S." (i.e., your subconscious) was trained from an early age to believe food makes everything better, that dream is doomed. Even though *intellectually* you know you should eat less, your subconscious is screaming for Ben and Jerry's. And soon, you're wondering why you're holding an empty carton of Chunky Monkey.

To overcome the "default" process of your subconscious, you have to do some things that people think are weird. For example, in Step 1, I asked you to write down your dreams and put them up all over your home.

Next, you must say your dreams *out loud* as often as possible but at least once a day. Just like an athlete trains to be the best at what he or she does, YOU are training yourself with these kinds of affirmations. The athlete repeats—over and over and over again—the kinds of physical moves needed to prevail in a specific sport or competitive activity. Nobody thinks the athlete is crazy—it's expected.

I started to say things that initially I really didn't believe myself, such as, "I have a million dollars," "The less I work, the more I will make," and "I'm making $10,000 per month in passive income." I used to repeat these affirmations out loud while I was driving, before going to sleep, just after waking up and even while I was praying. If I was somewhere in public, I would say them quietly to myself. Even to this day, I still do my affirmations by saying things like, "I am a multi-millionaire," "I am creative," "I have made 100 millionaires," and "I am the best real estate coach."

Remember, when you do affirmations, always use the present tense.

Don't say, "I'm going to be a millionaire" - say, "I AM a millionaire."

STEP #3: See It!

Visualization takes us further into the arena of the subconscious - and allows us to further implement real and lasting change.

Movies are visualizations of stories. A great one gets you emotionally involved, because you can actually see the characters come to life. You applaud and cheer—even though you know it's just a film.

Now, every time you watch that movie, you know it's going to end the same. It's already filmed, why would it change? But, say, you really *want* to change what happens. Would you try to change the screen? Or the projector? No, those are just tools—*the movie is still the same!*

Think of that movie as your subconscious. It replays the same scenarios and wants them to have the same predictable outcomes—*even though those outcomes may directly conflict with what you want to happen.* Even though you want your dream of success, you still force yourself to work hard, make less, live paycheck to paycheck, and never progress to fulfill your dreams.

That's because your subconscious always wants the movie to end the same way. *That's what it's used to.*

Visualization is the key to changing how your own personal movie ends. It allows you to substitute different outcomes for the expected ones. This is an extremely powerful tool, as we know from those Monks who can dry soaking wet sheets by raising their body temperature.

Here is my technique for making that happen: Imagine there's a video camera in your mind. You close your eyes and you see the video of whatever it is you want to achieve in your mind as if you already have it. Now whatever your objective might be—better health, becoming wealthy, having more quality time, a new career—you see yourself already having achieved it and enjoying it. For example, you could visualize watching your favorite movie or sports on your brand new 80 inch TV with an awesome 'surround sound' system with your friends and you see in your mind that everyone is happy, smiling, having their favorite beverage and then...

...STOP the video and freeze the frame.

Now the moving video becomes a still photo in your mind. Keep that photo in your mind for as long as you can. If your mind wonders off, bring your mind right back to that photo and hold it.

Now, it's not easy in the beginning to train your mind like this. Our minds are used to continual thought and movement—especially in this day and age. The sad fact is...

Everything in modern life works against meditation and visualization - even though these are the most powerful tools available to change our lives!!!

You can beat that trend. You can train yourself to freeze on images of your success and "download" those images to your subconscious. The more you repeat, the more successful images get implanted. The subconscious, quite frankly, doesn't know the difference between a real image and a made-up one.

Make believe you are successful *now*. Remember—the subconscious minds of most people create movies in which they're merely extras, not stars. Now that's crazy—why would you make movies and not be the superstar making things happen?

As a seminar leader and a paid speaker who has trained over 100,000 people, I do many presentations. I often visualize my students becoming successful real estate investors and wonderful coaches. That helps *me* help *them*.

You can make your success happen too. It all begins with your mind... because it's an inside job!

STEP #4: Attract It!
In this step, you automate your success—in a big way.

I'm sure most of you are familiar with the Law of Attraction. Basically, what you focus on is *what you attract*.

If your subconscious is convinced you're a loser, that you are never going to get anywhere in life, you attract the kinds of people and circumstances into your life that are going to cause negative outcomes. You become an expert at bringing bad stuff into your life automatically.

But...BUT...if you successfully write it, say it and see it, if you successfully rewire your subconscious, then you will make the *reverse* happen—*good* things will come to you automatically.

All you have to do is focus on your dream…almost become obsessed with getting it and not letting anyone change your mind. Know your main goals by heart and ask this question whenever you come to a crossroads—is this activity going to get me what I want?

If it is, go for it, if not, stop.

STEP #5: Do It Now!
This is the all-important final step...

YOU MUST TAKE ACTION IN THE REAL WORLD!

I am not one of those people who preaches positive thinking will bring you everything you want. The opportunities will present themselves—but you *must act on them*! Doing all those things in steps 1 to 4 and working with your coach will make it *"normal"* for you to take action when the opportunity presents itself, despite your fears.

Fear is the number one reason why people don't become successful. So, how do you overcome yours? By actually doing the very thing that makes you scared. You must find a way to move past your fears. Once you do that, the fear no longer exists.

Use this technique:

Make a list of all your fears and start "killing" them one by one. For example, speak up at board meetings, ask for a better table at the restaurant, negotiate a better price for something you actually want, etc. Also attend self-help seminars, where you do things like walk on fire, break a sharp arrow on your throat, pretend to be a rock star and sing in front of hundreds of people (all of which I have personally done, by the way). The idea is to not let your fears stop you from taking action. I sometimes say to myself, "If I can walk on fire, I can surely do this…"

Good luck—and I hope you will find a way to help many people and achieve lots of success.

About Sunil

➤ *"If you want to be successful, you follow people like Sunil."*

➤ *"His process has absolutely increased my net worth...it's been phenomenal."*

➤ *"He actually teaches what he does himself - and he doesn't hire others to do training for him."*

➤ *"He's a man of integrity who has helped many, many people and continues to help them to grow their investments."*

➤These are direct quotes from students of the man known as "The Wealthy Cop" - as well as "Canada's #1 Real Estate Investment Coach."

Sunil Tulsiani in a few short years has made an incredible journey from policeman to influential real estate mogul - and, as his coaching circle will attest to, his track record in profiting from property deals is only eclipsed by his passion for helping his coaching circle succeed beyond their wildest dreams in their own real estate deals.

Sunil's determination in achieving his dreams was evident from his childhood. Born in India and raised in the Toronto area, Sunil had an early ambition to become one of the cops he admired on TV, movies and in real life - and overcame almost-insurmountable odds by earning a spot as an officer with the Ontario Provincial Police (O.P.P.). His dedication to success in law enforcement led him to serve his community as a Police negotiator, Police Detective, an elite investigator and finally becoming the first East Indian Platoon Commander in the Greater Toronto Area with the force.

However, the long hours and rotating shifts that police work demanded interfered with his family's happiness - so Sunil set his sights on a different course for success. With no prior experience in real estate investment, he set out to meet his goal of making a million dollars within the first year of leaving the police department. He fell short – but only by $20,000 – buying and selling 77 properties along the way.

Realizing that the secrets he uncovered along the way to his record-breaking year could be valuable to others like him, Sunil decided to become a real estate coach and founded the Private Investment Club (www.privateinvestmentclub.ca).

Currently, he mentors many students who wish to become financially free part-time or full-time. Sunil teaches them his inside knowledge of this lucrative world, as well his own innovative and dynamic techniques for personal development.

Sunil continues to educate himself in the real estate arena as well as continue his own personal growth. He is an in-demand keynote speaker for events and is the author of two best-selling books, *The Success Secret,* co-authored with Jack "Chicken Soup for the Soul" Canfield and *The Wealthy Cop*.

Special Gift For You
Sunil also has an exclusive 30-day personal growth workbook called "Success Mind Set." It is a simple, step-by-step guide that can "re-wire your brain" and help you get what you want in life. The hard copy sells for only $100 but for a very limited time, you may get the digital version for absolutely free. To get your gift, go to www.privateinvestmentclub.ca/SMS

CHAPTER 33

Investment Secrets of the Ultra-Wealthy

By Rob Russell

"BILLIONAIRE INVESTING FOR THE MILLIONAIRE NEXT DOOR"

"If it is correct that 'You shall know the truth, and the truth shall set you free,' then is it possible that if you don't know the truth, its absence can place you in bondage?" ~Andy Andrews

CAUTION! The ideas I'm about to expose you to will most likely dismantle almost everything you've been taught about investing. If you still want to continue to use the investment strategies for those that are "less wealthy," then skip this chapter, otherwise read on. All I ask is that you approach this chapter with an open-mind as I promise to be candid and share real-life strategies.

"Real knowledge is to know the extent of one's ignorance." ~Confucius

If you can enter this chapter void of bad habits and without the common myths and misconceptions of how Wall Street and brokers *want you to think*, then you will be in prime position for success.

When I reflect on my experience of working with the ultra-wealthy there's one thing that stands out in my mind above all else: you're not doing what they're doing. To be blunt, they're doing different things, well, differently. I'm not saying it's because you don't run a Fortune

500 company or fly in a private jet. What I mean is that their approach to investing is significantly different than yours.

For example, many smart people like you are told to buy and hold and that stocks are the best place to invest to get the best long-term return. But what if that wasn't true? What if buy and hold is really "buy and hope?" Consider this commonly held belief when applied to the Japanese stock market:

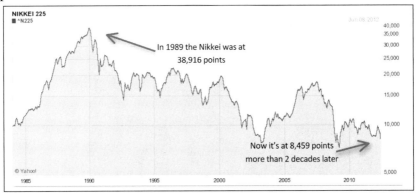

Do you think the Japanese believe "buy and hope" works? After all, the Nikkei is 78% off it's all-time high. Consider something a little closer to home:

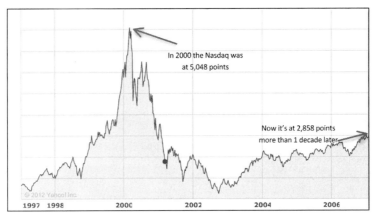

The Nasdaq closed at 5,048 points on January 2000, but more than 12 years later it's only worth around 2,858 points for a total return of -26.38%!

Now, do you still believe that "buy and hope" works?

The fact is you're probably being told to invest like those less privileged.

But how are you supposed to get ahead…far ahead? Why is it, do you think, that during the last market crash, the ultra-wealthy are still ultra-wealthy? Do you think they invest differently than you? Do they own stocks and bonds? Sure, but I've found they do to a relatively small degree. More importantly, they use strategies you may have never had experience with. So, now it's time to get you into the action, put you into "the know," and take a peek behind the curtain and see for yourself how "they" do it.

IT ALL BEGAN AT…

This story, my story, begins with some remarkable research I discovered from Harvard, Yale, and Stanford. Like you, I was told all the same things about 'buy and hold,' invest in the long-term, etc, etc. But I'm a natural born skeptic, always questioning, always struggling to discover the truth. Early on in my career I was determined to discover a better strategy than the old approach of holding stocks and bonds, and well, all roads led back to the Ivy League colleges and their unique investment models.

What I found by digging through all the performance data was superior annualized returns compared to the average investment portfolio of 60% stocks / 40% bonds. My personal favorite model is Yale's, because they have shown the most consistent performance even during bear markets:

	YALE MODEL	60/40 PORTFOLIO	YALE'S COMPARISON
5 YEARS	5.5%	4.9%	>12%
10 YEARS	10.1%	4.3%	>135%
20 YEARS	14.2%	8.3%	>71%

Source: Yale Endowment Fiscal Year 2011 & Harvard Management Company 12/2011 S&P500 / CITI US BIG. A mathematical comparison.

Obviously, over a 10-year period a 10.1% return is stellar compared to the average investors 4.3% return. Using basic math, a $1,000,000 account growing at 10.1% annually would be **worth $1,093,916 more** than an account growing at 4.3% annually. An extra $1,093,916 sure could come in handy during retirement! Take an even longer-term view over a 20-year period and the math gets real interesting. If the same

$1,000,000 earns 14.2% per year it becomes **worth $14,233,839** after 20 years! That's **almost $10,000,000 more** than what an average portfolio making 8.3% per year would've made during the same 20 years!

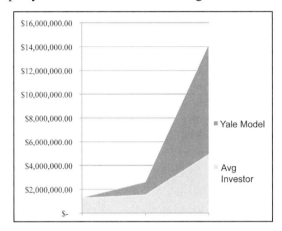

I certainly had enough common sense to realize that 10.1% per year is far from guaranteed, but I marveled at how the Ivy Leagues' investment management generated consistently superior returns to the average investor and advisor?

SO, HOW DID THEY DO IT?

Harvard, Yale, and Stanford collectively are responsible for managing more than $50 billion in investments, and have earned their reputation not by chance. It's common knowledge that one of the best ways to achieve portfolio diversification is through asset allocation, but the Ivy Leaguer's model took diversification to a whole other level! What they were employing was a diversification approach unlike anything I've ever witnessed before; I dubbed it **"Vertical Diversification."** It seemed like such a simple concept, almost as if the answer had been right in front of me for years, yet it took on a level of expertise and sophistication that would send almost any experienced money manager into a tizzy trying to duplicate the model.

Tragically, this strategy was secretly locked away from the majority of investors.

It wasn't until I completed considerable research, formed the right relationships, and hired the right people, was I able to endeavor to replicate and possibly build upon the success of Yale. The solution I found all hinged on this thing I called, "Vertical Diversification," which I define as *"asset allocation among truly non-correlated alternative investment strategies to generate an absolute return regardless of market volatility."*

I'm a pretty simple guy from a pretty small town in Ohio, and while I work with clients from all over the world, one thing every one of them has in common is that they desire a simple plan. While I could overwhelm you with all the details and research behind "Vertical Diversification" I rather choose to explain it to you the way I describe to all of our clients, because like you, I like to keep things simple.

BUILDING YOUR FISCAL DREAM HOME

I've never physically built a house, but I know from a rudimentary level what makes up the structure of a house—a Roof, the Walls, and of course, the Foundation.

It was from this simple premise, building your dream home, where my vision to deliver the Yale model of "Vertical Diversification" to aspiring retirees and retirees was born. This quantum leap to real asset allocation turned traditional investing on its head.

Imagine you were to build your dream home today. Would you start construction on the roof OR the foundation? The foundation of course, because no matter how fancy your roof is, without a solid foundation your home will crumble when the perfect storm comes. When constructing your ideal portfolio shouldn't you have a solid foundation on which to build?

PREPARING YOUR FOUNDATION

When it comes to your money, its critical mission is to have a rock-solid foundation. In terms of your fiscal dream home, I describe foundation accounts as "Protected Money." I define "Protected Money" as "money you cannot lose, unless you choose."

While every investment or savings vehicle has some sort of risk, foundation accounts are the closest thing to risk-free as it gets. In other words, these vehicles offer some level of principal protection.

There are really only three options to choose from here that meet this strict definition:

    1. CDs (backed by banks)

    2. Fixed & Hybrid Annuities (backed by life insurance companies)

    3. Government Bonds (backed by the Government)

All three of these vehicles provide principal protection as long as you hold them to maturity (otherwise penalties may apply). The principal protection of CDs are backed by banks and the FDIC, Fixed Annuities by life insurance company assets and state guaranty funds, and Government Bonds by the promise of the Government.

YOU CAN'T LIVE IN THE BASEMENT FOREVER!

While the basement is certainly the keystone of your fiscal dream home, it doesn't provide much in the way of big potential returns. This is where taking some calculated risk comes in.

The "Roof" of your fiscal dream home is where you're trying to shoot the lights out in terms of potential returns. "Roof" money is "Risk Money." I define "Risk Money" as "money you can afford to lose due to outside circumstances beyond your control."

There are several options to choose from here that meet this strict definition of "Risk Money":

    1. Individual Stocks & ETFs

    2. Mutual Funds (stock & bond funds)

    3. Variable Annuities

    4. Commodities

    5. Options

    6. Managed Futures*

7. Private Equity

8. Venture Capital

The "Roof" is traditionally where Wall Street, brokers, and advisors love to put your money. Understand that the "Roof" is critical to have for potential growth, but also understand it's exposed to all the outside elements that are beyond your control. Whether it's terrorist attacks, earthquakes, political mishaps, balance sheet fraud, high unemployment, or the ongoing European Union debt drama—realize you have no control over these events, but they certainly can affect your money that's invested in the "Roof."

When it comes to managing risk, it's important to not get so bogged down on world events that you cannot control or even influence, but instead focus on what you CAN control and that's how much to put into the "Roof" of your fiscal dream home*.

*Some Managed Futures seek to take advantage of world events, and as such, during volatile environments may help to lower "Roof" risk and increase return.

WHAT WOULD A PRUDENT INVESTOR DO?

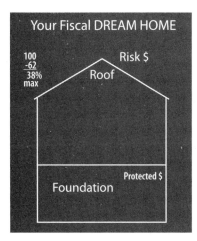

I've found that one rule of thumb to limiting risk, in particular, has served investors well for over 100 years... the "The Rule of 100." This rule states that a prudent investor would limit their exposure to "Roof" style investments.

Basically the "Rule of 100" says you should take 100 minus your age and the remainder is the MAXIMUM (percentage) a prudent person would have in what I term the "Roof."

So, if you're 62 years old the max you should have in the "Roof" is 38% (100 – 62 = 38%).

INSULATING YOUR DREAM HOME

The "Roof" of your fiscal dream home is only as good as the "Walls" that it's anchored to. And like the walls in any well built home you need good insulation. The "Walls" of your fiscal dream home are no exception.

The "Walls" are unique because they do not offer the "Protected Money" feature of the "Foundation" nor do they offer the risks of the "Roof," they are kind of in-between. The "Walls" are made up of investments that must meet three criteria:

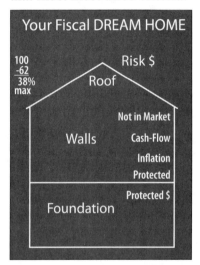

1. Little/No market correlation

2. Stable Cash-Flow

3. Inflation protection

Because the definition of "Wall" investments is so strict, in my opinion only a few pass the smell test in the current environment:

1. Opportunistic Real Estate (not mutual funds/stocks)

2. Secured Floating Income

3. Natural Resource Exploration (NREs)

WHAT ARE THE PROS, CONS, & "STRINGS ATTACHED?"

One of the most critical things you need to understand about investing is that there is no such thing as a perfect investment. Every investment has a pro, a con, and always a "string attached." Oftentimes advisors, brokers, and bankers tell you the pros and maybe some cons, but rarely do they discuss the "strings attached."

The vehicles that comprise your fiscal dream home are not exempt from this. They all have pros, cons, and "strings attached."

As you move from the "Foundation" to the "Roof" you move from safety to risk. But you expect a reward for that risk taking, don't you? So, generally speaking, the lowest returns will come from the "Foundation" because they are the lowest possible risk. The "Walls" are positioned to offer middle of the road returns because they are riskier than the "Foundation." While the "Roof" is where we look for the sizzle…the highest potential returns, which obviously involves the highest risk.

When was the last time you dug up the foundation of your house? Hopefully you never have. Same goes for your fiscal dream home. The "Foundation" is your longest-term money, which IS the string attached. In the "Foundation" you trade access to the money in order to receive principal protection (which is another reason we don't want everything in the "Foundation"). The "Walls" are intermediate term (generally an anticipated holding period of 5-7 years) and the "Roof" is by far the most liquid (and consequently the most uncertain) because you can always take the roof shingles off and put new ones on.

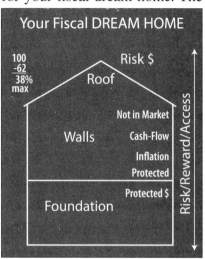

CONSTRUCTION BEGINS

If you were building your dream home you would have a hand in picking out the faucets, tile, carpet, paint, etc. In other words, it's tailored to

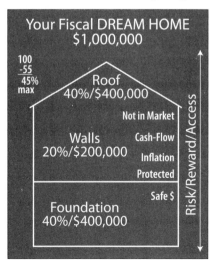

you. Your fiscal dream home is no different, it should be tailored to fit you exactly—your concerns, goals, tax sensitivity, income needs, etc.

To provide a hypothetical example, let's assume you're married, 55 years old, amassed $1,000,000 in retirement savings, want lower risk, and you want to be certain to not run out of money in retirement. Your allocations to the "Roof", "Walls", and "Foundation" may look something like this:

CAN YOU HANDLE THIS QUESTION?

For years, I'm sure you've been told to invest in the same approach of a hodgepodge mix of stocks, bonds, and mutual funds expecting that this recipe would provide ultimate retirement security. This old, antiquated, and unsophisticated approach provides only a limited degree of benefit and certainly lacks an element to create and preserve wealth in both good and bad times, not to mention the assurance that you won't outlive your savings.

Have you, at times, questioned whether you've made the right choices or decisions with your money?

Are you investing the same old way and expecting different results?

Have you had doubts about the direction of your investments?

You may have the "Forrest Gump Financial Plan." What do I mean? Remember what Forrest's mama said about chocolates?

"Life is like a box of chocolates...
...you never know what you're gonna get." ~Forrest Gump's Mama

Here's the BIG CHALLENGE for you:

Is your investment plan like a box chocolates? When you review your retirement accounts and investment statements do you know what you're gonna get? In other words, is your investment strategy like a box of chocolates?

IS KNOWLEDGE THE TRUE SECRET TO WINNING BIG?

In this book you've discovered all kinds of "Secrets to Winning Big" from some of the top experts in their respective fields. You've learned behind the scenes techniques and top-secret strategies from those at the top of their game. That's a lot of new information for anyone to absorb, but remember this:

"Knowledge is not power. Knowledge is potential power. It's what you do with knowledge that gives you real power." ~Robert Russell

[Disclaimer: The opinions in the preceding commentary are as of the date of publication and are subject to change. Information has been obtained from third party sources we consider reliable, but we do not guarantee the facts cited are accurate or complete. This material is not intended to be relied upon as a forecast or investment advice regarding a particular investment or the markets in general, nor is it intended to predict or depict performance of any investment. Past performance is no guarantee of future results.]

About Rob

In only nine short years, Robert Russell has amassed an impressive list of clients and credentials. He often contributes to *The Wall Street Journal*, *FOX Business*, *US News and World Report*, and also co-hosts "Retirement Rescue Radio" on 95.7 FM WHIO and AM1290 News Talk Radio.

Although, Rob's specialized advice is valued by the national financial media and the mass affluent, he is NOT Wall Street royalty. He is not part of the system. With a heart of a skeptic...from the beginning he set out to uncover ways to create and preserve wealth that didn't involve the failed strategies of buy-and-hope, mutual funds, CNBC, or divining the actions of the Government and The Federal Reserve.

Securities offered through Kalos Capital, Inc., Member FINRA, SIPC. Investment Advisory Services offered through Kalos Management, Inc., 3780 Mansell Rd. Suite 150, Alpharetta, GA 30022, (678) 356-1100. Russell & Company is not an affiliate or subsidiary of Kalos Capital, Inc. or Kalos Management, Inc.

CHAPTER 34

The Role of Business Ethics in the Success of Your Business

By Margaret Good

There is more to business ethics than individuals making good ethical decisions. Business ethics is organizational ethics. Companies have moral responsibilities and can exercise their influence on those they do business with simply by virtue of their being in connection with the organization. There are formal and informal mechanisms that either empower or discourage those we do business with – be they suppliers, customers or employees. These mechanisms will or will not cause them to follow the dictates of conscience.

Moral decision making in the context of an organization is much more complex than ethics decision making in ones private life. Analogies in business life can be very different than analogies in our private lives. So how do we in business set up formal and informal practices that encourage and support ethical behavior?

Tensions can arise from conflicts between an individual's ethical sense and the realities of business.

Most discussions of business ethics focus on ethics as a constraint on profits. The perspective is that ethics and profits are inversely related. The more ethics you have the less profitable you will be.

A more balanced view would be that there can be a positive relationship between ethics and profits. Ethics does enhance the bottom line rather than diminish it. Good ethics provides a money-making opportunity and gives you a competitive edge. Known for high ethics, a company can have above-average profits. All you have to do is look at various industries and ask yourself who you would rather do businesses with. A shop that is honest will do more business than one that does not. The important thing to do is keep a long range view and not simply look at short term gains. Dishonesty will get you the first sale, but diminishes the probability of future sales as the truth and conduct of the dishonest business ethics come to light.

Ethical behavior contributes to the bottom line by reducing the cost of business transactions, i.e., you only need to do it once. It helps establish trust among the stakeholders and creates better teams. Employee and customer theft go down. Employees diligently do their jobs. Issues such as security requirements are lowered and substance-abuse problems do not exacerbate the business environment. If they do, the high level of ethics will ferret out the problems and peer pressure will cause the unethical behavior to come out and be dealt with or eliminated.

In the 1980's, companies moved to the Midwest in the U.S., because they believed those living there had higher ethics standards and this could save them money. In Budapest, companies looked at hiring younger workers because they were more productive and not infected by the bad work habits of the communist era.

It is believed that those motivated by strong moral and religious values are less likely to behave opportunistically and will be more productive and more profitable.

Ethics builds trust with our customers and clients, our suppliers and with our employees. When we all trust each other, we are more likely to play fair and less likely to take advantage of each other. It is when one party has a sense of entitlement and greed enters the picture that we have serious issues affecting the bottom line. After all, isn't it more about having repeat sales from the same clientele that is most cost effective in a business than always having to go looking for new ones?

What is trust? It is defined as keeping one's word and not taking undue advantage or behavioral opportunistic acts when one has the capability of doing so.

Do you keep your promises? Do your products and programs deliver what they say they do? What percentage of success have those using your programs, services and products had?

Are you a mentor to your employees or a policeman? Do you build qualitative relationships with your clientele versus just quantitative measures?

With higher levels of trust, you can have better joint ventures between parties. The idea in joint ventures is to have a compensation package which requires the greatest cooperation between all parties to achieve the ultimate goal. Without trusting the other party to carry out their end of the process, how can these high levels be achieved?

A trustworthy partner is the best partner, and a moral one may be the most important decision to be made when setting up a joint venture. No one wants to be blamed for some shoddy product or service. Therefore, for all parties to cooperate together for optimal sales and results is extremely important.

Trust also allows employees and joint venture partners the freedom to be creative. Creative people need freedom and independence to stimulate their thought processes and therefore require a 'hands off' approach. As long as you can rely on them to deliver their part of the project as agreed upon, one will not have to continuously monitor creative people in an environment built on good moral ethics and trust.

Have you created a culture in your business that sustains and enhances good ethics? Have you put together a corporate credo for yourself, an ethical program and a code of conduct by which you are willing to do business?

Have you ever considered whether your zest and loyalty to your business has ever caused you to ignore or overstep the ethical boundaries by which you consider yourself to live by?

How do you see your personal character playing a significant role in your ethical behavior in all your business dealings? Do you believe your character – which is largely formed outside your business by your parents, religious background, education, mentors, and dominant peers – is more influential on your business transactions than your mission statement? Do you have business mechanisms in place to make sure you are not tempted to act unethically or are you relying solely on your character? Have you tested your personal virtue and the levels of trust others can place in you in the success of your business?

How as an individual in business do I infuse ethical principles into my business?

One way would be to create a corporate credo. A credo sets out your ethical responsibility to all of your stakeholders. Your stakeholders are your suppliers, your customers, your employees and your business partners. It is a succinct statement of the values permeating your business. They are objective mission-like statements. You want the credo to set out the principles and beliefs which provide guidance and direction in all your business transactions, both internal and external.

Your credo is your Ten Commandments.

Another way to infuse ethics into your business is to have a code of conduct. Such codes address things such as conflict resolution, conflict-of-interest situations, privacy issues, gift giving and receiving, political involvement, etc.

Each area of your business can have its own code which guides its behavior. Marketing, finance and human resource development will all have codes which deal with the specifics of their area of expertise. You can have these codes set up between you and your outside suppliers. For example, if you have an outside firm doing your bookkeeping, invoicing and collections, the code between you and this firm will be different than the code you have with your marketing company due mostly to the nature of the work involved.

You can introduce your code to all your clients, suppliers and employees as soon as you start or agree to work together. Consider the impact the code will have on your day-to-day activities.

A code of conduct will spell out what clients can expect from you in terms of performance, administration and delivery. It also lays out what you expect from your clients in terms of compensation, cooperation in information required to get the job done, access to their premises, training, counseling and effective communication.

The code spells out the limits to acquiring information and to using information confidentially. It talks about customary business amenities and what is regarded as undue influence and pressure on the recipient of gifts in terms of entertainment or other items and what is considered to be more than a nominal amount.

A code of conduct provides a clear set of guidelines by which all parties enter into business together. It recognizes that this relationship is voluntary and that each party has the freedom to move on at anytime with or without cause.

Once you set up your code, ask yourself, will you and the parties involved be able to live by those principles? Tailor the code specifically to your needs and treat them as a permanent guideline for you to consult on a regular basis. Make sure they are not too restrictive. Once you have developed them, take the time to reflect on them and discuss them with your closest mentors.

Remember, there is no one single ideal approach to business ethics. For business ethics to work, you must be committed to it. The process must become part of your business for you to succeed and not just some document in a drawer. You must communicate and let your business partners know about your code of ethics.

Developing a code takes a lot of time, discussion, revision and communication with various parties involved. It is not something developed quickly and in haste. It is also a living document.

So what do businesses as a whole think about mistrust? Many feel mistrust can be a self-fulfilling prophecy. Most think that people are trustworthy and innocent until proven guilty. This is a good rule of thumb to live by, and it isn't worth getting too hung up about other people's pasts. After all, people can change. Initiating a relationship on the assumption that the other party is going to try 'to get you' may induce them to do exactly that.

The next question then becomes, do businesses think retaliation is a good thing? Studies have shown that retaliation is considered to be a waste of time and a total distraction. It is a distraction especially to many business people if they have a lot of irons in the fire. Retaliation is inconvenient and causes inertia. Getting even is expensive and mentally debilitating. The motto many therefore live by is: forget the event and move on. The only time it is considered to be worthwhile is when patents are in question. For many, retaliation is a luxury businesses can't afford for several reasons.

Retaliation and an obsession with getting even takes a lot of energy and thus you lose your focus on the good things going on in your business. Instead of increasing your profits, you are stopping them from growing due to your retaliation.

Retaliation causes many stresses, and with stress comes physical and emotional illnesses. Your obsession will negatively affect everything and everyone in your life. You yell at your family. You will make lousy sales calls and miss great opportunities because of your negative focus.

Retaliation also sends a message that you are not to be toyed with. This message can in fact do more harm to you than good. You do not want to be seen as someone who is vindictive, and thus send even the most honorable business partners away from wanting to have close business dealings with you.

From the reading and research I have done, today's businessperson isn't interested in revenge and most consider it to be unprofessional and irresponsible.

The importance of moral, social motives and ethics in business can't be overemphasized. The fundamental basis of trust is, however, moral. We keep our word and do good things for everyone because we believe it is the right thing to do and not because it is good business.

Trust is the basis for many relationships. Good relationships lead to synergistic outcomes inside and outside of the business world. Good relationships enrich our lives when we all know what the rules of the game are. Credos and codes of conduct help lay the ground work on which to build those great relationships. They make the world stable and predictable. Contracts are honored and people bond. Great relationships built on clear understanding, trust and good ethics only increases the bottom line in the long run.

About Margaret

Margaret L. Good has transformed lives by showing people that success, wealth and living abundantly is not difficult when you learn simple life-altering principles. She is a Barnes and Noble two-time best-selling co-author, coach and speaker. She currently hosts the radio program "God's Financial Plan" on Joy 1250 AM.

For the past 30 years, Margaret has supported hundreds of people from many walks of life as a Certified General Accountant. Margaret is a unique and stand-alone speaker and coach. Her candor and ability to point out what your true gifts, talents and inspiration are can quickly help you live the life you have always dreamed of.

Helping you reach your fullest potential is Margaret's mission in life. A stellar businesswoman, wife and mother, Margaret shows her clients and audiences how to truly have it all and live the way you want to, aligned with God and never in scarcity.

Margaret's co-authored best-selling book Living in Abundance has become well-known. She has also co-authored a book specifically for the inspiration of women across the globe: *Wake Up Women Be Happy, Healthy and Wealthy* which reached #7 on the Barnes & Noble best-sellers list in January 2009.

Margaret is the wife of Rob with whom she has shared her life for the past 32 years. She is also the mother of Stephanie. She loves reading, knitting and quilting as well as enjoying the weather and its elements while attempting to play the game of golf.

CHAPTER 35

Principles Of RadicalWealth™ Leadership

By John E. Lang

Back in the mid-1950's, my father, my grandfather, and my uncle invented the flea collar for dogs. They designed this product and put it on sale in various locations like Woolworth's, Sears, and other small department stores.

Their flea collar sold for 69 cents. It was packaged in a clear plastic bag with a hole at the top, and it hung on a pin at the checkout counter. My grandfather, who was a marketing expert, had a number of connections in the business world. The product was not selling as well as he desired, so he went to a company in New York City that made custom boxes.

They worked with the box company to design a box that was approximately four inches by four inches by one-half-inch thick. They put a clear plastic cover on the box so the flea collar was visible inside and produced these boxes in volume at a cost of only four cents apiece. They took the exact same flea collar they were selling in the plastic bag and packaged it in the box, and they charged $2.98 for this newly-packaged product. Once the change was made, sales started to pick up, and soon the flea collar became so popular that Hartz Mountain eventually bought them out.

As we go through life, and we strive to be leaders, there are certain steps we must take to repackage ourselves. I am talking about a mindset and attitude that will serve to be a launching pad for your success as a leader.

Sometimes the cost of this is high; sometimes it's only four cents. But if we don't repackage ourselves the cost may be the fatal to our success.

Here are 7 principles that will help you repackage yourself for success as a leader:

PRINCIPLE 1 – HAVE A VISION THAT SERVES OTHERS

Do you know what the word maverick means? As with people, words live a life of their own. They start out seemingly innocent and simple, and then they change over time. The definition of a word develops and grows as it gathers worldly experience and new meaning over time.

According to *The Cowboy Encyclopedia*, by Richard Slatta:

"A maverick is a term, usually referring to cattle, for an animal that does not carry a brand."

This definition for the word *maverick* is probably pretty close to the original meaning intended by those who coined the word in the first place, but since the cowboy days, *maverick* has taken on several other meanings. In current times it has come to mean:

"A lone dissenter, as an intellectual, an artist, or a politician, who takes an independent stand apart from his or her associates."
~Dictionary.com

Beyond the definitions I have found in the dictionary, when I hear the word, here is my own interpretation of "maverick" as it relates to leadership:

A maverick is a cow that differs from other cows. Without a maverick, a herd of cows will huddle in a group, each cow with its back to the wind. When faced with extreme weather conditions, the cows put their heads down and shoulder together with each other to remain motionless. Sometimes the entire herd will freeze to death in a storm. A maverick, however, will lift its head into the wind and set out to lead the herd to new and better grazing grounds. It seeks out shelter from the storm in places where the herd can be safe. The maverick serves the herd in that way.

There is a parallel to this in life—with people. Certain individuals have maverick qualities that help them become effective leaders. When confronted by an adverse situation, if a person remains relatively inactive or huddles together with other inactive or negative people, that individual is likely going nowhere in life. Leaders leave the herd and serve others.

Our actions in serving others display who we are. The seemingly insignificant things we do for seemingly insignificant people can prove to be not so insignificant. Decide never to be too big to do the little things.

PRINCIPLE 2 – KNOWLEDGE IS POWER™

What you know influences who you are, which in turn, influences what you do. Permanent change takes place by altering how we think. When we absorb good information, it acts as a counter-balance to the background noise of the world.

To obtain massive knowledge, you must constantly further your education to better understand a changing world. It is important to realize that, in life, you are either moving forward or falling behind, and that new ideas and thoughts are as important as past experiences.

Teaching to Learn

One of the best ways to learn is by teaching. Teaching is an effective learning technique because during the teaching process, we are challenged to understand the information deeply. Before we can stand up in front of a live audience, we must _know_ the information, and during the act of presenting the information, we give ourselves the ultimate pass-or-fail test.

How many times have you studied the material for a course you will present or a speech you are about to give? You study and work very hard, and then all of a sudden you are up in front of a group to present the speech or teach the course. When you are finished delivering the material live, you walk away and realize that you mastered that material by giving it other people.

Learn from Failure

I believe failure can be a very good teacher, and in the act of failing, we can learn a lot of things about ourselves and about what is important.

In life, we choose our attitude, and it can be either one of letting failure consume us or one of uncovering the inherent opportunities presented in that failure, and then acting upon them.

PRINCIPLE 3 – SEEK GREAT FRIENDS

When I sat down and thought about the best way to describe this concept, I at first hesitated to use the term "great friends," because it's not a matter of having great friends, per se; rather, it is a matter of having people who are willing to invest in your life.

Friends will tolerate your weaknesses, but your "real" friends will remove them entirely. Friends are comfortable with your past, but your "real" friends are more comfortable with your future. Friends will always tell you what you want to hear, but a "real" friend will tell you what you *need* to hear. A "real" friend will stretch you just by being in your presence because they know and understand you better than you understand yourself. Know the difference between your friends and your "real" friends.

When you are seeking out a "real" friend who is going to help you, you want to get the very best, not just someone who is _good_, but the absolute _best_ person you can find. I will give you an example. Harvey Mackay is the international speaker and author of the best seller, *Swim with the Sharks without Being Eaten Alive*. I am honored to call Harvey a friend and I recently called Harvey up and asked him to mentor me.

He said, "OK, I'll tell you what. I'm going to send you six books that I have written, and here is what I want you to do. I want you to study them. Now understand what I am saying, John, I want you to _study_ them, not just _read_ them. Read each book, mark it, write in it, and put sticky notes in it and when you have studied all six books, you call me back and I'll mentor you...Oh, by the way, John, when you call me back after studying those books, basically your mentoring is finished."

What he did for me when he sent me those books was to inspire me. So I went out looking for the best, and I got exactly that!

PRINCIPLE 4 – HANDLE ADVERSITY WELL

It would be easy during these turbulent times to become discouraged by the wave of bad news that seems to flood us on a daily basis, and to let our fear of the unknown consume us. But allowing such discouragement to inform our decision-making would not only be a disservice to ourselves, but it would also cause us to miss the opportunity to see this economic crisis as a gift, and to focus on the more important things in life.

True leaders don't accept a serious setback or failure when it comes knocking on the door. We all fail at various things in life, but out of that failure, we can either just sink into the depths of despair or we can rise up from those depths and turn the failure into a positive outcome.

A friend once told me, *"To find out the true character of an individual, just bump them and see what spills out."* The true test of character comes when the stakes are high, when times are tough and fear sets in. People of integrity look past their fears with confidence and are at their best during the tough times.

Times of insecurity, fear, and chaos can be life's most teachable moments. Insights of wisdom, strength, and direction can be born in such moments. Failure is not your enemy! When your life unravels, embrace those times, look for the lesson, and expect greatness!

PRINCIPLE 5 – HEALTHY LEADERS ARE BETTER THINKERS

My friend and mentor Mack Newton is an 8th degree Taekwondo black belt and fitness instructor to the stars. Working out at Newton Fitness is no joke and is not for the timid. In 1998, I worked out with Mack and got into top shape for a man in his 40's. Several years later, I decided to take some time off from my workout regimen. In 2002, I was diagnosed with a 100% blocked LAD artery in my heart, which required a stent. The doctors told me that I beat the "widow maker" and that my past workout program had developed collateral arteries around the blockage. Mack Newton had saved my life...

Many of us who work hard often get myopic in our approach to our careers. We work hard and don't spend much time attending to our own health. Many of us put off working out because we are "stressed out." Exercise will help you deal with the negative effects of stress on several levels. Physically, it will act as a conduit for stress, providing endorphins, lowering blood pressure and provide an array of physical benefits in health. The average age for a "Type A" individual in the US is 54 years of age. Don't be a statistic!

Most of us are used to meeting schedules, making deadlines and providing service for others. Ask yourself this question. What have YOU done for YOU today? By disciplining yourself to exercise regularly and to eat carefully, you will promote health and fitness throughout your life and you will become a better thinker. Leaders need to be better thinkers.

PRINCIPLE 6 – HOLD YOURSELF ACCOUNTABLE

I have taught my children that a leader must "protect themselves against themselves," and as they have grown, they have found this to be a useful tool. It has to do with holding yourself accountable. This is a difficult process and requires honest introspection to be effective, but most of us are able to put this principle to work in the obvious areas of our lives. Today's world is cluttered with chores and tasks we must accomplish, and we are constantly impacted by the busy schedules that are commonplace in our society. Look for those areas in your life that you can organize and make more efficient and predictable. It may be as simple as making sure you "empty your brain on paper"—those tasks and schedules that you need to make. Part of holding yourself accountable is to find those people who you give authority to hold yourself accountable and put into place those systems that automatically keep you focused on your goals.

You need to decide whether you are a goal-setter or a problem-solver. Either you are ready to take control and change your life or you are being reactive to problems in your life! By holding yourself accountable you become a goal setter.

PRINCIPLE 7 – CREATE RADICALWEALTH™

The name of this chapter is *Principles of RadicalWealth™ Leadership*. To improve your mind without cultivation of your *physical* gifts would be a very hollow victory in life. Elevating your *mind* and *body* to the highest level without nurturing your *soul* would leave you feeling empty and unfulfilled. But when you dedicate energies to unlocking the full potential of all three of your human endowments, you will experience an enlightened balanced life of RadicalWealth™.

www.RadicalWealthInstutute.com is my member's only resource that has brought together today's greatest thought-leaders to provide answers to our current challenges by sharing insights and secrets with world-renowned authors, speakers and teachers such as Robert T. Kiyosaki, Blair Singer, Mack Newton, Chris Widener, Harvey Mackay, Jim Britt, plus many more! You can learn from them how to improve your spiritual, physical and financial health.

For effective leadership, living a balanced life is essential. Many of us who live fast-paced, overcrowded lives sometimes rob ourselves of "margin" in our lives and RadicalWealthTM living is compromised. Margin is defined as "The space that exists between ourselves and our limits." In today's world, progress has come at a high cost and the cost shows up in a margin-less life. We have seen more progress in the last four generations than the entire world has seen in its history.

With progress comes change, and we now live in an unprecedented period of change in our lives. The change that progress has brought, in many ways is good change. There are countless examples of change that nobody could have imagined years ago. Newspapers and magazine give us unbelievable amounts of information on a daily basis. The average Sunday New York Times newspaper contains more information than a 17th century person would have encountered in a lifetime.

As you read this, there has been more information produced in the world in the last 48 hours than has been produced since the beginning of time until 2003—Combined!

The world we live in today has brought immense pleasure and efficiency to our lives. However, along with the pleasure and efficiency has also come pain. People are tired and frustrated. People are anxious and depressed...people don't have time to heal anymore. Leaders are leaders —they are not super human. Leaders need margin. I suggest that every 90 days you take time away to recharge and create margin in your life.

The road to RadicalWealth™ leadership can be hard work, and sometimes costly because superfluous, unimportant things may need to be put aside, but the payoff is more effective leadership, happiness, contentment, peace, greater success and margin.

About John

John Lang is a bestselling author, marketing expert, successful Real estate developer and entrepreneur.

With over 30 years of marketing experience at the highest level, John has amassed a resume of some of the most successful projects in the United States and managed a personal portfolio of over $400 million worth of properties. His successful projects have received National and International acclaim for design, marketing proficiency and profitability. The Arizona Republic called him *"The Man with the Golden Touch."*

His most recent venture is RadicalWealth™, a member-only resource which brings together today's greatest thought-leaders to provide answers to current challenges by sharing insights, secrets and blueprints to a successful, fulfilling and balanced life. Contributors to RadicalWealth™ include Robert T. Kiyosaki, Blair Singer, Mack Newton, Chris Widener, Harvey MacKay, Jim Britt and others.

As a long-time business and coaching veteran, John has helped hundreds of people make powerful changes, helping them reach their personal and professional goals. John helps people create a plan that aligns their values and builds on their strengths while providing them the support they need to achieve the outcomes they desire.

To learn more about John E. Lang and discover how to grow your business, find your niche and leverage your strengths, visit:

www.RadicalWealthLiving.com

Or call toll free 1-888-240-9990.

CHAPTER 36

Winning Big Requires A Shift In Thinking

By Charles Anderson

What is it that makes people successful and I mean really successful, compared to you and me? Are they smarter or do they work harder? Are they risk takers or have powerful and influential friends?

This question has been on the minds of many people of late with the publication of Malcolm Gladwell's *Outliers* and Daniel Coyle's *The Talent Code*. If you have read these books, you might conclude that 'winning big' has little to do with innate abilities—intelligence or inborn physical capabilities— and everything to do with self-motivation and the right circumstances.

To win big, you must have it all: physiological gifts, the right circumstances, and finally, the psychological capabilities to take full advantage of them. However, if you look at these three contributors to performance, you really only have control over the last one: your mind.

Throughout the past decade, there has been much interest in the idea of how the mind influences success. How the mind and body work together is a question to which no one has found a compelling explanation, but one thing is crystal clear—the outer conditions of a person's life will always be found to be harmoniously in-sync with his or her inner thinking.

In 2009, a heart attack put me in the hospital. As I lay in bed recovering,

I was overcome with remorse—remorse for not taking better care of myself and remorse for missing my oldest daughter's college graduation. I worried about making it home. I've never been known as a quitter, but maintaining a positive outlook wasn't easy. Especially knowing that just six months earlier, my mother had died from a sudden heart attack at the age of 77.

But that setback, as unfortunate as it appeared, had sown the seeds for my rebound. Those seeds sprouted when my cardiologist explained to me that despite my continued anguish, my post-attack tests looked normal.

He said, "There isn't anything I see that would cause the pain you're experiencing. Healing after a heart attack has a lot to do with your mind and how you think. Your mind and mental state can have a profound effect on the way the body responds after a heart attack. The mind and body are interconnected. When one is affected, the other suffers."

I embraced his advice and decided it wasn't my time to die. After I shifted my thinking around, in three days I was back home and, two weeks later, at work training 75 insurances salespeople in Chicago. It took that heart attack and my doctor's words to turn me from a skeptic to a believer of this dictum: "Thought is the greatest and most powerful force on earth."

Thomas Sikking, author of *Creative Responsibility*, said, "You're not the product of a broken home, a devastated economy, a world in the upheaval of a war, a minority group, a family of drunkards or a poverty-ridden neighborhood. You are the product of your own thinking processes, and whatever you're thinking about today is the cornerstone of your tomorrow."

There are many things in your life that you cannot control, but you can control what really matters: your mind—and how it directs your thoughts, attitude, and actions. Because we can notice and observe how our mind reacts, it means we actually have a choice in modifying our behavior.

An exciting result of the last 20 years of brain research is that, as our brain gets rewired, we can improve many aspects of our lives. In his widely-acclaimed book, *The Brain that Changes Itself: Stories of*

Personal Triumph from the Frontiers of Brain Science, Norman Doidge, M.D. states plainly that the brain has the capacity to rewire itself and form new neural pathways.

Keep in mind, all success comes from behavior (from doing something), but all behavior starts out as thought. So if you're looking for different behaviors, you first need to develop different thoughts. As Dr. Wayne Dyer writes, "All of our behavior results from the thoughts that preceded it…so the thing to work on is not your behavior, but the thing that caused your behavior, your thoughts."

When you examine the logic of this connection, it is apparent that if you become what you think about, then performance and behavior changes can be affected by altering the way you think. Your thought process, therefore, is the point where changes need to happen.

Albert Einstein said, "The significant problems that we have cannot be solved at the same level of thinking we were at when we created them." In other words: It's impossible to 'win big' with the same thoughts that you currently have. If you keep thinking the same thoughts, you will continue getting the same results.

Thinking is the most advanced mental activity present in human beings. Yet, most people don't pay attention to what they are thinking. Do you consciously think, or is it more like breathing—you do it naturally, without much thought.

How aware are you of the things you keep thinking about that are not working for you? How many of your thoughts today have been about winning big? How many of your thoughts today have been about joy? How many of your thoughts today have been about frustration, lack, scarcity, impatience, loss, or fear?

The challenge for most people is not producing more thoughts, but producing better thoughts. We have between 30,000 and 60,000 thoughts a day, and most of those are thoughts that come to mind involuntarily and effortlessly. This is all mental activity but it isn't thinking.

George Bernard Shaw said, "Few people think more than two or three times a year; I've made an international reputation for myself by thinking once or twice a week."

Most of us believe that we are always thinking; it's not true. The bulk of what we consider thinking is just the mind going through its normal process.

Only when you become aware of your thinking skills can they be directed, steered and improved for the future. Just paying attention to what we are thinking can help us identify 'thought patterns' that we need to change and actions that we need to take.

HERE ARE FIVE STEPS TO HELP YOU PAY ATTENTION TO YOUR THOUGHTS AND WIN BIG:

1. Stop and think about what you're thinking about. Before you can ever hope to win big, you need to understand just what's going on with your thinking and how it's contributing to the situations in your life. If you want to win big, your first act needs to be reclaiming time to think about what you're thinking about. Nothing will change for the better until you do that.

2. Identify thoughts that are helping you achieve your goals. (Good thoughts).

3. Identify problematic thoughts. If you think thoughts such as "I am not happy," "I am poor," "I will never be successful," or any other negative statement, you are telling your subconscious mind to bring these ideas into your reality.

4. Select an empowering replacement thought. Take the negative thought and re-channel it into a positive written affirmation. Affirmations have the potential to help you change your mindset and your emotions. By repeatedly feeding yourself positive thoughts you can make yourself more motivated, happier, more relaxed and more confident.

Every morning I read the following passage out loud:

I like myself

I love my work

I am going to be happy today

I will make today a great day.

5. Practice visualizing a new outcome for 30 consecutive days. Visualization is the intentional process of creating a mental image of something you want.

What separates successful people from the rest is not talent. Surely, this plays a role. But it doesn't fully explain why some people with marginal talent win big and others with extraordinary talent never make it.

I've studied successful people for 23 years, and though the diversity you discover among them can be astounding, I've found that they are all alike in one definable way: how they think! And here's the exciting news: *how successful people think can be learned.*

HERE ARE FIVE COMMON THINKING PATTERNS OF PEOPLE WHO WIN BIG:

1. They Think Success, Not Failure
Ironically, no one wins big until they believe they can. Success begins in the mind with the belief that you can be successful.

Your success is only partially related to your potential. It is largely a function of your deep-seated beliefs – which create expectations about results and future outcomes. Beliefs help you discover what you want and energize you to get it.

Robert Collier, author of the bestselling book *The Secret of the Ages*, said, "There is nothing on earth that you cannot have – once you have mentally accepted the fact that you can have it."

Here are a few steps to help you develop the power of positive thinking:

- Use only positive words while thinking and while talking. Use words and phrases such as, 'I can', 'I am able', 'it is possible', 'it can be done', etc.

- Disregard and ignore negative thoughts. Refuse to think such thoughts, and substitute them with positive thoughts.

- In your conversations, use words that evoke feelings and mental images of strength, happiness and success.

- Before starting with any plan or action, visualize clearly in your mind its successful outcome.

- Read at least one page of an inspiring book/magazine every day.

- Associate with people who think positively.

2. They are Good Thinkers.

No matter what your current circumstances are, you'll be more success-ful if you become a good thinker. Good thinking – using the best think-ing you are capable of – is the seed that gives birth to unprecedented achievement. It is the make-it-or-break-it skill that separates big win-ners from the "you-came-so-close" people.

How good a thinker are you? Are you open-minded or closed-minded, curious or indifferent, aware of possibilities, judicious or impulsive, systematic or careless, rational or irrational, gullible or skeptical?

If you develop poor thinking habits, all sorts of impure thoughts join together to trip you up and keep you from becoming your best.

If poor thinking is reinforced, it becomes stubborn. Initially, it will be difficult to release negative thoughts from your mind. They will struggle to exist. But they cannot sustain the constant attack of good thinking.

A good thinker:

- Looks at both sides of every situation.

- Looks for hidden assumptions

- Looks toward solutions rather than problems.

- Looks to build explanations and understandings.

- Looks to make plans and be strategic.

- Looks to be intellectually careful.

- Looks to evaluate reasons.

3. They Practice Possibility Thinking

Striving for the impossible is your birthright. You are on this earth to grow, to discover, to change and to better yourself.

Throughout my career, I've met many people who have accomplished things that others were convinced they could never do. They believed in achieving the impossible, making the improbable happen through hard work. Vowing to do the impossible requires effort and courage and these qualities help make the impossible suddenly possible.

The history of science clearly demonstrates that things are only impossible until they're not. By looking for possibilities and working on new things, you can break free from your limitations and discover your power to win big.

Richard Bach in his book Illusions wrote, "Argue for your limitations and sure enough, they're yours." If you think about hardships and failure, then this is what you will reap. If you think about possibilities, you will be able to create miracles in your life.

Here are six ways to start practicing possibility thinking:

    i. Begin with clear thinking. Ask yourself, what do you really want in life/career?

    ii. If you know what you want…ask yourself, why do you want it?

    iii. Where do you want to see changes in your life and career?

    iv. Stretch your possibility thinking a little bit every day.

    v. Create a list of all the things that might make having what you want possible.

    vi. Open your mind and visualize the best possible options and solutions coming your way.

4. They Challenge Their Fears

There is no greater impediment to your personal success than fear. The dictionary defines fear as: "A distressing emotion aroused by impending danger, evil, pain, etc., whether the threat is real or imagined."

Fear is a master seducer as it shamelessly robs you of everything good and preys on your vulnerabilities. It is the biggest obstacle that stands between you and the greatest desire of your heart.

Fear itself is neither positive nor negative; it is neutral. Fear, like nuclear energy, can provide the electricity to light a city, or it can fuel the bomb which has the potential to destroy any large city.

The fears that keep you where you are do not generally reflect reality. They reflect the reality you create in your head. And a large part of that reality doesn't really exist. You are being held captive by imaginary barriers that originate in the mind.

Fear isn't your enemy; it is through fear and hardship that we grow the most.

How to conquer fear:

    a. Know the source of your fear.

    b. Face your fears and become stronger.

    c. Understand what causes you to be afraid.

    d. Don't let fear impact you on a personal basis. Otherwise, it will defeat you.

    e. Shift your thinking. If you feel anxious or uncomfortable about a particular activity, find a way to reframe your thinking to make it a learning experience.

    f. *The best way to reduce fear and build confidence is taking action.*

    g. Keep a journal to record your achievements. And look at it at least three times a day.

5. They Accept Responsibility

Great leaders, great athletes, and great business people all have one thing in common—personal responsibility.

If you want more success, you have to accept 100 percent of the responsibility for whatever happens in your life. That means giving up all your excuses and all your pathetic crybaby stories as to why you can't do something.

The hallmark of mediocre people is to blame others for all of the things that go wrong in their lives. When you blame someone else, you are not taking responsibility for yourself or your circumstances.

Dr. Wayne Dyer, a popular self-help advocate, author, and lecturer, said, "All blame is a waste of time. No matter how much fault you find with another, and regardless of how much you blame him, it will not change you."

Key Points:

i. You will never accomplish anything of value, without first accepting complete responsibility for your life.

ii. Be brutally honest with yourself.

iii. You must take credit or blame for where you are today.

iv. Everything you are and everything you become is up to you.

v. You choose the direction of your life and career.

vi. You are responsible for what you choose to think, feel and do.

Winning big is not a gift from God, and if you insist on seeing it that way, you're simply giving yourself an excuse not to live the life you were meant to live.

You have more control over winning big than you may think. To win big, you must cultivate the habit of successful thinking and take action toward your goals. This is what separates the big winners from all others.

About Charles

Charles Anderson is a sales consultant, author, keynote speaker, and personal sales coach. He has close to twenty-three years of sales and entrepreneurship experience. He is the President of the Selling Skills Institute, an innovative sales training and personal development company located in Massachusetts. Charles Anderson has worked with thousands of top performing salespeople and hundreds of companies across the United States.

For 12 years, he and his family owned the Reporter Newspaper Group – A group of newspapers in the greater Boston area. After selling the Reporter Newspaper Group, he began his sales training and coaching career with Sandler Sales Institute. In 2001, he founded the Selling Skills Institute.

In 2002, Charles Anderson developed and trademarked the propriety Shift Thinking™ Selling Methodology. This 'outside the box' approach to training and coaching provides the innovative thinking, knowledge and sales skills that help trigger record-breaking results. Its basic principle is that your ability to create an extraordinary sales career is much more an issue of what you think and do, than what you know and say.

In December of 2008, Charles wrote, *The Secret to Sales Greatness" – How to Unlock Your Full Potential and Skyrocket Your Sales*. In 2009, he wrote, *Opportunity Calling –The Easy Way to Double Your Number of New, Qualified Appointments*. This book is helping salespeople identify and breakthrough internal barriers that hold them back from telephone prospecting. And in 2011, he wrote, *Shift Thinking – 40 Key Principles to Rewire Your Mind And Skyrocket Your Sales*. In this inspirational book, Charles offers his readers a roadmap that will guide them through the process of rewiring their brain – so they can change their life and be free of self-imposed limitations and finally become the success they were born to be.

Shift Thinking™ changes the whole concept of what it takes to be successful. Our objective is to teach salespeople how to set more qualified appointments, close more profitable sales, shorten the sales cycle, and earn more money.

You can contact Charles Anderson via email:
Charlie@shiftthinking.net
Or call 339-927-2746.
To reach the Selling Skills Institute visit their website at: sellingskillsinstitute.com

CHAPTER 37

Trust, Accountability and Responsibility

By Derek Loose

"Did you do it?"

"No I was waiting for you to do it?"

"Why were you waiting for me to do it? I always wait for you to do it."

"Not always; I wait for you to do it all the time. Are you going to do it?"

"Maybe we should wait and see if Bob does it."

AAAAAAAAAAAAAAAHHHHHHHHHHHHHHHH! These are real conversations that we are having every day. When are we going to start living in a society where people understand what needs to be done will start going first!!! Is it a regular occurrence in your life to have these types of conversations with other people, and yourself, about why something didn't get done, and then all the reasons why you were waiting for somebody else? This is our society, this is where we live.

"Can you please make sure that the client gets that package by Tuesday?"

"I will get that package out when I have time, I do not take orders from you!"

"Sorry, I was just making sure."

"Why don't you make sure your job is taken care of and I will make sure of mine."

"You don't have to speak to me like that, I just was passing on a request from the client."

"I have been doing this for 20yrs, I think I know how fast a client would need the package by!"

Want to hit that guy? Have you ever responded in a fit of insecurity because you know you are not doing your job to best of your ability? Or because you are totally oblivious in that moment to how you are being perceived? The truly unaware are always the ones that seem to act in a fit of defensiveness.

"Sorry about the other day. I didn't mean to yell at you for no reason, but I had a head ache!"

How about, collectively as a society, we stop giving ourselves a free pass because we had a bad day or a headache or were stressed. You never get a free pass to treat somebody poorly. Let's bold that one: **YOU NEVER GET A FREE PASS TO TREAT SOMEONE POORLY!**

"I am sorry your honour, I wouldn't have drop kicked that nun but I was having a bad day…oops.!!"

In order to maintain great relationships, both personally and in the business world, you have to take a few things into consideration: trust, being aware of yourself and surroundings, taking action by going first, and accountability.

When I am talking about trust, I don't mean the type of trust that keeps you out of jail. *"I can really trust that guy he would never stab me with a sharp object for no reason, he is built with the highest of integrity!"*

When talking trust, I mean deep character trust. I mean total awareness and respect for the people around you. See, in our world we have entered into a society in which, if we can justify it in our own minds, we deem it acceptable or close enough to honesty and integrity. We tend to peg others with a bad trait to justify us not following through with a promise we made or breaking a deal. We also view trust quite selfishly, as in trust always applying to how others react to us and not how we react to them.

"I disagree with the direction we are heading and was hoping we can take a closer look. I would like to explore all the options."

"Are you questioning me? You don't trust me? This is going to be best for the company, and I trusted that you would see that! Maybe I was wrong."

"I just think we haven't done enough exploring of other options to make a final decision, and would like to go over it so I can get on board, or we can discover any adjustments that may be possible. I am just asking for clarification."

*"F****! I can't believe it. We have been in business together for years, and now I find out you have no confidence in me? You think you can do a better job? The decision's been made, so you either back me up or move on!"*

This is a variation of the most common breakdown of trust. The problem is: Most of the time, we are totally unaware it is happening. Having a highly trusting relationship with someone means you feel anything can be discussed no matter how tough the subject. Now, here is the key to being trustworthy. How you respond to somebody will determine how much they can trust you. In the above example, the person wanting to explore the options has not broken the leader's trust, the leader has broken the trust by responding poorly. If people are not able to speak of their concerns in a safe and free environment with *you*, then you are the one that is breaking *their* trust. We often look at people bringing up mistakes we have made or errors in judgement as not being supported or, in fact, being betrayed. This is because, selfishly, we don't want to deal with those topics, and we feel that people close to us should just look the other way. If you have a truly trust-built relationship, all communication should be welcome, if done in a respectful and caring way.

"IT"S NOT ME! ITS YOU AND THEM!"

We hate being accountable for anything. Think of all the times you have reacted poorly to somebody. It usually stems from being held accountable for something you said, you did, or you didn't do. When have you ever been furious at somebody for making a mistake? Now many of you will say you have, but I guarantee that the mistake was not what made you furious. It was the lack of accountability of the person who made it. All we want is to not have to guess; we want to know the answer. In my experience with businesses, taking responsibility for your actions, or anyone's actions for which you are responsible, is extremely important in maintaining a strong relationship with anybody. Always pointing the finger shows you are a coward and you have the inability to stand up for the truth, even if it means you would have to take some heat. Not being accountable shows a lack of character, honesty, and integrity – which are the foundations of every successful relationship.

> *"Beginning today, treat everyone you meet as if they were going to be dead by midnight. Extend to them all the care, kindness, and understanding you can muster, and do it with no thought of any reward. Your life will never be the same again."* ~Og Mandino

Here is the key. We have, as individuals, become very selfish and lazy. We want everything to be done for us, and we want others to do all the work without us actually having to be in the trenches with them. Our whole planet has been evolving based on successful relationships. Happiness is at its greatest height when you have strong relationships. Changing the world has happened with people believing in people. So why is it, when we know one of the most important tasks that we have for our business and personal health is successful relationships, we spend very little effort and time on them?

"I could call my client and make sure they are happy or I can do nothing and assume everything is fine!"

The problem is that we might not get the review we were hoping for, or we might have to take time out of our "very busy" day to care about the most important vehicle in our lives. To be successful in relationships we have to get rid of the "what's-in-it-for-me" attitude and start coming from a place of truth. Here is a simple rule for the "busy" excuse. WE ARE ALL BUSY! There, now I have taken that away forever. That is no longer an excuse for incompetence, laziness, lack of effort, or carelessness. By taking that away from yourself, I promise your relationships will improve exponentially.

Here is a quick list to go through when you are maintaining, building, or starting relationships in business and personally.

1. AWARENESS

Where are you on the awareness scale? Do you know how you are being perceived? How is your energy level? Are you being lazy and careless, or are you alert and focused? How is your attitude towards others and events around you? Are you living 'full out', or are you standing around with a miserable look on your face? Do you react emotionally, or do you take all information into account, even if it is not going your way? Are you being authentic with yourself and others, or are you just being a "yes" man?

"Hot out there, isn't it?"

"Yes, it is hot out there. I am sweating!"

"Actually, I mean cold. It's cold out there!"

"Yeah, cold. Someone get me a jacket!!"

Knowing these answers are crucial to great relationships. Being upbeat and an enjoyable person to be around and work with attracts other great people. Being unaware will be a slow death in any relationship business —which is essentially all business.

2. TRUST

Are you trustworthy? Can people be themselves around you without you judging them? Are you capable of doing the right thing when nobody's looking? Do you give 100% regardless of the effort in return? Do you act unselfishly when doing your job? Are you concerned about serving people, or what your commission is? Are you reliable?

Trust is deeper than just staying out of prison, not stealing, or not screwing somebody over. Trust and integrity are a total package. You either have character or you don't – there is no in-between. You won't have people give you a review that says: *"He is a great guy and usually, most likely, won't screw you over, and almost always sometimes tells you the truth."* You are or you aren't, period.

3. ACTION – GOING FIRST

Do you take action by initiating contact? Do you do your job first, with no guarantee to get anything in return? Do you help before being asked? Do you try to make things better before they are bad, or do you wait until it is necessary?

Going first is a lost practice in today's world. We are all waiting for people to initiate contact or care before we are willing to put ourselves out there. We want a guarantee that somebody is going to pay us before we will put 100% into building a relationship with that person. Our marriages are failing because we get lazy and don't want to deal with issues head on. Our businesses are losing credibility because we get defensive when someone wants us to prove our worth. Go First! I promise you will be rewarded!

4. ACCOUNTABILITY

Can you take full responsibility for your actions, good or bad? Can you take full responsibility for your team member's actions? Can you put down the finger and be more solution-oriented? Can you be accountable to yourself to do what is required of you?

Accountability, or the lack thereof, is also hurting our society today. We live in a world where we can sue somebody for burning our lips on a coffee cup or a fast food chain for making us fat. We blame others for absolutely everything we can. If a husband cheats, it's because the wife wasn't active enough in the bedroom; it has nothing to do with his lack of character or integrity. We take this personal lack of accountability and apply it to our relationships. We don't admit to mistakes or lack of communication. We just find an excuse or explanation to let ourselves 'off the hook.' In building great relationships, being accountable shows your character and encourages people to do business with you. Take responsibility for your actions, good and bad.

We can change the way we all deal with one another if we take it upon ourselves to pay attention to these topics. Be Aware! Go First! What's the worst that could happen with that philosophy?

About Derek

Derek Loose has been in the Finance Industry for over 10yrs. Currently, he is the co-owner of a Dominion Lending Franchise in Lethbridge, Alberta. Derek has spent the last 6 years guiding home buyers through the mortgage process so they can enjoy the experience of home ownership. Derek was recently awarded one of three Dominion Lending Centres Top Performer awards out of 2200 agents across Canada. His mortgage brokerage is ranked in the top 10 of Dominion Lending franchises.

Derek is passionate about helping his clients with integrity, as well as honest and open communication, so they can trust that their best interests are being looked after.

To learn more about Derek and his services, please visit:

www.derekloose.ca

Or email: dloose@dominionlending.ca

CHAPTER 38

Winning Big In Relationships

By Bernadette McGree

The Secret to Winning Big, is to win big in relationships. The secret to winning big in relationships is to win big in your most important relationship—that with yourself.

At some point in our adult life, a situation presents itself with an opportunity for us to delve deeply into our relationship with ourselves, our I-relationship. We may not see this as a gift. It is. This gift may present as a serious illness, accident or a tragic loss. As painful as the situation is, how we move through it determines how our I-relationship evolves.

Here are two examples to illustrate the point:

Back in 2000, something propelled me to make a change, a big change. I had been suffering form chronic depression, though I didn't know it. If there had been an academy award for being depressed, I would have won it. I was utterly miserable. Every day was a struggle. I was so used to this struggle, I didn't know anything else. Even during the moments when I felt happy, there was an underlying heaviness.

At some point I started drinking every night, and one glass of wine became two or more. I don't know how many glasses I drank. I didn't count. All I knew was that there was a point where I was so intoxicated I was numb. The best part was when my head hit the pillow each night and I lay there, with the room spinning, until I soon fell asleep in a stupor. This was fine, until I started to wake at about 3 a.m. and was unable to get back to sleep. I lay anxiously for hours, worried I would wake up exhausted. Funny, that's what happened.

The mornings were very stressful. I managed to get the family out the door with the children to school, and the rest of the day would proceed in an overtly 'normal' way. I functioned fairly well and drank only one or two cups of coffee a day. By early afternoon, productivity reached an all time low and I was exhausted. By school pick-up time, I was functioning better. It was a lot easier to be bright and bubbly with the children and other people around. Somehow the heavy, aching, sad me inside would become smaller and the bright, bubbly, organized part of me would show up and lead the way.

I'm not sure how long this pattern went on. One day I said to myself "I've had enough." I called my doctor and made an appointment. I had to wait two long days to see her on Friday. I said to her I was completely convinced that I had lost my mind and needed serious intervention, "Get the men in the white coat. I'm ready for electric shock therapy. I'm going mad. I've had enough." She listened, validated, made me feel good about myself and at the end of an hour made up an herbal concoction of liquid lavender and St John's Wort. She had told me I was depressed though not that bad (could she be serious?). She referred me to a psychotherapist whom I worked with for a few months, until such time as we felt I no longer needed therapy.

There were two interesting outcomes from my treatment with both professionals. The first was that after three doses of the liquid herbs, Friday night, Saturday morning and Saturday night, despite that I still wasn't sleeping well, I awoke on Sunday morning and the cloud had lifted. My husband and I remember this so clearly, twenty-three years later. It was an enormously empowering feeling. I felt free-er than I had in a long time. As I gradually climbed out of *The PIT*, as Terry Hawkins calls it, life became less of a struggle. The other important point to note is that my psychotherapist introduced me to meditation. It was a guided meditation. Every day after lunch, I would lie down and relax with my eyes shut for half an hour and be guided into a deep, relaxed state. I introduced my daughter and other people to this meditation. It was especially helpful for my daughter two years later when she was suffering anxiety and bullying at school; she was then only eight years old.

Alongside this regular meditation practice, I resumed regular exercise. I ran and lifted weights five days a week. In three weeks, I could feel the difference in my mood and my resilience.

It took many years and constant work to keep climbing out of *The PIT*. There were times when I'd regress and feel like I was never going to be happy again. Other times I would feel light and liberated from my sorrow. In hindsight I can see there was constant gradual progression, mostly in small steps, towards a more balanced, enjoyable existence. Betsey Downing, PhD calls this gradual progression – successive approximations. It's important to note that no matter what work we are doing in the area of self-improvement, consistent effort enables these successive approximations.

Over the years that followed, I felt that I regained my joy for life. Whenever I felt myself slip down, I would take time to stop and meditate. Sure enough, that would right me. I felt much more capable of leading a "sane" life, though I was directionless. Other than being a wife and mother and working as a teacher, I didn't feel I had a purpose. I wasn't sure when this was going to come. In effect I still didn't know what I wanted to be when I grew up!

At Christmas in 2005, just as I was feeling really good about myself, my world was turned upside down. No, it wasn't cancer, a car accident or some physical manifestation of chaos. I received no Christmas presents. Not one. Laugh. It IS funny. What was not funny was that it threw me into a swirling mix of internal drama. To make it even more challenging, my husband had bought himself a new motorbike – a custom Harley Davidson. I had encouraged him to fly to Boston from Chicago the weekend before Christmas to purchase the bike. I guess he'd not thought to take the children shopping to get a gift for me.

Some years later, I learnt from Zhenja la Rosa and Douglas Brooks PhD that "We don't choose the situation, we choose the experience." I chose to go down the path of attaching meaning to that giftless Christmas. I told myself that I had moved halfway round the world with my family to further my husband's career. He was able to buy himself a motorbike for Christmas, but nothing for me.

What was so great about this event was that I could no longer pretend my marriage was ok. It's not that it wasn't. However, it's not that it was.

I was forced to look at my marriage and see it without pretense. I had become a regular yoga student for some months, having flip-flopped in and out of yoga for many years. However, now I found myself seeking out a practice every day. Teachers had often said at the beginning of the class "and if you haven't set an intention for your practice, now's the time to do so." Initially, I had no idea what they meant. Nevertheless I developed a pattern of saying something positive to myself that related to what I was going through. I would repeat this phrase over and over as I moved and breathed throughout the class. Over a few weeks to months, I began to feel better about myself and able to see more clearly what had transpired. It soon dawned on me that I had allowed myself to not receive a Christmas present. It's not that the gift or lack therof was really that important, it's the meaning I attached to being giftless that was important. I realized that the simple act of moving my body and breathing while I spoke positively to myself had incredible power to change the way I saw, felt and experienced life. If this was true for me, then it would be true for others.

There were some key realizations that occurred during this time. Firstly, Grace gave me the sense to know that despite feeling my marriage was in question, the best thing to do was to wait. I knew I could not do anything that would impact my family too greatly, like leaving the marriage! This would have been a 'knee jerk' reaction and despite wanting to, deep within I felt it wasn't the right move for now. I knew I needed time to "figure things out." This was such a gift. I am so grateful for this gift of Grace.

Secondly, I had to be honest with myself. I realized I was totally responsible for what had transpired. I created that giftless Christmas. Because of my own feeling of unworthiness, I had no gifts. My practice on the yoga mat became one of looking for that worthiness, in a wholesome way, so that others would benefit too.

I realized that my relationship with my husband was a product of my relationship with myself. If I was to work on my marriage, then I had to work on myself. It's the same for all of us. I started to take notice of the voices in my head. I had heard them for many years. They were full of destructive, self-deprecating words and phrases. Many of the intentions I created for my yoga practice were (as Brian Tracy says), simple "I like myself"- type statements.

One day I noticed the voices in my head were positive. There were consistently no negative voices talking. Instead the positives were loud, clear and joyful. The day I realized this was indeed a great day.

Over time as I healed, my relationship with my husband improved. It continues to grow and change to this day after over twenty-three years of marriage.

So after this deeply revealing discourse, how can I help you find the secret to winning big? There is no one secret. There are many. We each have to find our own secrets that give meaning to our lives. However there is a way to develop an intimate, honest relationship with yourself. Learn to love yourself in all ways, for always, for everything. Learn to love every aspect of who you are, especially the gringly bits – the parts of yourself that you'd rather not have. They offer the greatest opportunity for personal growth and empowerment.

I offer these steps as a way to develop an ongoing relationship with yourself and to allow it to grow and blossom.

STEPS

1. The Situation is a Gift - We Choose the Experience
Remember we don't choose the situation. We choose the experience. In our personal and work lives, situations always present themselves. When we see the situation as a gift, then we can respond in a way that uplifts us and the people involved. This impacts our relationships dramatically. As Madan Kataria MD says, "When we change, the whole world changes."

2. Be Aware of Your Inner World
For us to respond, we need to be truly aware of what's going on in our inner world. Tara Judelle calls this inner world the "Innerverse." Are we going through the motions of living or are we fully engaged in what we're thinking, feeling and doing? Are we living a life of joy and purpose? Do we know what our purpose is? Do we really know what joy is?

Anyone can go through the motions of living. Being aware means being awake to the constant conversation between our "true" and "false" ego, as Alice Christensen calls them. Meditation, conscious breathing, yoga and laughter yoga are great tools for getting in touch with our inner world.

3. Invite Grace in

Grace is a wonderful gift. It involves submitting to what is, allowing and accepting that we cannot control everything. Grace begins with a pause, then a conscious breath. Pause. Breathe consciously. Don't rush into decision or action if this will impact on other's lives negatively.

Grace is like exercising impulse control. When we allow Grace to enter a situation, we invite truth in and open the door to life-affirming decisions. We wear our big girl or big boy underpants.

4. Set an Intention

In that moment when you pause and breathe, set an intention. In yoga this is a *san kalpa*. What I learnt from my practice is that our intention has three vital components.

1. It's an "I statement"

2. It's in the present tense

3. It's phrased positively

Examples: I am relaxed. I am healthy. I am a really nice person.

5. Move Your Body Regularly

Our bodies store the history of our lives, our ancestors' lives and even threads of the whole human race. Much of this is essential. Some of it we no longer need. This unwanted "baggage" can block our creative energies, which are essential for realizing our purpose. Our bodies are a gift for life. A good gift is one that is used again and again. Through regular physical movement, we can release that which is trapped and no longer needed. We can free our spirit, so that it can soar creatively, for the good of all concerned.

Yoga is a great way to move the body and manage stress. It is fun, therapeutic on many levels, and often playful. It is also hard work. This hard work helps us tune into the conversation of our innerverse. "Exertion of the body leads to quietness of the mind," says Mac McHugh.

The physical practice of yoga has also been designed to quiet the mind It's a practice for all ages, temperaments and abilities. Regardless of perceived limitations, Christina Sell says, "Yoga welcomes you just as you are."

When you move your body while repeatedly saying your intention, you create opportunity for powerful, rapid and lasting change.

6. Meditate

Meditation is a wonderful way to just be. Beginning a practice takes patience, dedication and commitment, which is quickly rewarded. The easiest way to begin is by practicing Yoga Nidra. This is a guided relaxation and visualization technique, which brings you into a deep state of relaxation where your mind becomes calm, quiet and clear. Yoga Nidra is a very effective way to manage stress and to learn to listen within.

Beyond Yoga Nidra, there are many ways to meditate. Keep exploring different techniques until you find one that works for you. Make time every day to meditate. Be patient. You'll soon experience the benefits. Remember the mind is designed to think. Can you reach the stillness underneath the chatter?

7. Laugh Daily

Of all the tools we were given at birth, laughter is one of the simplest and most effective for managing stress, staying healthy and feeling joyful. Laughter is as old as the human race. It enables deep, energizing breathing. It boosts the immune system and releases endorphins that make us feel good. There are many other benefits of laughter that have been scientifically researched. Research into the benefits of laughter in the workplace is increasing, with the latest study coming from Deakin University in Australia.

A daily laughter dose of 15 minutes can bring about rapid transformational change. Some people have experienced cathartic release from their first session. Yet, as we become older, we tend to laugh less. One of the great benefits of laughter is that it instantly changes how you feel. Have you ever come across a person who is sad while they're laughing? Laughter is the most cost effective, instant, natural way to reduce stress. Another great benefit is that it is universal in its appeal and ability to unite people. Have you ever been in a tense situation such as a meeting, and experienced a profound shift when someone cracked a joke, resulting in a room filled with laughter and everyone smiling at each other?

Many people find it difficult to laugh. Children laugh as a natural result of their play. Adults usually laugh depending on their mood, how good a joke or gag is and their sense of humour. When you practice Laughter

Yoga, laughter is not left to chance; using certain techniques we simulate laughter to stimulate laughter. The body cannot distinguish between real or pretend laughter. The psychological and physiological benefits are the same.

One of the outcomes of laughter is increased play. "In order to adapt successfully to a changing world, we need to play. Play is not frivolous. Play is essential," according to Isabel Behncke Izquierdo, PhD.

8. Take Action Aligned with Your Intention

Ultimately we need to take action. When we have prepared well and our actions are aligned with our intention, then we are integrated – body, mind and spirit.

9. Let Nature Take its Course

One of the most challenging things to do is to let nature take its course. Once we have done our work, then we need to let the results unfold. It is time to rest and trust, knowing we have done the right thing. Others may not see it this way, because of their perspective. Neither is right nor wrong. We are all facets of the one diamond.

Each facet needs to be seen from a slightly different angle for its true brilliance to shine optimally.

When we engage in an intimate, honest relationship with ourselves, we empower ourselves and enable continual personal growth. This impacts all relationships in our lives. When we shine, then by association, those around us shine.

About Bernadette

Bernadette McGree is a Joy and Wellness Consultant specializing in time-tested practices of yoga and laughter yoga. She has presented and taught in the US, China and Australia.

Bernadette works with individuals and groups, helping people connect with their own heart as a gateway to find inner joy and personal purpose. Her goal is to help individuals and the organizations they work with, to realize their highest vision.

Founder of mukti bhukti (mook-tee book-tee) and the Lindfield Laughter Club, Bernadette's sessions are packed with laughter, fun and warmth. She empowers people to release stress, feel great about themselves and live a life they love.

Bernadette lives in Sydney, Australia with her husband, daughter and son.

"When you live a life of joy and purpose, then you live a life you love."

www.muktibhukti.com.au
...live a life you love...

CHAPTER 39

From Baby Steps to Giant Leaps: The Three P's for Maximizing the Performance of Your Sales Team

By Rajiv Mathews George

People often think I am the ultimate sales expert, simply because of my track record. After all, as an Executive Performance Coach, I've spent thousands of hours in one-to-one coaching and another 1500 hours of team coaching in the sales and leadership arenas.

That's extremely flattering—but it just reminds me of when I knew absolutely nothing about sales…and yet, I *had* to be a salesman. It was my first real job and I was desperate to succeed at it.

Let me explain. When I arrived in the United States as a young adult, I was still very shy. That only changed during my years at Wartburg College in Waverly, Iowa. There, I decided to become very involved in school activities. I even ended up running for Student Senate and I became very well known on campus, much to my surprise. Apparently, there was a leader inside me that made himself known not only to others, but to myself as well.

After college, I intended to return to my homeland in Malaysia. I wasn't sure what career I would pursue—but then one was forced upon me. My father tragically passed away three days before I was to graduate;

that meant I needed to make money immediately. If I went back to Malaysia, however, I would lose my American student Work Visa and my opportunity to start earning a good salary.

I was fortunate in one respect—my college achievements had been sufficiently high profile to attract the interest of several companies. This was unusual for a foreigner on U.S. soil— and life-changing for me personally. I accepted an internship in a sales position that was offered to me by a firm in San Jose, California.

And that's how I suddenly found myself becoming a salesman *who had no idea how to sell*. I obviously survived and even prospered. But back then, I was incredibly unsure of how to proceed—and very puzzled by my new employer's approach to me.

They didn't really try to develop my sales skills so I could be successful in my sales functions. Technical or product knowledge or basic sales training is far different from learning how to develop one's selling skills.

Now, even if you go to work at a fast-food outlet, they show you how to put together a sandwich. Too often, however, when a salesperson is hired, the pressure is immediately on to deliver results—without ever helping that person develop the skills, process or behaviors to *achieve* those results.

That's why I felt a strong calling to become a sales coach; I saw so much waste of potential in people who were never able to acquire the proper training. I felt I could make a significant difference in the business world —especially here in the Asian region and particularly in Malaysia, where I am based and where coaching is a relatively new concept.

In this chapter, I'd like to share my "Secret of Winning Big" in sales, by revealing "The 3 P's for Maximizing the Performance of Your Sales Team," to give you some insight into how salespeople can be developed for winning results.

P #1: PURPOSE – FOCUS ON THE PROCESS AND NOT THE OUTCOME

To initiate and improve the performance of the sales force, a common process and language is required. Most sales managers come from the ranks of top salespeople; they're self-motivated "doers." That means they're much better at *performing* than *developing* the people working for them.

A baby does not learn how to walk the first time it tries. And a parent certainly doesn't expect the child to succeed right away. Instead, the parent is gently encouraging and holds onto its arms to support it. And because the parent nurtures these first baby steps, eventually the child can grow up and run and play with abandon.

Now, imagine if the parent just expected the child to get up and walk on its own, without any assistance—and then looked down on the baby because it wasn't capable of doing that. Crazy, right?

Well, sadly, sales people and other lower level staff too often are told what to do—without knowing how to do it. Obviously, good salespeople must show initiative and keen minds—*but basic skills can be best transferred and developed through coaching.*

At its core, development should always **focus on the process and not the outcome**. For instance, you may be obsessed with the goal of making a million dollars in sales - it may be all you ever talk about. But you'll never get to a million dollars if you don't take the time or make the effort to figure out how to get it. You need to achieve a target of $100,000 first, $500,000 next and *then* finally a million.

When you nurture the baby steps, you make giant leaps.

P #2: PROCESS – ENGAGE TO MAXIMIZE PERFORMANCE

Having the right "Process" in place is crucial to achieving your team's goals and objectives. In my coaching process, I use the **4D Engagement™ Model** diagram that follows for coaching sales leaders. A deep partnership between the manager and salesperson is essential for the process to be effective.

Let's examine each step in turn.

• (a). Design the Agenda

Each salesperson is unique and has different challenges. When a sales person comes back from a sales call and discusses their specific challenge, it's time to decide the objectives they want to meet. Those goals should be in line with both their own personal development and corporate objectives.

Some of the questions that the sales manager can address include:

* What is important to you right now?

* How many client appointments do you want to achieve in the next seven days?

* What do you want to achieve in this appointment with a particular client?

* How do you bring more value into your appointment?

When there is a clear goal for discussion, the agenda is established and engagement is launched.

• (b). Discover the Gaps

Sales situations are dynamic and challenges vary day to day. Coaching is not a single event but a continuous push for improvement. Problems result from self-limiting beliefs, lack of proper skills training, lack of awareness/knowledge or the absence of sales/marketing tools. When the real gap is identified, solutions can be found.

Some of the questions that the sales manager can address in this step include:

* What makes it difficult to work with this prospect?

* What's stopping the prospect from sharing more information with you?

* What needs to happen for the prospect to accept your proposal?

• (c). Discuss the Solution

Here, the salesperson commits to new actions based on feedback and co-creative steps agreed on by the salesperson and the manager. Through co-creation, the salesperson takes ownership of this commitment to new behaviors that will bring the desired solution.

Some of the questions that the sales manager can address in this step include:

* What can you offer the client at your next appointment? How will it satisfy the client?

* How does your ideal client profile assist you in marketing your services?

* If you commit to three appointments every day, how does that help you achieve your monthly target?

• (d). Decide the Game Plan

Now, the salesperson takes purposeful action. The coach guides and supports the salesperson in committing to promises and helping the sales manager to meet goals. The manager, seeing improvement, continues to develop the salesperson by moving them up to the next level.

Some of the questions that the sales manager can address in this step include:

* How do I know that you will keep to your commitment?

* On what day will you achieve your goal? How will I know you've succeeded?

* What action will you take now? How can I support you?

P #3: PRACTICE – MASTERY COMES WHEN THE GIFTED PRACTICE

Even though problems and solutions have been determined, Practice is still required. An athletic coach can't just teach a player the basic skills of the game and walk away. No, he must observe the player putting those skills into practice—so those skills can be constantly adjusted and upgraded to an acceptable level.

In the sales world, Practice involves observing sales calls, conducting role play exercises and simulations; this enables the salesperson to fully develop, much the way a caterpillar transforms into a butterfly. Let's look at how the two "life cycles" compare.

• Stage 1: The Egg

A butterfly begins life as an egg, a stage at which it is only beginning on its path to full development. So it is with the new salesperson, who starts with only the **awareness** that performance needs to be developed and improved. This involves digging deeper into one's true motivations.

For example, once I signed up for a gym membership. A trainer interviewed me to see why I wanted to come to the gym. My initial answer was a silly joke—I said that I wanted to check out the women, since a lot of beautiful actresses went there.

Well, he didn't want a joke answer, he wanted the real answer. And he kept pushing until he got it. The fact was my grandparents both lived to be 100, because they were farmers and, physically, they were in great shape. As I mentioned, my father passed away at a relatively young age (62). He wasn't in such great shape, as he spent most of his time sitting at a desk and didn't do much in the way of exercise. I was at the gym to be more like my grandparents—and avoid my dad's sad fate.

A great coach will tap into the salesperson's real motivation for why achievement is necessary and will take that into account in the development process.

• Stage 2: The Larva (Caterpillar)

Here, the butterfly egg hatches and out crawls a caterpillar. Movement towards development finally begins. In our salesperson's case, the coach will create a series of small **improvements** for them to work towards.

To continue our gym analogy, if a person wanted to be able to press 200 pounds, you wouldn't simply move him up to that weight from 50 pounds; you would slowly raise the amount of weight as the person got stronger. Similarly, in sales or leadership coaching, you want to help the client get better in incremental steps by reaching a series of small attainable goals.

• Stage 3: Pupa (Chrysalis)

At this stage, the caterpillar stops growing and forms itself into a pupa. From the outside, it looks as if the caterpillar is not doing a thing—but inside, it is undergoing a remarkable transformation. Our salesperson is also achieving significant internal **breakthroughs** at this point—due to the prior work and effort to improve one's skills and attitudes.

- **Stage 4: Butterfly**

The butterfly emerges from its pupa fully formed—and, at this stage, the salesperson has also finally accomplished a real **transformation**. He or she can consistently and reliably perform at a higher level without thinking about it or second-guessing. High performance becomes the default "norm."

THE THREE KEY AREAS OF SALES COACHING

There are three specific areas where coaching is applied as salespeople progress and improve. Let's look at each of them in turn:

- **(1). Skills Coaching**

This coaching is very specific and focused on improving certain abilities. For instance, a salesperson may not have the right level of confidence on phone calls. The coach might monitor the salesperson's calls, listen to their recordings and/or work on specific techniques to enhance the approach.

- **(2). Performance Coaching**

This is a more general coaching approach, designed to improve overall performance, rather than specifically-defined skills. For example, the coach might shadow the client during in-person sales appointments to see how the salesperson performs in the room—and suggest what issues might be getting in the way of sales conversions.

- **(3). Developmental Coaching**

This level creates the conditions for reflective learning. The coach creates a space which allows clients to stand back from the workplace and gain perspective on their experiences and themselves through a challenging and supportive dialogue with the coach. The end result allows them to move past more substantial roadblocks and develop a more fundamental sense of leadership.

SMILEY SAM – A CASE STUDY

I'd like to conclude this chapter by sharing an actual case study that illustrates just how effective coaching can be when the client is serious about learning and growing. I'll call this particular client "Sam," as he prefers not use his real name.

Sam joined my coaching clinic, which was sponsored by one of the leading insurance companies in the country, several years ago. He had moved from a rural community to the big city to work for the insurance company as an agent. But there were immediate problems: His commission income was small, he had conflicts with his boss and he lacked the necessary discipline to succeed.

What he did have, importantly, was the genuine desire to achieve—he just had no idea how to reach his goals ("Egg" Stage). That's when he decided my coaching clinic might be just what he needed.

Through the coaching process, Sam articulated his objectives clearly and in detail—he knew exactly what he wanted when it came to his job, his family, and his lifestyle. Over the next two years, we got Sam to commit to specific daily and weekly goals that built up to bigger breakthroughs along the way ("Caterpillar" Stage).

He dedicated himself to all his goals, big and small, and put in place a positive attitude that served him well. As a matter of fact, it was his new, friendly smile that attracted clients to him; he discovered how to tap into his newfound strengths to build his business. Real and lasting transformation began to occur (Pupa Stage).

Three years later, Sam is a very successful insurance manager with fifteen agents reporting to him. He's won many awards and received some amazing incentive trips from his company for his outstanding performance. He has his own office, drives a beautiful car and recently bought a beautiful condominium; both of his kids are attending International schools (Butterfly Stage).

Sam went from being dissatisfied and frustrated to being an incredibly happy person who continues to build towards even greater dreams. His early coaching "baby steps" enabled him to take "giant leaps" forward down the line.

When you perfect the process, you enable the outcome. And that's what successful sales coaching is all about.

Finally, consider your own sales team - and ask yourself these questions:

1. What is greatest challenge in developing your sales team?

2. *What is your engagement process and how effective is it?*

3. *In what stage of the performance journey are your salespeople and in what areas do they require development?*

About Rajiv

As the founder and Chief Engagement Officer of Harvest Global Resources, Rajiv Mathews George enjoys a growing reputation as a top executive performance coach, sales strategist and mentor coach. The Kuala Lumpur, Malaysia-based company's mission is to help their clients achieve more and realize their goals through high-level coaching, expert mentoring and advanced training.

Charismatic and committed, with a passion to help both individual leaders and teams achieve personal, professional and business success, Rajiv show his clients how to amplify their natural strengths while removing the ceiling of limitations. He works as a coach full-time, specializing in sales coaching, leadership coaching and inner game coaching. With over 15 years of global leadership experience in the corporate and business worlds, he combines high-level, real-world understanding with the most innovative and productive coaching models to help clients throughout the South East Asian region find and implement sustainable solutions.

Rajiv earned a Bachelor of Commerce Degree from the University of Kerala, India, and a Bachelor in Business from Wartburg College, Iowa in the United States. He launched his career in San Jose, California, first as a sales intern and then as a sales account manager, and later served as a General Manager for Rubber Development, Inc. an Iowa-based manufacturer specializing in polymer based OEM products, then as Vice President of Daniel International, a Chicago, Illinois-based mergers and acquisitions firm. His expertise grew to include sales leadership, business development and International business.

Rajiv has over 2,500 hours of hands-on experience in executive, group and team coaching for clients from industries including Banking and Financial Services, Telco, FMCG, Hospitality, Government and others. He has been accredited as Professional Certified Coach (PCC) under the International Coach Federation USA (ICF). He is an ICF-ACTP licensed coach facilitator for coaching skills workshops with Corporate Coach Academy. He is a member of the Asia Pacific Association of Coaches as well as the founding member of ICF Malaysia, the leading organization for professional coaches in the area.

Rajiv also works as a mentor coach for certified coaches in leading organizations and private practices throughout the Asian region, and launched the Win Daily Coaching Clinic to help sales teams boost performance.

Rajiv is a co-author for the book, *The Path to Riches in Think and Grow Rich*, which was published by the Napoleon Hill Foundation in 2011, and has been listed in the International Who's Who among Professionals in 1995. He is active in social media and may be reached via LinkedIn, Twitter or on Facebook via his Harvest Sales Coaching Café page.

For more information, contact Rajiv at: rajiv.mathews@harvestglobalresources.com

CHAPTER 40

Life Is Better When You Are Prepared

By Daanish Memon

Mike and John are good friends and both are decent athletes who meet up once every three months to share milestones in their lives and what they have learned since their last meeting.

One October in 1994, Mike came into the Tim Hortons in Etobicoke (Ontario, Canada), excited to announce that he had decided to start a training and fitness service. John was a little late to the meeting. He had just finished his university degree the past April, and had not secured a job as yet. Today John slept in and woke up about a half hour before the scheduled time, sprang out of bed like a jack-in-the-box and rushed to get ready.

Before heading out the door, John read a text on his phone 'Hey, I am here what do you want me to get you? 'Dude, I got up late. Sorry man, be 15min. late.'

Mike sipped through his first bottle of apple juice while waiting a half hour before John showed up. The buddies exchanged pleasantries and immediately started their catchup meeting.

"Dude, man its so hard to find a job, I sent out so many resumes that I probably used 5 trees, I don't know what I am going to do. I slept in watching movies just to help me fall asleep. I am so worried. My parents are telling me to find a job and a career because I will have to support my family and kids, on and on, sorry for complaining dude, what about you Mike?"

"John, I am starting up a personal fitness centre, I am calling it FIT TEST. I want to help people to transform their lives totally, starting with their health. I want to help people understand their body and enhance it so they can live in peak state, you know, at their best."

"Oh really, hmmm…are you sure you can make it happen. That takes a lot of courage man! How are you going to start it up? How did you get the idea, dude? Wow man, that's interesting! Where are you thinking about getting the money?"

John and Mike discussed the new business startup idea for the next couple of hours when Mike excused himself for his next appointment with his mentor Danny.

"Hey John, lets catchup in January, ok? I will let you know how the business comes along. Hope you are able to get a job by then. And if you need any help with the goal setting technique I talked about, I will hook you up."

"All right Mike, yeah thanks, good luck with the business. Business is tough, so just be careful, OK? Later…"

****

When Mike left the October meeting he rushed to meet Danny at the local cafe. "Hey Mike, you are early aren't you? Remember the first time we met about a year ago and you were almost an hour late. You have come a very long way."

Mike laughed out loud and said, "Yeah Danny, it's hard to believe how far I have come and yet I know I have a long way to go. Can I just update you about my friend John, I told you about him."

"Oh yeah, the one who graduated with you 6 months ago and has not found a job that he really enjoys?"

Mike updated Danny on his meeting with John and then they started their monthly mentoring meeting.

"OK Mike, I think you are ready to supercharge your goal setting skills. I am going to give you a recap on what I have taught you so far. Remember success is a process which happens in inches even though we measure it in miles.

Since you joined the Learning Effective Attention Program (LEAP), I have taught you 11 little steps to Purposeful Goal Setting and today I want to recap them before I teach you the big one, the 12th one!"

Danny took out a piece of paper on which were written down the steps that Mike learned so far and had put into practice over the past year.

1. Build your creativity muscle by setting goals and tracking your progress - Recognize that life is a creative process and you have creative powers (intentioning, conditioning and attentioning).

2. Understand what is working against your creativity. Identify the F/O/Ls (fears, obstacles and limitations) and how they impede your creative processes.

3. Understand what is supporting your creativity. Identify the F/O/R/C/Es (Faith, Opportunities, Resources, Compelling Reasons, Expertise) and how they enhance your creative process.

4. Understand your obligations arising out of your spiritual beliefs - who are your constituents and what kind of life experiences do you want to create for them so that they are living in alignment with your spiritual beliefs? What values do you want to live by?

5. Understand that obligations are fulfilled through exercising our creative powers to create experiences for our constituents. What steps do you have to take to create the kinds of experiences you have identified for each of your constituents? What resources do you need? What knowledge do you need? What kind of expertise do you need?

6. Understand the timeline for delivering the experiences for each constituent. Time zone the dates when you want the creation of each of your experiences to be complete and delivered. When do you want the house built, the car bought, etc.?

7. Understand the strategies that will create each of the experiences identified. Each experience that we want to deliver needs different strategies to prepare. The steps we go through to arrange a wedding

are different than the steps to arrange a university degree or the purchase of a car.

8. Understand the timeline for preparing the experiences for each of your constituents. Break your strategies down into steps and identify a rough timezone (month/year) in which you would like to have taken a step by or have a percentage of the strategy completed. Make an intention to take each step that you have identified. Making an intention sends out a powerful signal of desire and attraction to the creator which is reverberated in the universe.

9. Timeblock the paying of effective attention to each of the steps timelined towards the creation of experiences you want to deliver for each of your constituents, including yourself.

10. Add your timeblocking steps to development of your F/O/R/C/Es so that you may overcome your F/O/Ls. Remember that our FORCEs and FOLs have a huge impact on whether or not we will follow through on taking the steps we have already timeblocked.

11. Carry out weekly and monthly planning to keep the steps towards creating the experiences you identified fresh in your mind and to keep the desire, passion and hope for creating those experiences alive. Time block specific time in each day.

"Mike, are you ready? The new lesson I want to share with you this month is this…read no.12."

12. Every day, as much as your mental and physical strength allow, follow through on the steps you have time blocked. It is in the follow-through or execution of our well laid out plans towards creating the kind of life that we want to see for ourselves and our constituents, that we will see our intended experiences become a reality. For those items on your schedule that you did not get to in any one day, re-schedule or time zone them to ensure that they are not forgotten, and that they are attended to effectively. Expect that initially you will be behind in paying attention to your life creation steps. And as time proceeds, you will get more and more effective. The more you condition yourself to pay effective attention, the stronger your muscle will become. Enjoy the process of creating the life experiences you want for your constituents!

"Danny, wow, you know what I like about that last step. It helps me understand the obstacles I might encounter along the way. And it also helps me understand what to expect in terms of challenges, and that by being persistent I will eventually get there. When trying something new, it's so easy to get overwhelmed. The steps you taught me made it easy for me to craft the kind of life I want for myself and my constituents. As I have completed the 12 steps of the LEAP program, what is next for me?"

"Mike, thanks for your compliments. You have done so well and I will always be here to support you through the last of the 12 steps and to refine each one of them. The next program we have is called Live-Effective-Attention-Refined-Nurtured or LEARN for short. The purpose of the next program is to enhance your own skills at living attentively, nurturing it in yourself and in your friends. It will involve digging deeper for your FOLs and removing your blocks by conditioning your FORCEs. Now that you have taken a huge leap forward, I want to help you learn how to keep the momentum. And the best part of the LEARN program is that I will help you coach any one person of your choice to go through the LEAP program I have taken you through."

Danny and Mike exchanged warm hugs as Mike left the meeting a bit overwhelmed and a bit tingled. Mike knew who he wanted to coach and bring into the LEAP program. He couldn't help but think of what he would say to John when he met him next time.

****

After the October meeting with Mike, John spent the next three (3) months doing everything he could think of to get and keep odd jobs to pay the bills. He tried working at a gas station, at a supermarket and a carwash to name a few places. All of those jobs made him some money, but none of them made him very happy at all. It was about 3 weeks away from their next quarterly meeting and John started feeling a downward emotional spiral – resulting in him quitting his jobs and spending time at his local coffee shop to find himself. His friends would always find him drinking coffee and John was struggling to find himself.

***

It was late January and the day had arrived for John and Mike to meet together. Mike walked into the meeting beaming, wondering how he would explain to John that he will take him through the LEAP program with Danny. John entered the coffee shop where they usually meet and looked a little mellow. Mike on the other hand had started the LEARN program with Danny a month earlier and was more pumped up than at their last meeting in October.

"Hey John, how is it going? I have so much to tell you!" Mike started the conversation as usual.

"A-a-a-m-m…nothing much, how is your business idea going?" John asked looking a bit sad.

"Oh, the business idea is going great. I am about 20 percent through my business plan; I will show you what I have done. Listen, remember that mentor I spoke to you about who helped me figure out what I want to do with my life? I told you about Danny and his program called LEAP? "

"Yeah, how is that going? Does it really work?"

"Well, Yeah, it worked for me, and I actually graduated to his second program and guess what?"

"What?" Asked John.

"Well part of graduating to the next level, I get to help one person by becoming their mentor and taking them through the same program I went through. And I was thinking that maybe you would be the person I can mentor and teach this program to, seeing as we are such close friends and all. What do you think?"

About Daanish

Daanish Memon is affectionately known as Dan the Land Man. He is an expert in helping people understand how their land is from a development perspective.

He is regularly sought after by land developers who are considering whether they should invest in properties and those who want to get their developments approved.

Although Daanish specialized in land development, his passion lies in people development. Daanish has conducted numerous practical skills training workshops in the fields of construction engineering, teaching youth and personal development.

Daanish is known to ask, "What will it take for this land (or person) to be successfully developed?"

He founded Terra Firma Plus Inc., a company that helps its constituents to understand their land and the development process, so they are able to complete their projects more effectively and economically. Terra Firma engages in the investigation of property owned by development prospects to help them and their designers, financiers and partners understand their land and what procedures and cost consequences are required to successfully develop it.

To learn more about Daanish and Terra Firma Plus Inc., and to receive a special report entitled: *Dig Deep – How to help prospective buyers understand your land and make land deals more attractive for development,* send an email to: info@terrafirmaeng.ca

CHAPTER 41

Go F.A.R.
—Three Principles For Running Your Business And Your Life

By Kiersten Gelfand

Think of the last time you had something to do that had the following characteristics: the project would take a month or two to complete; it was something you were dreading; no one was going to hold you accountable if the project was done or not; there was no prize, victory, or forward motion if you completed the project.

I bet if you had a project that was defined by these characteristics, there is no way you would complete the project. Or, perhaps, if you indeed bit the bullet and got it done, you wouldn't feel that rush of the "win" at the end—because no one noticed nor did it produce progress in your work or life.

There is no reason to go through life feeling defeated as you would if your life was one pointless project after another. Instead we are going to learn three (3) principles—the **FAR** principles—to build your day, life, and business so you can ensure the "win" every time!

Before I define the FAR principles, it is important that you recognize that there will be circumstances that will come up outside your control that you will need to deal with and adjust to, but the "win" is still within your reach if you adhere to these principles. Also, I would love a commitment from you, that you will not just read this, but will take the steps to apply the FAR principles. One effective way of applying and getting on track is using the monthly and daily Go FAR Fast forms for 21 consecutive days. It is one thing to know all the best practices and habits of those who have achieved what we would like to achieve. But unless we have the discipline to apply these principles day in and day out, I guarantee you will lose steam and not get the "win" you want!

Drumroll please....

(A) — The first principle with which to run your business and life by to win big and keep winning is: Fun. Life is too short not to have fun. Stay with me type A's and focused achievers that are ready to skip this section. You need to build fun into your business, with your clients and staff, and into your life pursuits in order to have a happier and healthier business and lifestyle.

Building fun into your business means using attractive marketing (real, not a smoke-screen) and making sure your product or service is an experience that customers WANT. Adjust your business practices by brainstorming a few ways you can amp up the fun-factor and leave your customers with a great "feeling" so they will remember the great experience they had with YOU and your business.

It is essential that this sense of fun extends as well to your staff. You cannot WIN without a great team around you. Thank them, liven up their work environment, make them realize they are a part of something bigger than just themselves, and celebrate successes as a team. As with customers, smile often, increase your positive energy and gratitude, and emphasize a sense of community.

Are YOU having fun? It is imperative that you apply this principle in your business and your life! I used to wear the "work hard and play hard" on my sleeve like a badge of honor. I felt that in order to earn the rite to play hard I had to either work ridiculous hours, or not have all that much fun in the long run. Don't spend another day living to work. Take an inventory. Look at the monthly Go FAR Fast form to discover your talents, what gives you energy in your work and personal life, and, in general, what makes you happy. Spend MORE time doing these things and this will in turn produce a better work environment, leave you doing the things you are best at (which will increase your revenue), and you will enjoy your work, clients, and staff exponentially more! Make sure you have "carrots," that is, rewards, for yourself, your staff, your family, and your clients. Give them something they can look forward to, some FUN they can have in their reward, to keep you and them motivated to push through towards the winning outcome.

(B) — The second principle to run your business and life by is Accountability. This is huge! It is important to use several levels of accountability to help you go from mediocre to winning big. When you are going to school or working for a boss there is much built in accountability to accomplish their set objectives. However, if you want to take the reins and win your life and your profession by your objectives, you have to make sure you have an accountability system built around your goals for all areas of your life that are important to you.

I want to encourage you to use as many levels of accountability as possible in all the areas of your life – your business, your clients, your staff and you. If one fails you, you can count on another level to catch the slack.

i. The first level of accountability is you. Do this by making deadlines, putting goals in writing, filling out your monthly and daily Go FAR Fast form, and belief in yourself (do not let your mind be what's holding you back).

ii. The second level of accountability is your team, your family, and your biggest supporters. Include them but identify: what's in it for them? How can they share in your victory? Verbalize your goals, objectives, and projects to them, and include them in the decision of a reward attached to a particular goal/win.

iii. The final level is social support. Remember there will be naysayers and saboteurs as well as supporters in this group. But knowing that all these people know your goals will give you the social pressure to achieve what you set out to do. Whenever possible, have all three levels of accountability in place for all important goals and life pursuits.

Apply accountability to your business as a whole by having a written business plan, mission, annual and quarterly goals that are specific. Share the appropriate ones, if possible, to all three levels of accountability. Accountability in your business can be strengthened with, to name a few, a mastermind group, professional organization(s), mentors, or a professional accountability buddy. Having some "greater purpose" (e.g., a charity, local sports team) to which your business contributes adds an additional level of accountability.

Build accountability with your staff by including them in the process of attaining goals that are relevant to them. Distribute "carrots" (i.e., bonuses and recognition) and hold celebrations when you achieve specific goals and projects. Lead by example and reinforce whenever you "catch" your staff doing something correct in order to shape your entire team's behavior.

Hold your clients accountable. Do this in marketing by calls-to-action, and have systems in place to check and reward them for completing the action you have assigned. Let your clients hold you accountable too by including them in certain activities, such as voting, piloting, or feedback on a new product or program. Sharing "the scoop" with loyal customers will make them better customers, keep you accountable for launching new products and programs, and it will improve word of mouth marketing because the clients feel invested in the outcome.

Accountability in your life as a whole is especially challenging. It is harder to measure categories such as relationships, environment, spirituality, and so on. However, it is important for you to identify all the areas of your life that are important to you. Make sure you have them listed and apply the levels of accountability, especially the first two levels.

*(C) — The final principle of the **FAR** plan is Results.* In order to win big and keep winning you need to be results-oriented. Learn what the steps are to get the results you want. You need to define, in writing, your outcomes (the results you want). Are you achieving the results you seek in your business, with your clients and staff, and in your life? Remember that the results you desire, in all areas of your life, need to be defined regularly (I suggest you do this monthly with the Go FAR Fast monthly form). You need to assess and continually repeat the process. Realize that your priorities may change or your focus can shift. But you

can still achieve the goals that will allow the wins you want in your life.

In your business, write your goals out annually. Then break these goals down further with quarterly and monthly goals. Once you have developed your measurable goals, go out and educate yourself on the best way to get the outcome you want and commit to a program with a proven track record. For example in my fitness program business, Fitness Inspired, people sign on and commit to a program with the track record for the results they want—including: weight-loss, lose inches, lose body fat, get stronger, and improve health indicators. To "win" your business and life in general on your terms and desired outcomes, you need to apply these principles in a results-focused program. In the FAR 21 day challenge, you will break down each goal into projects. Work on these daily to WIN every day. If, when you are re-assessing, and you still are working hard towards a particular goal and not moving towards the outcome for that particular goal, you might have to do more research. Try some different paths to the outcome which could change your projects the next month. Don't give up on a project without trying it in your win-your-day list for a full 21 days.

The results of your product or service are what keep you winning in the long run. They build sustainability and sell themselves through testimonials. Are your clients getting the results they want? Listen to your customers and decide if you can give them the result they want in the way they want it. You may have to educate and market to them in ways that teach/tells them the result they should want with your product or program. Get them to own it. They will give you the credit you deserve. You have to celebrate and allow them to experience the fun of the "win." You will have returning, loyal customers.

In my own business, I find I can apply all three principles simultaneously through the Fitness Inspired results parties. At the conclusion of each Fitness Inspired program, a party is held for the clients (F). It is also here that the clients discover to what degree they have succeeded. The fact that they know this will happen in advance provides a measure of accountability (A). Finally, the clients see the results (R) of their participation—something which also serves as accountability for the staff. The parties provide a strong sense of camaraderie among clients and instructors, everyone looks forward to them, and, in the end, serve to strengthen the bottom line. Here it is in one exciting and fun evening:

Fun, Accountability, & Results!™ for everyone involved.

I love the energy and celebration of the win, which all the participants experience when the Fun, Accountability, & Results!™ all come together as they **go FAR** in their Fitness Inspired goals!

In all areas of your life, make sure you stop frequently and see if you are living the life that you desire. As you are achieving and going FAR fast, make sure you are running down the right path. That is why if you list out every area of your life that is important to you, and make measurable commitments to grow and get better in those areas, you will be successful. I know you will be happy that you took the time to assess each month to go FAR in the right direction, surrounded by a great team of people to share in the excitement and reward of discovering and living the secret to winning big!

I cannot wait to hear your success using the three principles of Fun, Accountability, & Results!™ to run your business and life to win big. I am confident in you that you can stay motivated and inspired by a daily and monthly commitment to application and action of what you learned. Strive to think and win big daily! Remember, you can and will **go FAR**.

About Kiersten

Kiersten is the founder and CEO of Fitness Inspired (FI). She holds a Bachelor's Degree in Psychology and a Master's Degree in Exercise Science. She is nationally certified with the American Council of Exercise (ACE), Aerobics and Fitness Association of American (AFAA), Turbo Kick®, and Schwinn Cycling. Additionally, she is a fitness coach for BeachBody® and enjoys helping other fitness entrepreneurs. Her business is physically located in Mt. Pleasant, MI, with another location to be soon open in State College, PA. In addition to her studio programs, Kiersten teachers a number of on-line classes and has developed numerous FI videos. She is a member of IDEA Health and Fitness Association and was a member of Rotary International in Mt. Pleasant, MI.

A few words from Kiersten:

"I am a passionate, adventure-seeking, fitness entrepreneur. I love helping people succeed by living inspired and more specifically Fitness Inspired. I know and have seen the positive impact that can be had when your body gets stronger and fit, and you develop the mental toughness to adhere to a Fitness Inspired program. I believe and have seen how living fitness inspired improves all areas of your life. One of my greatest joys is to connect and coach people towards a happier and healthier business and life.

I have built every single program for Fitness Inspired around these 3 words: Fun, Accountability, & Results!™. I have helped people lose thousands of pounds, drop multiple clothing sizes, and get stronger by feeling the positive improvement in their lives from the inside out. I am fired up to help YOU apply these three principles to your professional and personal life with this plan that works! If you are committed to winning, whether it is in a sports competition, in the business world, and/or your general health and fitness, it is imperative that you structure your life and days with a results-focused plan; a result's focused plan that can be adhered to.

Winning doesn't happen by accident and it doesn't happen without daily preparation. If you are reading this book, I know you have the passion and desire to win. I am excited for us to conquer our goals and the games we set out to win together!

Please connect with me, share your goals and successes, and if you are up for it, step up to the FAR 21 Day Challenge. Win in your business and life with a 21 day challenge tailored to the application of what you learned here."

Fitness Inspired ~ Fitness Business Coach ~ Live Inspired Training

For more information, visit:

www.FIKiersten.com

www.LiveFitnessInspired.com

Social Media:

www.Facebook.com/LiveFitnessInspired

www.youtube.com/FIKiersten

www.twitter.com/FIKiersten

www.pinterest.com/FIKiersten

CHAPTER 42

Secrets And Tools Of The Millionaire Mind

By Lisa Christiansen

In life you will find two things... a way and an excuse. For what you want enough you will find a way, for what you don't you will find an excuse...Rewards await those who choose wisely, it is when you continue to fight when you know all hope is lost that miracles happen...

Mastery in one's career and self-growth simply requires that we consistently and constantly produce results beyond the ordinary into the extraordinary by producing outstanding results. Mastery is attained by consistently stepping outside of our comfort zone, going beyond our limits with the knowledge that the only limits there are in life are the ones we set for ourselves. Open your eyes, listen to hear, feel your achievement and breakthrough your limits to the success you deserve.

For most people, this starts with technical excellence in a chosen field and a commitment to that excellence. This needs to begin with a clear vision and the decision to do what it takes making success your only option. If you are willing to commit yourself to excellence, to surround yourself with things that represent excellence, your life will change because you are your five closest friends. (When we speak of miracles, we speak of events or experiences that go beyond the ordinary into the extraordinary.)

It's remarkable how much mediocrity we live with, surrounding ourselves with daily reminders that the average is the acceptable, we

375

must decide this behavior of mediocrity is UNACCEPTABLE. More often than not you will find the common belief is limited thinking with a mindset of 'go to school to get a good job to retire comfortable and then you die.' I urge you to look inside yourself and identify the things that are keeping you powerless to go beyond any "limit" that you have arbitrarily set for yourself.

Take a moment to assess all of these things around you that promote your being "average," now take action to remove these things from your life even if this means making new friends, because often your friends will bring guilt to your dreams by saying, "Oh, you think you are better than me?" or "What makes you think you can do that?" These are dream thieves and you need dream achievers in your circle of friends. With that being said, you must reach up to those that frighten you and cultivate friendships which you once thought were impossible. You will be surprised how many will be excited to mentor you.

To begin mastery is to remove everything in your environment that represents mediocrity, removing those things that are limiting. Again, one way is to surround yourself with friends who ask more of themselves than anyone else ever would, because these are the ones who step up to defy the odds, to set new standards and to be the change they want to see in this world by being the example. It is this recipe for success that you must emulate to achieve your success, because if you find someone who is successfully doing what you are passionate about, you simply have to follow his or her formula to achieve the same result.

Another step on the path to mastery is the removal of resentment toward masters—whether on your level, below or above your level. This action is very important because these are your potential mentors. We are always learning from each other so respect is critical; if you don't respect the person please respect their gifts to contribute to others even if you don't agree. Develop humility so that while in the presence of masters you are emotionally available with an open heart and an open mind to grow from the experience. Do not compare yourself to others and do not resent people who have mastery, remain open, respectful and receptive; allow the experience to enrich you like the planting of a seed within you that, with nourishment, will grow into your own individual unique mastery.

We are all created equal; mastery is learned through education, life experiences and the examples lay before us. A true master will embrace their flaws and weaknesses as a tool to relate to others with a genuine appreciation of their circumstances. A master recognizes this fault as a foundation for building the extraordinary instead of using it as an excuse for inactivity; use this as a vehicle for growing, which is essential in the process of attaining mastery. You must be able to learn, grow and accept criticism without condemning yourself to accept results and improve upon them. Growth is essential to power and mastery because if you are not growing you are dying.

One of the most important things you can do is to reprogram your success blueprint. What are the strategies that will do so?

ELEVEN STRATEGIES TO REPROGRAM YOUR BLUEPRINT

Success Blueprint #1

Confidence, Self-esteem and Self-image
 The key to confidence is acquiescing a heightened level of positive self-esteem by believing that you are intelligent enough, good enough, and deserving to succeed your desired results.

Ask yourself "who do I need to become to achieve the life I am committed to living?"

When you mirror the self-image of a person who easily does what you desire to do, this action will almost guarantee that you will achieve your outcome.

Success Blueprint #2

Driven By Your Purpose – Your Why
It is not enough to be motivated to reach your outcome; you must be driven by your why. Your 'shoulds' become 'musts.' You must decide to live on purpose and show up for your dreams with a compelling reason. It is impossible to be this driven unless you are being pushed by something more than just surviving. You must have a passion so intense that it consumes you from the core of who you are. You must be motivated from within and maintain momentum through ups and downs. It's critical to constantly focus on your purpose, why you want the outcome must be the fundamental focus with every decision. A weak purpose means failure 99.999% of the time.

Success Blueprint #3

What You Focus On Is What You Get
Your brain does not know the difference between fact and fiction, and equally, your brain will not make you a liar. Visualize your outcome in the present with clarity because Clarity is power. When you visualize what you want with intense emotion, your psychology will control your physiology and in turn control your environment.

Just as a dream can seem so real, you have the ability to bring it to fruition by visualizing your desire with belief. When you live your dream in the present in your subconscious, your mind will continually move you in the direction to make it happen. Everything that was ever accomplished by anyone was first seen in the mind's eye. It is no different for you because you have the ability to live life on your terms. When you see it as real, accomplished, as done, as a storming success in your mind, … then you will bring it to fruition.

Success Blueprint #4

Tenacity
The will to succeed can overcome every limitation no matter what your challenge is. The only limitations are the ones we set for ourselves. Get out of your own way.

Success Blueprint #5

Decide
Once you make a decision you will succeed because to decide is to cut off, to sever, bringing success is the only option.

"Yes, I Can," will become your new mantra.

And as your self-confidence grows, your stress levels will plummet and your willingness to take action will soar.

Success Blueprint #6

Follow Up With A Plan
You must know that exactly what you need to do to reach an outcome or make a change in yourself is vital. Inconsistent actions lead to failure. It is essential to follow through on whatever actions are required of you each and every day. Review your why every day in every decision

and ask yourself, "Is what I am about to do getting me closer to my outcome?" Before you reach your outcomes, have new ones in place to continue the momentum of your growth.

Keep a vision board or journal and cross off each accomplishment as you move forward in your victories. Your thoughts are what create your life. If you simply do what is required of you each day, you'll get to your desired outcome. Just like the other people who always get what they want in life.

Success Blueprint #7

Enjoy The Journey
Anything worth having is a challenge, if it were easy everyone would do it, you are extraordinary because you are willing to set new standards and defy the odds. Is the activity of accomplishing a challenging outcome always fun? No. If it were fun, everyone would be taking action? Wouldn't you look forward to the next challenge? Wouldn't you experience your mistakes, setbacks, delays, and criticism differently than you do now? Yes, you would.

Instill in your mind an alert awareness of the fun and satisfaction you can have all along the path toward reaching your desired outcome. For example, in areas where you don't now enjoy the tasks, like exercising, with the statements steering your consciousness toward a love for all things physical, you'll easily see the activities as enjoyable, or at least gain a greater appreciation for the tasks just like the millions who see it that way already.

Discover new ways to make it more pleasant. You'll look at the situation in whatever way you need to see it – so that you feel good instead of depressed over your fate of having to do this set of tasks or activities related to your outcome. Your stress levels will go down considerably, and you should be able to reach your outcome easier than you could ever have imagined just a short time ago.

Success Blueprint #8

Be Teachable And Trainable
Duplication is the key. The most important outcomes in our lives often don't fall within our natural abilities and current level of knowledge. We usually need to do some research, explore options and learn new

ideas, techniques, facts, skills, or principles. The problem is that most people don't want to be bothered to learn anything new. It's viewed as too much work, as boring or unpleasant, or cuts into relaxation and recreation time.

You need to be ready and willing to learn what you must to reach your outcome and love doing it.

Success Blueprint #9

See Things Better Than They Are
Whatever your outcome is, the truest test of how you are progressing toward it lies not in how you function when you are moving along smoothly, but in how you act and react when problems are presented to you. Bad decisions, mistakes and setbacks are simply part of the process to get where you want to go, and absolutely no reason to quit, to get upset, or even slow your progress.

So whether you're trying to gain a habit, lose a habit, reach success in business or relationships, or overcome depression or anxiety, flood your mind with self-instructions telling yourself that you are optimistic and level-headed through your setbacks and moments of challenge. With conditioning, your desire and determination will grow and stay high even after bigger, more serious setbacks. You'll become one of those people that always knows or figures out what to do and makes sure it gets done without delay.

Success Blueprint #10

Appreciation
One of the biggest frustrations most people experience is to experience success in reaching a big outcome or status level only to see it all go away. To watch yourself stop doing what you did to reach your success in the first place. The strong tendency is to forget what it took to succeed. This is why people who have been good at something for years can make mistakes and correct them fairly rapidly. People who are just gaining a skill, attitude, or habit can very easily mess up once and quit, or they can fall back into old routines without even knowing it.

When changes are desired, conditioning is critical. One of the things you MUST do to make your changes stick is to pay attention and appreciate what it took to get there, to enjoy the end result, to enjoy the rewards, to acknowledge your success and efforts so that when temptations arise you can understand how you came to succeed. This way, you'll keep your new ways and continue to succeed when 19 out of 20 are failing, predictably going back to old ways of thinking and acting within days, weeks, or months.

Success Blueprint #11

Gratitude

Most people who reach some long-term outcome or who quit some bad habit self-sabotage after they worked hard to reach their outcome. They don't see in their own mind that they have accomplished anything. When you accomplish anything, whether it is large or small, give yourself a boost by rewarding yourself for it. Accept other's praise for what you have accomplished. It's time to give yourself and accept from others the credit you deserve.

EIGHT SECRETS TO WEALTH CREATION

Rewards await those who choose wisely...Procrastination is the abortion of success!!! Choose and be happy...

Do you want to live in wealth? These are the eight secrets that all masters of wealth have in common. Do you have what it takes?

Wealth Creation Secret No. 1

I know one thing for sure and two things for certain...To create exponential wealth today, you must own your own business and here are the two reasons why.

Your belief may be that the corporate executive with the $100,000 a year job has a net worth more than the small shop owner, but the truth of the matter is that the executive will be challenged to double his/her income and with the expenses of having a family, this will limit the amount of savings not to mention that the taxes will eat up most of any profits that are left.

What I have found through my own personal experience is that the smallest home business owner has unlimited opportunities to expand his/her business and income, as well as how many employees. In most cases, the owner is even able to write their own paychecks, and has the control to increase sales whenever they choose. Did I mention they also have time freedom?

Wealth Creation Secret No. 2
Remember the three levels of mastery

1. *Cognitive Mastery:* understand what you have learned.

2. *Emotional Mastery:* Link what you learn to emotions

3. *Physical Mastery:* you have done enough repetition to make it natural, now anchor these together! You must be passionate enough to have a working knowledge of your chosen business when you start, and continue to take steps to be a professional student expanding your knowledge as you master your skills. (It is better to live by example than to lead by ignorance).

What I have learned through my personal and professional life experiences is that if you don't know what you're doing, your mistakes will be many as well as costly, and more often than not, they will be unnecessary. You will not be able to keep up with the ever-growing technologies in any field. Start smart and stay that way. Information linked to emotion is retained.

Wealth Creation Secret No. 3
Saving money in your personal life and in your business venture is equally important.

Always remember it is not how much you make when you are right. It is how much you save when you are wrong. Self-discipline is the key to saving money. You must develop the will power to deny yourself instant gratification or the temptation of the "get-rich-quick" thinking. Resources will be needed for growth and should be guarded carefully.

Mitigate your risks and always protect yourself.

Wealth Creation Secret No. 4
You must take risks with borrowed money, your own money or both. Your number one resource is your resourcefulness.

Taking risks is essential to the growth of your business. Some of the richest women and men have staked their entire life savings and lost, several times over, before the risk-taking paid off. When you back risks with good judgment, experience, commitment, and the right support, you have a formula for wealth creation. Now the most important step is to follow through and follow up…Did I mention follow up?

Search out for advice on risk-taking from the wealthy who still take calculated risks with successful returns, not from your friends who risk nothing more than a few bucks on a lottery ticket; and remember, you are your top five friends, so think about that and seek wisely.

Wealth Creation Secret No. 5
Do you know the difference between a piece of coal and a diamond? YES, the answer is pressure! Right now you are a diamond in the rough; you just need a little more pressure…It is important to not only learn to live with tension, you must passionately seek it out.

Learn to thrive on stress! Begin getting physically fit, have a psychological overhaul and ingrain new anchors. What will it take for you to handle it? Start now! Once you make the decision to thrive on stress, you will enjoy it; you will begin seeking it out willingly and enthusiastically, and wonder how you ever lived any other way.

Women and men of wealth look at making money as a game much like a child playing monopoly—which they love to play passionately.

Think about this…your biggest problem isn't that you don't know what you don't know, it's that you don't know what you do know.

Keep things in perspective and you will be in control of your stress level, once you learn to master your emotions, you will be in control of your life. What will it feel like to live life on your terms?

Perception is everything, we give things meaning. You decide what things mean. Information linked to emotion is retained.

Wealth Creation Secret No. 6
Create wealth as a positive side effect of your business success. If money is your only outcome in business, you will more than likely fail. The money is the bonus of the game. If you win, the money will be there.

Remember if you lose, and you will every now and then, keep in mind if you play long and hard enough, it must be fun or it isn't worth it.

Success is living life in fulfillment and money can't buy that! I know lots of people that have millions of dollars and are very empty. I know plenty of people that live from paycheck to pawnshop and are the happiest people I know.

Money doesn't define success, if you focus on your passion and love what you do, that is where you will find fulfillment.

Wealth Creation Secret No. 7
You Must Have Patience.

The greatest business asset you can have is patience, although sometimes *(I have challenges with this one, I'm still learning patience)*…You must wait for the right time to make your move, if you are in the right place at the wrong time you will have pain. You must learn to adapt to your environment and act accordingly.

Learn to trust yourself, do what you do best and let your business grow naturally. Pay attention and recognize opportunity.

Don't procrastinate when opportunity knocks answer the door.

Wealth Creation Secret No. 8
You must Challenge yourself, one way is to diversify your time and assets.

When you accomplish your outcome, you will find the need to be challenged once again. One way to fulfill this need is to seek out other ventures to grow and contribute.

I like the three-bucket game:

My first bucket I have a SNF (sleep-at-night factor) or some people might call it a security bucket. This bucket has 40% of my investment money in it in the form of CD's, Money Market, etc.

My second bucket is my growth bucket. This bucket has 60% of my investment money in it in the form of real estate, buy-and-hold, etc. this is my momentum or high return, which is a little more of a risk.

My third bucket is my dream bucket or my play money. How this works is that every time the other buckets show a profit, I take 10% of the profits and give it to tithes, another 10% goes into the dream bucket,

30% goes into the growth bucket and 50% goes into the SNF bucket. If I want something I must wait until my dream bucket has enough for me to buy it with.

Now to diversify my time, I love to ride my bicycle in events all over the world. So that takes care of that need, and I am living my dream with this formula. Now you have the formula, what is your dream?

I'M NOT TELLING YOU IT'S GOING TO BE EASY, I AM TELLING YOU IT IS GOING TO BE WORTH IT! NEVER LET YOUR DREAMS BE GREATER THAN YOUR MEMORIES!

First we make our choices then our choices make us...

What decision will you make today to create the tomorrow you are committed to?

This has been and still is the single most important action I take everyday. I have found that success is achieved more efficiently when this action is taken seriously. This may also be the most impactful action you can take immediately to start living your dream today.

Before you choose to make any decision ask yourself these 10 questions:

1. What am I doing today to get what I want?
2. Will this behavior improve my situation and move me towards what I want?… or am I settling?
3. How would the person I want to be do the thing I am about to do?
4. Who do I have to become to attract the success I want?
5. Am I willing to accept the consequences of not changing?
6. Who is in control?
7. Am I practicing to improve or doing just enough to get by?
8. What don't I SEE?
9. If my Board of Directors could see my level of effort, focus and intensity, would I get a raise or get fired?
10. Am I willing to do whatever it takes?

Never leave the site of a goal without taking at least one action toward achieving your outcome...

About Lisa

Creator of extraordinary lives, Lisa Christiansen has served as an advisor to leaders around the world for the last two decades. A recognized authority on the psychology of leadership, organizational turnaround and peak performance, Lisa has consulted Olympic athletes, world-renowned musicians, Fortune 500 CEOs, psychologists, and world-class entertainers such as superstar Patrick Dempsey.

Lisa's strategies for achieving lasting results and fulfillment are regarded as the platinum standard in the coaching industry. Lisa captured the attention of heads of state and the United States Army.

Christiansen has impacted the lives of millions of people from 30 countries. She has been honored by: **Cambridge Who's Who** as one of the "Top Business Intellectuals in the World."

Lisa has helped millions of people create extraordinary lives globally. Her expertise and guidance has enriched the lives of icons such as pop superstar Kelly Clarkson, Olympian Dara Torres, and the members of the rock band *Journey*.

CHAPTER 43

Brand Big, Win Big

By Gus Kaloti

BIG IDEAS

The idea for Inovia Health came to me like most great ideas: unexpectedly. I was busy at the time. I owned and managed fifteen successful dental practices, developed and administered an industry-changing dental discount program, and created a nonprofit group called the Elite Academy to inspire entrepreneurism in children. I had a growing family, business success, and didn't need to start another venture. I didn't *need* to, but wanted to—the idea literally called to me. I deliberated, imagined the idea in action, and envisioned the business it *could* be. Rather, *would* be: rule one is to start from a position of confidence. Seasoned by the many lessons I'd learned in my career, I was determined to make Inovia a model for startup success.

While there's no *secret* to big success, no specific formula to make a business grow and flourish, there are specific strategies for taking those critical first steps. Researching, defining the objectives, putting together a great team, visualizing success and starting with the goal in our sights. Inovia plunged ahead and I shared my vision with the team. The next move was crucial, even more pressing than the mountain of work inherent in product development and an operational launch. For a startup, taking the time and energy to do this critical step right is the difference between creating a business and creating an entity that can long endure. What is the key step? Branding.

Branding your startup effectively is imperative. Startups are exhilarating. The possibilities seem endless and the power of setting a direction is heady. But the margin for error for startups is thin—success or failure a hair's width apart. As Inovia formed, I directed my team to create more than a business, but a brand. Bigger spoils go to the victor that dreams bigger. Inovia as a brand refuses to follow, we aim to lead. We plan to redefine success in our industry. Inovia will dominate the niche market we target, with a name whose sum lives up to its parts: innovation, vision, and action. That's the goal. How to get it done?

BIG EXAMPLES

Learn from the best. Name a brand you admire, and find out their approach. A very familiar and successful brand is Starbucks. There's a good chance that you or someone on your staff swung by to start their morning, they've become so synonymous with coffee in our culture. That's no accident. Howard Schultz, CEO of Starbucks, fronts a force that since going public in 1992 has grown exponentially to 17,000 worldwide stores and revenue of $11.7B. Howard Schultz's mission was to make Starbucks the most recognizable brand in the world, a big goal. They are succeeding, serving approximately 8 million cups of coffee a day, even as competitors as formidable as McDonald's attack. Starbucks still manages to grow, and their big results stem from the power of branding. So, how'd they do it?

Shultz didn't brand Starbucks alone. Stanley Hainsworth is the man behind Starbucks the brand as we know it. In Debbie Millman's book, *BRAND THINKING*, she interviewed Hainsworth about his portfolio. Hainsworth's work with Nike is legendary as well, one of the best at what he does. While branding is complex, the key steps as prescribed by Hainsworth that I've outlined can be implemented by smart startups on a shoestring. Hainsworth compares a common trait of his two high-profile brands: vision. As a company, Nike had it. Starbucks had it. That's the starting point.

Next? Create an emotional connection. "No one is going to pick up your product...if they don't want to buy into the experience." says Hainsworth. Starbucks CEO Shultz concurred, and says in his book *POUR YOUR HEART INTO IT:* "The success of Starbucks demonstrates the fact we have built an emotional connection with our customers."

Being able to leverage that connection is a key takeaway. Schultz continues: "Starbucks represents something beyond a cup of coffee." For its millions of customers, it does.

How to get to that meaning? Hainsworth spells that out, too. He says "the best brands are those that create something for consumers that they don't even know they need yet." Starbucks clearly did that. Prior to its rise, most Americans might have a cup of coffee at home in the morning, but it was unfathomable that grabbing a premium priced coffee drink could become part of your morning routine. It has. How to similarly motivate that?

Says Hainsworth, it comes down to an idea of the "end state." Even more than the product's details, express the results of using said product. Great brands offer great products, and equally create experiences of the brand—both elements are important. But, to paraphrase Hainsworth, … experience first, …product second. Why? As Hainsworth says, "No one is going to pick up your product and try it if they don't want to buy into the experience." Starbucks is more than coffee, it is community, culture and experience surrounding the product.

To communicate that experience, brands must tell stories unique to them. It could be the brand's reason for existence, or the founder's story, but must be clearly plotted, and everything the brand does becomes a part of the story. "Everything that you do, everything you release, everything that you say—everything is the cumulative expression of the brand." say Hainsworth.

Starbucks lives the brand. Their attention to detail is emphatic. They ensure that every store you walk into demonstrates the brand's quality and consistency. When branding Starbucks, Hainsworth identified some of key filters as criteria: artistic, sophisticated, and enduring. These are characteristics the brand embodies and imparts. The mythos of Starbucks is one consumers not only recognize, but actually want to be a part of. Starbucks mastered communicating to customers with their in-store atmosphere, all of it evoking a feel-good response. Starbucks is successful because they tell their story and personify traits that customers themselves strive for within. "We have no patent on anything we do and anything we do can be copied by anyone else. But you can't copy the heart and the soul and the conscience of the company."

The heart of Starbucks is that their heart, soul, and conscience are all a part of that story and they embody it inside out, they tell it, and they make their customers want to be part of it. That's the secret.

THE BIG LIST

So what are the key takeaways from Hainsworth, Shultz, and Starbucks? Here are your action steps:

1. Identify: What's the vision?
What is your vision for your company? Starbucks wanted to be the world's largest coffee seller and they achieved it. Maybe your goal is to be the most successful cosmetic dentist in a given market, or to take a chain of car washes nationwide. Start by plotting where you want to go and working hard to get there.

2. Reach: What's the connection?
For Starbucks, the connection is more than the coffee. Starbucks is about a sense of community. What they do in-store and out, tells that to the customer. Inwardly, the stores function as office space, meeting space, or as respite from a hectic life; whatever the customer needs. The space is alive, housing the community. The idea of community is reinforced outwardly by the stores "giving back" and partnering with charities, then deftly publicizing these acts in-store. Starbucks might be branded a luxury, but to its customers it is an *altruistic* luxury. Customers reward themselves with a product they enjoy and also feel as though they're helping others. That's a powerful connection, deep in consumer psychology. It's effective.

3. Necessity: What's the need you fill?
It's about filling a need that consumers didn't even know they had. Nike convinced a nation they needed high performance shoes (and we do - back it up with product and fact). Starbucks proved we need high-octane caffeine and an indulgence that's within reach. Fill a like need for your customers.

4. Outcome: What's the "end-state?"
The end state is how a customer *feels* when using the product. Nike commercials feature powerful athletes that illustrate resonant health. In those shoes, customers imagine feeling powerful, healthy, and accomplished. How you want your customers to feel? The above-

mentioned dentist should brand by considering how a cosmetic dentistry patient wants to feel. These are consumers hungry to make a change and concerned with appearance. Show them how they'll feel *after* they've invested in themselves: changed for the better and beautiful. In branding, work with that end state, in this case life-changing and beautiful.

5. Communication: What's the story that informs the customers?

Says Hainsworth, "... products were all created to fill a niche. Why? That's where you'll find your story." What's the need you are filling? Say your startup is the car wash example, and you're targeting thrifty but image-driven customers. The story you tell is one of upward mobility. Take care of the car you have today (with us) and you're on your way to the Benz. Give the consumer something that they are working towards. The story you tell makes the customer excited to buy into your product or service.

6. Planning: Market research or gut?

Starbucks CEO Howard Schultz joked that if he'd gone to customer focus groups and asked them if Starbucks should sell $4 cups of coffee, of course the answer would be no. Starbucks branded largely by gut, at least initially. To be successful, most companies now do both. Know the market, know the needs of the consumer, trust your instinct, and come in somewhere in the middle with what you offer. If your brand is higher end and you're reaching for the top of what's feasible in pricing, everything about the brand must support that premium. The consumer must feel amply rewarded. If you are branding as the least expensive alternative in a market with the aim of capturing big volume, everything about the brand must clearly and sincerely communicate that value. By going with gut and knowing the market in combination, you can better achieve this.

7. Execute: What other way but flawlessly?

A company that brands deliberately and thoroughly will execute their business strategy with precision and excellence. Product quality, operational quality, all of this reflects on and is part of the big picture of the brand. Be your brand. Two of Hainsworth's brands are great examples. Starbucks does it. So does Nike. Nike is famous for saying "Just Do It." It's good advice, and to paraphrase, *just take it.*

OUR NEXT STEPS

Coming back to the story of Inovia, as someone who had already found success in business, I wanted my newest venture to be not just more than good, but great. I wanted a prototype for startup success. To that end, Inovia was branded systematically. The initial idea is big, a company that serves to cover the myriad needs of dental practices with a thoroughness they had never known. The vision is equally big: be the best and take it globally.

What's the connection to our customers? Using us for their educational, management, staff development and branding needs will make them more successful and enrich their lives. The yet-to-be-discovered need? Merge those disparate aims under one trustworthy umbrella and change the way they think about efficiency, an under-developed skill set in their rigorous professional training. What's the end state? We instruct our clients to imagine life if their workplace was everything they dreamed it could be. They'd be making more money, with less stress, and more time to enjoy it. That's a persuasive end state. What's the story? We're still writing it, the story of Inovia as a leader in innovation, vision, and action.

These are the same traits we know our clients strive for in their practices and personal lives. We are a brand that embodies the managerial success and positive mindset that our customers seek. Market research or gut instinct? It's a lot of both. And finally, executing flawlessly: it's the only way Inovia knows how, because it's the only way I know how.

About Gus

Author and president of Inovia Healthcare, Gus Kaloti redefined dental practice success, smashing old barriers to maximize efficiency and skyrocket profitability. Kaloti's entrepreneurial and industry-specific experience turns around underperforming practices and delivers quantifiable results with his proven combination of sound management, penetrative marketing, and emerging technology-based solutions.

Gus Kaloti is set to be featured in *USA Today, The Wall Street Journal*, and on ABC, NBC, CBS and FOX. His skilled dental coaching develops your team, increases your reach, grows your practice, and gives back what Kaloti realizes is most valuable asset: your time.

To do business with Gus, and to take your first step towards unimaginable success, visit: www.GusKaloti.com. See his vision in action at: www.inoviahealth.com. To learn more about branding excellence, visit: www.inoviahealth.com/branding today for solutions-based marketing that delivers amazing results.

Gus Kaloti — A Leader in Innovation

CHAPTER 44

Success Is A Lot More Than Luck

By Peter Sorrells

We can go a long way with the right knowledge, hard work, and luck. But there is another element that shapes our success, peace, and destiny more than anything else. I'll talk about that element in this chapter.

In the spring of 2005, we were flooded with news and advertisements about opportunity in real estate. Lots of companies offered investment courses, which cost more than my bachelor's degree. I jumped in with both feet and a suitcase full of my life savings.

That financial risk was more than enough. But for the next two years I borrowed…and borrowed again…and borrowed even more. I was betting that the properties would return all my capital investment plus a profit of several hundred thousand dollars. Fast.

It all looked perfect on paper.

What I didn't know was what even most big investors did not know: real estate values had become a house of cards. Easy loans for homeowners and investors ramped up extra short-term demand by both groups. The real demand was much smaller. When all those new houses flooded the market, property values dropped faster and further than anytime in U.S. history. I was part of the problem, and one of the casualties.

I sold some properties short of their mortgages for 30 to 50 percent of the purchase price. In fact, I sold some parcels of land for 5 percent of their purchase price. That's not a typo. I do mean a selling price of $2,500 on lots that I had bought for $45,000 three years earlier. At one point I owed close to $2 million on assets valued way below $1 million.

Around the same time in late 2008, the semiconductor industry was cut nearly in half. Major players laid off 30 percent of their employees and closed some of their factories. The salary that had been keeping my family afloat was cut severely. I couldn't carry the payments on anything, even our own home. We were essentially bankrupt.

When we look at the principles of success, how and where did I fail?

Was it lack of education? My degree in engineering had served me well, and I worked for one of the most successful high-tech companies in the world. In real estate, I learned from multimillionaire investors and followed their teaching and example. One friend owned 99 homes with a net worth of more than $10 million; some of my instructors were wealthier than that.

Was it lack of preparation? Besides multiple investment courses with live instructors, I signed up for one-on-one coaching and met with the instructors privately. I studied all the material thoroughly and researched the best locations to buy property before investing. I personally visited the locations and inspected the properties.

Was it lack of wise counsel? I spoke with other successful investors and double-checked my location choices with my instructors and others. I discussed all the data with my wife, Lori, and we decided together.

Was it lack of work ethic? I didn't sleep much for the next few years, as I tried to make this goose lay some golden eggs. I worked my high-tech job all day and into the night, and then worked on real estate until 2 a.m. and through the weekends. There were calls to make, faxes and emails, stacks of documents, research, tenants, contractors, inspections. At the same time, I managed the global marketing team for a $100 million division of a high-volume semiconductor company. I worked harder than just about anyone I knew.

Was it bad luck? Yeah, I had some pretty incredible bad luck and bad timing.

But as Paul Harvey might say, what about the *rest* of the story?

Education. I ignored what I had learned from my parents and some of my friends about conservative and careful money handling. At the time I was making the choices above, my friend Tim was saving tens of thousands of dollars for his kids' education. Years earlier, my parents, on a teacher and preacher's income, had put three of us kids through college. But when the dust settled after my real estate venture, my retirement and kids' college funds were gone. And now I owed hundreds of thousands of dollars. I might have considered that earlier real-life education in my decision and invested more cautiously.

Preparation. At the time I jumped into the deep end of the pool, the fastest-growing real estate markets were Arizona and Florida. Wow, the faster and higher they rise, the harder they do fall. Those two states, where I had six properties each, then endured some of the worst battering of property values in the country. The properties I mentioned losing 95 percent of their value...Florida. Empty rentals? Arizona. I could have learned lessons about fast rise/fast fall from history and other markets.

Counsel. I didn't mention the voices that told me to go slower and to be careful—those of my family, friends, and in the middle, when I could have avoided about half the problem, my wonderful wife. I figured that they hadn't been through this training, that they didn't know real estate. So I didn't listen to that counsel. With all this expensive training, how could I fail? Big mistake—fail I did. They had what is called common sense, which I was apparently lacking at the time.

Work ethic. There is a line between strong work ethic and workaholism, ...between working steadily and strongly, and overwork, ...between doing what's necessary and right, and that thing becoming your god. My god. That last sentence makes it so personal, doesn't it? *My focus was on the wrong god.*

In the spirit of full disclosure, I am a Christian. That means I believe in a God who is alive and sees, hears, answers, and acts. So we must consider what I omitted from the questions above: prayer.

Prayer could have prevented several years of financial disaster. It's hard to describe the situation to someone who hasn't been there, the absolute misery of digging out of a giant financial hole. Angry calls from creditors ten times a day; lawsuits; deciding which bills we could pay and which would be late; telling my wife and children no—a lot. I lost nearly all of the investment property and some things that used to matter to me (a Chevy Avalanche, a motorcycle, musical instruments, jewelry, and more). We nearly lost our own home. We received certified mail from attorneys almost every week—sometimes every day—for *years*. It was one of the most painful experiences of my life.

Did I mention that, in the middle of my real estate mess, when the high-tech crash caused my salary decrease, we paid more than $10,000 each year in out-of-pocket medical expenses? Several years in a row. Everyone in my family, including me, had some kind of surgery.

It would have been wise to consult the Creator of the universe, the only One who truly knows the future, before dumping all my money and a ton of debt into any venture. You think? If I had listened to *that* voice— God's voice—I'd have saved myself a lot of heartache. Instead I ignored my core beliefs and cut myself off from the power that was available to me.

I didn't even ask Him!

That was hard to write. If I had asked and couldn't discern an answer, OK then. But since I didn't ask, it's all on me.

He knows the future. We don't have to look any farther than early parchment copies of the Bible. There are dozens of prophecies (predictions) that came to pass exactly as they were foretold – hundreds of years later – in astonishing detail. God was able to accomplish His plan amid the utter chaos of human history—that is the most amazing part to me.

And His plan is *perfect*.

Believing in God does not mean that I am free from the difficulties and challenges of life. A lot of bad things did happen to me and my family between 2006 and 2010. But if I'd consulted Him before jumping into real estate, I would have avoided most of that mess.

He's not going to prevent a nationwide real estate crash to protect me from my own poor choices, misplaced focus, and lack of common sense. But I am convinced that He tried to protect me with warnings from friends and family, and direct messages to me. My receiver was turned off.

Expensive events (such as surgeries, broken cars, and pay cuts) would have been easy to cover if I had followed sound biblical advice:

"Invest in seven ventures, yes, in eight; you do not know what disaster may come upon the land." (Ecclesiastes 11:2, NIV). That little verse alone should have kept me from putting all my eggs into one highly-leveraged basket.

Well, then, how did I survive and even prosper after the crash? The way I should have started in the first place:

Prayer, work, and—well, something very different from luck.

1. PRAYER

If I didn't pray before jumping into the real estate pool, I certainly prayed when I began to drown. Nothing like a crisis to drive a person to his knees and get serious about talking to God. It seems to be human nature that we talk to Him less when things are going well and a lot more when we're in trouble.

My Great-Uncle Ray, who fought in the trenches of World War II, said he didn't know anybody who *didn't* pray in the foxholes. When we come to the end of ourselves and our resources, we naturally turn where we should have gone first, to the One who *"loved us and gave Himself up for us."* (Ephesians 5:2, NIV).

Indeed, when things are going great, it's only an illusion that we have control. Consider anyone who's been at the top of his game, then struck down with an incurable disease or devastating accident. Or when things go unexpectedly well—you receive a windfall of cash that you didn't expect, or a disease goes away with a suddenness that surprises even the doctors. We only have just so much control. I'm reminded of two wise teachings from the Bible:

"Every good and perfect gift is from above, coming down from the Father of the heavens." (James 1:17, NIV).

"Remember the Lord your God, for it is He who gives you the ability to produce wealth." (Deuteronomy 8:16, NIV).

We can create wealth by our thought, creativity, and work. But He gives us the life, ability, and opportunity. He can also influence our decisions to avoid traps, multiply success, even redefine success, and accomplish His plan. His plan is better anyway. It's bigger than we are, or what we want. His plan—is to save the **entire** *world*.

2. WORK

During the years I invested in real estate and dug out of the aftermath, the quality and quantity of my work for my employer did not suffer. In fact, I produced some of the best work of my career. My employer liked it; I just enjoyed my 20th anniversary with the same company and continue to help drive revenue growth and influence major business there.

At the same time, I completely revised a book I had written 20 years earlier, based on new technology and new lessons learned. I published *100 Ways to Save and Grow Your Money: Financial Fitness for Regular People* in the middle of my own crisis. Now that little book is helping lots of people get control of their money, and avoid some of the mistakes that I made.

While most advisers told me to file bankruptcy, I decided instead to repay my creditors, or come to an agreeable settlement with each of them. I negotiated and managed seven short sales and numerous payment plans and settlements, and I endured a foreclosure when one bank refused to cooperate in a short sale.

Would bankruptcy have been easier? Absolutely yes. Would it have cost less money? Oh, yeah. A *lot* less. But I had signed for all that debt, and believed it was my responsibility to pay or settle with my creditors. What I'm saying should not reflect poorly on anyone who's had to file bankruptcy; it is a difficult decision. Sometimes there is no other way. But because we decided to work our way out rather than file our way out, I believe that God helped us to succeed. And I don't have to wonder if I did the right thing.

3. LUCK?

Today most of the debt is gone, and we are back to building wealth. 100 Ways hit four bestseller charts on Amazon.com, including No. 1 in the Money and Values category. My salary, which had dropped significantly due to the tech downturn in 2008, has been restored. I've been asked to participate in excellent new business projects.

Lucky? Yes, I am a very lucky man. But more than that, I am *blessed. Luck is random; blessing is action by a living God.* I was lucky to be born in this country, with so much opportunity. But following biblical guidance and engaging God in daily life and decisions? That has definite rewards. Not random.

God has *chosen* to put me back on my feet and to restore my family's security, as we've prayed and worked our way from the depths of crisis to new success. That, my friend, is a blessing—nothing to do with luck. He responded to my new connection with Him and my change in direction: **doing things His way**.

If you've ever read the story of Job in the Bible, you know it's a difficult read. He was a good guy, doing all the right things, and very wealthy by the standards of the time. Then he lost nearly everything. Wealth, children, health, possessions…gone.

But read the rest of his story. *"The Lord blessed the latter part of Job's life more than the former part."* (Job 42:12, NIV). After the crisis, Job's wealth and family multiplied several times over. Looks like some prayer and work were involved—but it was certainly not luck. It was God, acting for a definite purpose.

This may be hard to understand, but part of my blessing was in the crisis itself. I learned more from the experience than from all my college courses and real estate courses combined:

• living by faith

• perseverance

• tapping into reserve strength

• goal setting in the face of disaster

• closer relationships with both God and my wife

• seizing new opportunities to help others, which means participating more fully in *God's* plan

Would I want to repeat the experience? No. But I wouldn't trade the education and blessings.

Create success by praying and working, working and praying. Tap into the power and love available from God. You might run into some luck; but you'll definitely be blessed.

About Peter

Peter Sorrells holds eight patents and a Bachelor of Science in Electrical Engineering (BSEE) degree from the University of Arizona. He has held successful engineering, marketing, and management positions in a half dozen high-technology companies, and is currently in his twentieth year serving Microchip Technology, Inc. An accomplished speaker and author, he teaches large and small audiences on technical, business, financial, and biblical subjects.

His book *100 Ways to Save and Grow Your Money: Financial Fitness for Regular People* has been an Amazon.com bestseller in four categories:

#1 in Money & Values,

#2 in Budgeting & Money Management,

#10 in Self-Help/Motivational, and

#10 in Christian Living.

It has also been endorsed by bestselling authors Steve Chandler, Loral Langemeier, and Scott Alexander. The book is available from: www.amazon.com, www.BarnesandNoble.com, and any local bookstore.

Visit its Facebook page at: www.facebook.com/MoneyHelp.

To learn more about Peter Sorrells and download a free e-book of *10 Ways to Save Your Money Right Now!*, go to: www.BestBooksLLC.com.

For speaking engagements or volume discounts on book orders direct from the publisher, send email to: Manager@BestBooksLLC.com

Or call +1.480.656.9683.

CHAPTER 45

Inspired By A New Life – You're Never Too Young To Grow Up

By John Escano

My kids are my guardian angels.

I met my wife at the tender age of 16, and she got pregnant at 18. Most would think this is a recipe for disaster and divorce, and at first, it started out that way.

I had a great girlfriend. I came from a good family. I was a karate guy —disciplined and strong. Even with all this going on, for some reason I still thought about ending my life. I even tried a couple times. To this day, I don't know why I had these terrible thoughts. I needed a savior, and I needed one fast.

What snapped me out of this horrific mindset was my daughter, plain and simple! Once I got confirmation that my wife was pregnant with our little baby girl, I snapped right out of it.

Luckily for me, once I decided life was a gift not to be thrown away, the sky was the limit for my success. I always look at my children and know they were meant to enter my life, just so I could touch others the same way they touched me. You may not believe in guardian angels, but I have seen their work firsthand. It's indescribable. My two children continue to amaze me every day.

Now, a lot of people go the other way when in my situation. They find out, at a very young age, that children are on the way, and they tell themselves, "I can't be a parent. My life is over!" Sometimes, these people aren't ready to be parents, but sometimes this responsibility can be the greatest miracle.

Let me tell you what happened next in my life.

At 18, I had to work two jobs to provide for my family. At 20, I turned up the intensity and began to become extremely aggressive in the health club industry. Within two months, I got my first promotion. Another two months later, I got promoted again.

I went from making $15,000 to $39,000 a year from those promotions. I eventually went over six figures, which allowed my wife to quit her job and stay home with the kids.

My parents always told me you'll never make something of yourself without a college degree. I still think that's great advice; you just can't be handcuffed by the degree or lack thereof. If you're passionate about your work, you will overcome and excel in any field. I know I did.

Fast-forward to today. My wife and I just celebrated 26 years together on July 4, 2012. People always marvel that I met my wife so young, but it is possible to make it work. It's not easy though. Couples that got married in their 20s and 30s end in divorce more often than not these days. So, how did two teenagers make it work? Through personal growth, networking, and masterminding that I want to pass along to you here.

And remember those two little angels that brought me back from the brink of extinction. I couldn't be prouder. Our daughter graduated from a great university, and now she is a nurse going to graduate school. Our son is 20, and he actually already has his degree. They told him to stay one more year, because he is going on to medical school. When I do my speeches, I tell this story. I tell this NOT to impress you guys, but to impress upon you that you too can do this. You can make it work.

The cause of my new company, my upcoming books, and my seminars is to help mentor young parents to achieve financial freedom for their families like I did. The greatest satisfaction I get is seeing my young parents stay together and raise intelligent, motivated children. I focus on the kids too, because if you can achieve financial success, you have a better chance of raising successful kids. They learn so much from their parents, and you can be their rock.

Where does this guy get off telling me about personal growth?

Remember that 20-year-old kid making good money and getting promoted? I left something out of the story. Something magical happened around that time that I will never forget. A woman at work recommended this tape – it was a Tom Hopkins tape. I said, "Pop it in!" She put it in the tape player, and from the first minute I listened, I was hooked. I never looked back.

Ever since that first moment, I have spent the past two plus decades studying the personal growth craft. I have seen Tony Robbins, Brian Tracey, Tom Hopkins, and many others. I have spent close to a college education on all my classes. I am probably up to $75,000 now, but to me it's worth millions.

From reading countless books to getting certified as a coach, I am an example of how the system can work for you. It's more than what you see on TV. It's about finding out who you are as a person and growing into a leader. I believe in this so much that I quit my job in the health club industry after more than 20 years and created my own program.

"Get your MBA life coaching certification, it's the new degree for success" is the motto for my company, the Mastermind Business Alliance (MBA). I stand by that statement everyday, and get to see its positive influence on my members.

After my programs, I get a ton of testimonials, and a lot have the same message. "John, I really did think about killing myself, and I can honestly say that if I hadn't been to your seminar, I might have done it that night!"

This is my mission that I feel privileged to carry on my shoulders. This is what drives me.

I even created a nonprofit, the Young Parents Mastermind Group, to help those unprepared parents I have been talking about that I hold so close to my heart. This work is what gets me out of bed in the morning. Well, enough about me. Let's focus on you.

Let's focus on how: (1) personal growth and development, (2) masterminding, and (3)

networking can help reshape your life – starting today!

I. PERSONAL GROWTH AND DEVELOPMENT

"Empty the coins of your purse into your mind, and your mind will fill your purse with coins." ~Benjamin Franklin.

Know Thyself
This is where we start, because without confidence in knowing yourself, you can't even begin to Network or Mastermind. I'm a father first and foremost. It took my daughter, both my kids really, to sharpen my focus and shoot for my dream of helping others.

One of the young parents I am working with now was ready to give up her baby for adoption. She may not be ready for parenthood, but neither was I. Who is really ready at 16 or 18? She ended up keeping the baby. She took it upon herself to save the child from abandonment. She grew by stepping up to the plate and taking responsibility.

She looked inside herself and knew she was a fit mother. If the opposite were true, she would have given the baby to a loving family. But she knows herself and what is best for not just the baby, but her future too.

The same goes for any profession or relationship in life. I want to help people grow to acknowledge their strengths and work to accept their weaknesses, so they can face them everyday.

Bob Proctor always says, "We are either growing in life or dying in life." Get to know yourself, what you need to grow, and go after it!

Accept Help
"When the student is ready, the teacher will appear." ~Buddha

Everyone needs a coach, but you have to be ready. You have to be able to accept the help and not fight it. Be open to others who might know more about a certain situation than you.

The aspect I love about mentoring young parents is I have a bird's eye view of the entire process and how great things can turn out. They are in the thick of things right now. They can't see 26 years into the future.

I can. I'm living proof.

I love being able to guide these lost people to sit alongside me on top of this illustrious mountain called success. It's lonely at the top, and I love company.

Study
"Those few souls who are actually studying their craft attempting to perfect it, stand out in a crowd like a giraffe in a herd of field mice."
~Bob Proctor

I am throwing in a third topic under personal growth and development, because I believe so strongly in the search for knowledge. I always say if you study an hour a day, it's worth 7 hours of the physical. If you study that one hour a day, that gives you the ability to stand out in a crowd.

Don't assume everyone else is studying. In fact, they're probably not. Don't accept the *status quo*, and never become the status quo. For example, my last year working at the health club, I studied my butt off. I hit my last 11 out of 12 profit quotas. The next manager, who didn't have my drive, only hit about 4 of 12.

It's so true. If you think about the Michael Jordan types of the world, those people who practice more than the average person—they stand out!

II. MASTERMINDING

Something We Do Everyday
"No man is an island." ~John Donne

Another way to think of this is brainstorming—a group of two or more trying to better the cause. This concept was the focal point of the book *Think & Grow Rich*, which came out in 1937. Masterminding is something that you do everyday. You just don't know you are doing it.

It's a very, very powerful concept. Napoleon Hill, author of *Think & Grow Rich* basically said the sum of two brains is almost as valuable as having a third brain.

A couple is a mastermind, a church is a mastermind, a phone conversation, where a friend calls to get your opinion on an important decision, is a mastermind! It's a retro-term that is making a comeback, and a simple concept that is crucial in any venture.

Two minds are always better than one.

Joint Venturing
"Alone we can do so little; together we can do so much." ~Helen Keller

Like Synergy, Joint Venturing is taking my talents and your talents and creating something neither of us could have alone. The whole is greater than the sum of its parts!

There is always something I know that you might not, and vice versa. Coming together on any project, concept, or initiative is always better than working alone. This action is something I always stress in my programs. Get together, talk, and find out if someone standing right next to you could be the key to finishing your dreams.

I can only imagine all the great works of art, literature, or personal growth material that may never have seen the light of day if it was not for joint venturing.

III. NETWORKING

Extend Yourself
"Word of mouth and evangelism are gifts that customers give you, but you must first earn them." ~Ben McConnell

Networking has done wonders for my life. Since I started in the physical fitness industry, networking came naturally through the art of working the exercise floor. People need to network and build contacts, and be in the right environment to meet other like-minded professionals.

What drives me are the young parents and surrounding them with other people who want to network and be successful. The goal is to create joint ventures, so that through networking, my members can create multiple streams of income. By networking, you build an extension of yourself and your company.

Industry statistics don't lie. If you have 30 people in a group, you are actually passing along an average of a 150 referrals a month. With the 20 minutes of personal growth and development at everyone of my meetings, we surpass those statistics. Think about it. You are getting your message out to not only those in the meeting, but their friends and family. You are exponentially getting your product out there to the masses.

I call it "Facebook Live." I am not here to sell my product to you guys. I am here to sell to your network. Networking is taking word of mouth and exploding that concept.

There's No 'I' in TEAM

"It is the spiritual inspiration that comes to one when he discovers that someone else believes in him and is willing to trust him."
~Ralph Waldo Emerson

If you have seen the acronym TEAM, it means Together Everyone Achieves More. Don't be afraid to ask others to tell their network. Their friends or family would much rather turn to someone they can trust, rather than a stranger.

For TEAM, I like my own variation—Together Everyone Achieves Miracles. The power of this team is also squared. For example, if you have 10 people, that's 10 squared, which equals 100. Every extra person adds in an exponential way to the power of the team.

That's why prayer groups are so strong, because 100 people praying for somebody is the equivalent of 10,000 people. I am not here to debate religion, but it's just about the power and belief of a group.

I think this power is grossly understated. Just look at Facebook and what happened to that company. They took the power of TEAM and joined together billions of people.

About John

John Escano is the founder and president of Mastermind Business Alliance. For the past two decades, John has not only been a professional star in the health club industry, he has also been a personal growth and development junky.

With his 20 plus years of training under the best in the personal growth industry, including Bob Proctor, Mastermind Business Alliance is different in that John doesn't just provide networking for his members. He has infused 20 minutes of personal growth and development, and 20 minutes of masterminding into his seminars and meetings. With the goal of taking this program nationally and internationally, John wants to reach 200,000 members in the next 10 years.

This is a lofty goal, but with just his first 20 members, investors were so impressed that he was given $100,000 in investment capital. Now his funding is well over $400,000 and growing. "I knew I was going to be getting into joint ventures, but I didn't think I could raise that kind of money in such a short time," he adds proudly.

Escano, a Licensed LifeSuccess Consultant, is so proud of the new MBA program he designed that he calls it "The New Degree for Success." With networking, inspirational education, and planting the seeds for meaningful relationships, John is poised to help thousands grow their business and improve their lives.

His meetings and seminars are not his only outlet to reach the masses. John is currently co-authoring a book, *Close the Gap Between Knowing and Doing*. This inspirational book will address secrets for lasting change that will help create action from knowledge.

John was recently identified in *USA Today* as a top business leader in America and as a "Game Changer" in today's business world. He was also featured on the "America's Premier Experts" TV program.

John Escano is grateful for all the gifts life has blessed him with, so he organized the non-profit Young Parents Mastermind Group. Having gone through the struggle of being a young parent himself at the age of 18, John knows the doubt this age group faces internally and from a judging world.

For more information about John Escano, Mastermind Business Alliance, or the Young Parents Mastermind Group, visit:
www.johnescano.com
and: www.mastermindbusinessalliance.com

CHAPTER 46

Becoming A Smooth Operator

By Laura Smith

Planning ahead and thinking through the process of your event makes all the difference in the results you achieve. In everything I do that will touch the lives of others, whether it's a simple dinner party or a 4000-person seminar, I am a planner. I visualize my event, walk through it, see it through the eyes of those attending, and prepare and tweak accordingly. I have found that this process has several benefits for me, those who are helping me, and those who are there to receive. The result is a smooth event with very little room for mishaps and errors, thus, producing greater value for the guests.

I've been to several seminars that others were hosting and I couldn't help but notice that this was one treasure many lack—when it came to helping people receive the value intended. When the guests were arriving, they were still trying to set up equipment and some wire was missing from the sound system. The speaker was running from one person to another trying to answer questions about registration or the book tables, searching for the bottled water for the guests, or testing the microphone for a sound check.

By the time the event started, usually late, the guests felt unappreciated, the workers were nervous about their jobs, and the speaker was not very focused anymore. My thought for them is always, *"If they would've planned for at least one day, they could've been a smooth operator and their guests would've had a greater experience to take home with them."*

You can always tell when someone is a planner. When the guests begin to arrive, there are smiling faces there to meet them and there is no confusion about what will carry them through to their good-byes. The people working are secure in their roles and can help with any normal or unexpected situations. The speaker can mingle with the guests and create personal connections that draw people in to want more. The guests are able to experience a safe place to receive and learn. They can also experience what I call relaxed energy, where there is anticipation for what they will be hearing.

Relaxed energy is that feeling when a planner has taken care of all of the details beforehand and the guest can enter knowing that there is something exciting ahead, and they can sit and wait for it in a calm and safe place. The other extreme would be when a person haphazardly puts together their event and the guests arrive excited and their tension rises when they see the confusion of the mishaps going on with the leaders of the event. That would not be relaxed energy for me, but rather nervous energy. The guests may still learn what they came for but the atmosphere for receiving it has changed dramatically, and it could change your success for future event invitations even more.

VIZUALIZE IT!

Would you buy a house without walking through it? Would you go on vacation without researching your trip? Would you have a baby without preparing the nursery? Planning pays off when you take the time to just do it. I can't imagine that poor day when a mother would come home with her newborn baby if she hadn't prepared for the arrival. Wow! The baby would need so many things, and going to get them at that point would be horrific. The mom and the child would struggle to get through it.

But every single mom I've ever known has planned for her baby ahead of time, almost in excess, to make sure that the arrival of her baby is smooth and easy. Whether the labor was hard or not, she has relaxed energy about getting that baby home to its cute little nursery full of everything it will need. It's the same, I have found, with anything that you want to do in your life. Planning ahead will make you a smooth operator.

Think about that new house you have looked at and have to decide whether you want it. You picture each room and how you would use it, right? I think we all even picture ourselves eating in the kitchen or think about where the television would be. I even begin to pick out color schemes and bathroom décor in my head when I look at places. It's a normal process for us to use our planning skills.

And how about that vacation you want to go on? Would you just show up at the airport or get in your car and drive without knowing your destination or length of stay? Would you leave without going to get the money or credit cards you would need for your trip? You know, it actually sounds like kind of fun to me, but it would be a disaster if you only had enough time to get there or only enough cash for one meal.

Let's run an event through your head the same way we would plan for other major things we do. Let's look at it in our mind and watch it unfold. This process helps us to see needs and concerns before they happen, but also it helps us to see how great it will turn out. I have certain things that I walk through in my mind every single time and I will admit it…I'm a smooth operator! And to tell you a secret, it's because of my planning that people think I'm really good at what I do. It makes it look very easy for me and that's key to a great event. If you can make it look easy, people will want to do what you do.

OVERALL PICTURE

So, let's start with an overall picture of your event. You can be planning any kind of event and this will still work and you will be on your way to being a smooth operator yourself.

You and I both have special talents and gifts within us that give us our specialized fields of expertise. You may already be doing something in your life that is almost second nature and other people are asking you questions about the how-to's of it. It could be anything from specialized knowledge to hands on building of technical equipment to decorating cakes to business mentoring to a comedy show. I don't know what you're made of, but you have something that you do better than anyone else and you need to share it with others.

If you are just getting ready to launch yourself out there or have been doing this for a long time, my strategy for planning can save you thousands of dollars in event planner fees. You can do it yourself and have the assurance that everything is taken care of so you can relax and have a great time doing what you do best!

So first of all, take a few minutes and write down everything you love to do and what people think you're amazing at. You may look at your list and think there's nothing there, but there is. You could take something like building a chicken coop and turn it into something fantastic. And if it was done well enough, you could launch yourself into being the premiere chicken coop builder in the whole country, selling chicken coop books, plans, supplies, etc.! You've got something to share in you!!! Start your list and run each and every thing on it through a money making adventure. Narrow it down to your favorite scenario and let's run with it!

VISUALIZE AN EVENT

I love this part because it takes very little effort and lots of (don't let me scare you with this word!)...creativity. In other words, daydream, brainstorm, let a really fun event come passing through your mind and let yourself change parts of it until you have a perfect day for yourself. If you just happen to be the person who makes a darn good chicken coop, you might have seen yourself surrounded by bales of hay and speaking from a platform that looks like a farm. Maybe you had tons of chicken jokes and could make them all laugh their way to buying your books and blueprint plans. You are the chooser of your fate and your event.

Make it grand and don't be afraid to expand every thought and see it as something that will blow people's mind, because...YOU ARE THE PREMIERE CHICKEN COOP BUILDER! Be creative and make it an event they will never forget. Have a little chicken coop with your business card in it and have a few teasers in it so they will order from your website. Or give them all a book of chicken jokes. Make them remember you because your event was well thought out and made them feel special.

Now take your ideas and write them all down. Begin to organize your event from your creativity. Make your list come to life on paper. Add your ideas to the different segments of your meeting. For example, if you had a great idea on how to market the event, put that down for that segment. If you had gift ideas for the registration table, write them down for that segment.

A simple list of meeting segments would be as follows and plug your ideas into them:

1. Marketing your event.

2. Theme for your event at registration table, book table, and speaking platform, etc.

3. Guest comps at registration.

4. Refreshments.

5. Special effects, audios, videos for the seminar.

6. Marketing your products.

7. Technical issues.

8. People who will help.

9. Whatever your creative mind comes up with.

WALK THROUGH YOUR EVENT

Once I have most of my list together, which so far might've taken about an hour or two, I will start to run it through my head again. Only this time I'm picturing the sections of the event as coming together and what it will actually look like all dressed up for my subject. I might have gone bonkers in some area and overdid the theme while I lacked completely in other areas. I just do a plain old walk through in my head and look at the room and the people and the speaking content and all the bells and whistles I just added from my daydreaming.

Am I happy with it, and do I think it will be a knockout success? If so, I write it down in detail as if I had to explain it to someone else who would read it. This not only helps keep your ideas from being lost, but it also helps you remember it visually by writing it down.

Now that you know what it will look like, prepare your words. Pen out your message and reread it and tweak it. Make it natural to you. When I first started putting messages together, I would type it over and over until I thought it was just right. Then I would read it out loud several times and sometimes I would even time myself so I wasn't speaking for 15 minutes when I thought it was going to be an hour.

When I had my message completely done, I would read it out loud about a gazillion times until I eventually could start ad-libbing when I would get to certain parts. This practice helped me so much at first. I am naturally a very shy person but it allowed me to build my confidence for speaking my message in my own living room instead of in front a crowd. Now when I write a new script for a meeting, I don't have to think about the words and content so much and I'm down to writing or remembering my speeches through simple outlines. The meetings I did frequently became so much a part of me that I could present them in my sleep after awhile, so just work at it and practice at first.

If you plan out a great meeting where people are getting great value and it goes very smoothly because you have planned well, you will get invitations, and that message will eventually become one you know very well and are so comfortable with, that you will have tons of fun with it.

BE YOUR OWN GUEST

You are preparing. You are getting closer to making it happen. You have people in place that will make sure your equipment is running right and the room is set up before the first guest shows up. Your people are ready with simple instructions to register, feed, and sell if you are using those options, and you are amazingly ready for the people to begin to show. Having everyone and everything in its place, you can become a guest alongside them and enjoy the time of arrival with them, exciting them, making connections, and building them up to receive your great information.

When you step up on the platform, people will see you as someone put together, in the know, and they are ready to listen to your message, buy your products, and send others your way. You've become a planner and it will show in your presentation. You will be more relaxed, more professional, and more people will follow you because of it.

You have become a smooth operator.

About Laura

Laura Smith is a jack-of-all-trades, and a master of most! Living life to the fullest is her passion. Having and accomplishing a huge bucket list since she was 10 years old, she has been on a mission to learn and do everything possible in a lifetime. Her discoveries and adventures have led her down many roads and have taken her around the world. From hugging babies in small African villages and Russian orphanages to staring at Mona Lisa in the Louvre in Paris, she has never lost her zeal for what's next. People wonder that one woman could own a chocolate shop, a variety store, a greenhouse business, a restaurant, a water company, and a bakery while earning degrees in Applied Technologies, Christian Ministry, and Master Gardening. And after that, she became a Pastor, Counselor, Teacher, Author, and an International Speaker.

The people who have known Laura well can attest that she always has something in the works, and in her funny and light-hearted manner, she will draw you in to help you see there is more to life than work and play. There's adventure! "The more you try, the more you can achieve, and the more you achieve, the better you are at everything you do," is what rings from her heart. Her passion now and always is to help people add zing and zeal to their life as well.

You can find Laura on her website at: www.expert-gardening-advice.com

List of Entrepreneurial Endeavors: Chocolate Shop, Restaurant, Variety Store, Produce Center, Bakery.

International Christian Speaker, Pastor, Counselor, Teacher, Author, Master Gardener, greenhouse grower, bedding plants, hydroponics, victory gardens Degrees in Applied Technologies and Christian Ministry Local Television Personality.